Tolstoy's *War and Peace*

OXFORD STUDIES IN PHILOSOPHY AND LITERATURE

Richard Eldridge, Philosophy, Swarthmore College

EDITORIAL BOARD

Anthony J. Cascardi, Comparative Literature, Romance, Languages, and Rhetoric, University of California, Berkeley
David Damrosch, Comparative Literature, Harvard University
Moira Gatens, Philosophy, University of Sydney
Garry Hagberg, Philosophy, Bard College
Philip Kitcher, Philosophy, Columbia University
Joshua Landy, French and Comparative Literature, Stanford University
Toril Moi, Literature, Romance Studies, Philosophy, and Theater Studies, Duke University
Martha C. Nussbaum, Philosophy and Law School, University of Chicago
Bernard Rhie, English, Williams College
David Wellbery, Germanic Studies, Comparative Literature, and Committee on Social Thought, University of Chicago
Paul Woodruff, Philosophy and Classics, University of Texas at Austin

PUBLISHED IN THE SERIES

Ibsen's *Hedda Gabler*: Philosophical Perspectives
Edited by Kristin Gjesdal

Shakespeare's *Hamlet*: Philosophical Perspectives
Edited by Tzachi Zamir

Kafka's *The Trial*: Philosophical Perspectives
Edited by Espen Hammer

The Oedipus Plays of Sophocles: Philosophical Perspectives
Edited by Paul Woodruff

Jane Austen's *Emma*: Philosophical Perspectives
Edited by E. M. Dadlez

Murasaki Shikibu's *The Tale of Genji*: Philosophical Perspectives
Edited by James McMullen

Dostoevsky's *Crime and Punishment*: Philosophical Perspectives
Edited by Robert E. Guay

Joyce's *Ulysses*: Philosophical Perspectives
Edited by Philip Kitcher

The Poetry of Emily Dickinson: Philosophical Perspectives
Edited by Elisabeth Camp

Proust's *In Search of Lost Time*: Philosophical Perspectives
Edited by Katherine Elkins

Albert Camus's *The Plague*: Philosophical Perspectives
Edited by Peg Brand Weiser

Tolstoy's *War and Peace*: Philosophical Perspectives
Edited by Predrag Cicovacki

Tolstoy's *War and Peace*

Philosophical Perspectives

Edited by
PREDRAG CICOVACKI

OXFORD
UNIVERSITY PRESS

Oxford University Press is a department of the University of Oxford. It furthers
the University's objective of excellence in research, scholarship, and education
by publishing worldwide. Oxford is a registered trade mark of Oxford University
Press in the UK and certain other countries.

Published in the United States of America by Oxford University Press
198 Madison Avenue, New York, NY 10016, United States of America.

© Oxford University Press 2024

All rights reserved. No part of this publication may be reproduced, stored in
a retrieval system, or transmitted, in any form or by any means, without the
prior permission in writing of Oxford University Press, or as expressly permitted
by law, by license, or under terms agreed with the appropriate reproduction
rights organization. Inquiries concerning reproduction outside the scope of the
above should be sent to the Rights Department, Oxford University Press, at the
address above.

You must not circulate this work in any other form
and you must impose this same condition on any acquirer.

Library of Congress Cataloging-in-Publication Data
Names: Cicovacki, Predrag, editor.
Title: Tolstoy's War and peace : philosophical perspectives / edited by Predrag Cicovacki.
Description: New York : Oxford University Press, 2024. | Includes index.
Identifiers: LCCN 2024015179 (print) | LCCN 2024015180 (ebook) |
ISBN 9780197625880 (paperback) | ISBN 9780197625873 (hardback) |
ISBN 9780197625903 (epub)
Subjects: LCSH: Tolstoy, Leo, graf, 1828–1910. Voĭna i mir. |
Tolstoy, Leo, graf, 1828–1910—Philosophy. | Philosophy in literature. |
LCGFT: Literary criticism.
Classification: LCC PG3365.V65 T68 2024 (print) | LCC PG3365.V65 (ebook) |
DDC 891.73/3—dc23/eng/20240403
LC record available at https://lccn.loc.gov/2024015179
LC ebook record available at https://lccn.loc.gov/2024015180

DOI: 10.1093/oso/9780197625873.001.0001

Paperback printed by Marquis Book Printing, Canada
Hardback printed by Bridgeport National Bindery, Inc., United States of America

Contents

Series Editor's Foreword by Richard Eldridge	ix
Contributors	xiii
Translations and References	xv
Introduction *Predrag Cicovacki*	1
1. Tolstoy on War *Robert L. Holmes*	18
2. Overcoming System and "Science" in *War and Peace* *Gary Saul Morson*	43
3. *War and Peace* as a Historical Novel *Marie-Pierre Rey*	63
4. Denis Davydov's Truth in *War and Peace* *Donna Tussing Orwin*	82
5. Moscow's Urban Form and Spatial Politics in *War and Peace* *Julie A. Buckler*	112
6. Life Immersed in Love: Natasha, Andrei, and Pierre *Predrag Cicovacki*	140
7. *War and Peace* and the Origins of Tolstoy's Religion *Lina Steiner*	165
8. Death and Infinity *Jeff Love*	194
Index	223

Series Editor's Foreword

At least since Plato had Socrates criticize the poets and attempt to displace Homer as the authoritative articulator and transmitter of human experience and values, philosophy and literature have developed as partly competing, partly complementary enterprises. Both literary writers and philosophers have frequently studied and commented on each other's texts and ideas, sometimes with approval, sometimes with disapproval, in their efforts to become clearer about human life and about valuable commitments--moral, artistic, political, epistemic, metaphysical, and religious, as may be. Plato's texts themselves register the complexity and importance of these interactions in being dialogues in which both deductive argumentation and dramatic narration do central work in furthering a complex body of views.

While these relations have been widely recognized, they have also frequently been ignored or misunderstood, as academic disciplines have gone their separate ways within their modern institutional settings. Philosophy has often turned to science or mathematics as providing models of knowledge; in doing so it has often explicitly set itself against cultural entanglements and literary devices, rejecting, at least officially, the importance of plot, figuration, and imagery in favor of supposedly plain speech about the truth. Literary study has moved variously through formalism, structuralism, poststructuralism, and cultural studies, among other movements, as modes of approach to a literary text. In doing so it has understood literary texts as sample instances of images, structures, personal styles, or failures of consciousness, or it has seen the literary text as a largely fungible product, fundamentally shaped by wider pressures and patterns of consumption and expectation that affect and figure in non-literary textual production as well. It has thus set itself against the idea that major literary texts productively and originally address philosophical problems of value and commitment precisely through their form, diction, imagery, and development, even while these works also resist claiming conclusively to solve the problems that occupy them.

These distinct academic traditions have yielded important perspectives and insights. But in the end none of them has been kind to the idea of major literary works as achievements in thinking about values and human life, often in distinctive, open, self-revising, self-critical ways. At the same time readers outside institutional settings, and often enough philosophers and literary scholars too, have turned to major literary texts precisely in order to engage with their productive, materially and medially specific patterns and processes of thinking. These turns to literature have, however, not so far been systematically encouraged within disciplines, and they have generally occurred independently of each other.

The aim of this series is to make manifest the multiple, complex engagements with philosophical ideas and problems that lie at the hearts of major literary texts. In doing so, its volumes aim not only to help philosophers and literary scholars of various kinds to find rich affinities and provocations to further thought and work, they also aim to bridge various gaps between academic disciplines and between those disciplines and the experiences of extra-institutional readers.

Each volume focuses on a single, undisputedly major literary text. Both philosophers with training and experience in literary study and literary scholars with training and experience in philosophy are invited to engage with themes, details, images, and incidents in the focal text, through which philosophical problems are held in view, worried at, and reformulated. Decidedly not a project simply to formulate A's philosophy of X as a finished product, merely illustrated in the text, and decidedly not a project to explain the literary work entirely by reference to external social configurations and forces, the effort is instead to track the work of open thinking in literary forms, as they lie both neighbor to and aslant from philosophy. As Walter Benjamin once wrote, "New centers of reflection are continually forming," as problems of commitment and value of all kinds take on new shapes for human agents in relation to changing historical circumstances, where reflective address remains possible. By considering how such centers of reflection are formed and expressed in and through literary works, as they engage with philosophical problems of agency, knowledge, commitment, and value, these volumes undertake to present both literature and philosophy as, at times, productive forms of reflective, medial work in relation both to each other and to social circumstances and to show how this work is specifically undertaken and developed in distinctive and original ways in exemplary works of literary art.

Richard Eldridge
Swarthmore College

Contributors

Julie A. Buckler is Professor of Slavic Languages and Literature at Harvard University, where she regularly teaches courses on *War and Peace*. She is the author of *The Literary Lorgnette: Attending Opera in Imperial Russia* (2000) and *Mapping St. Petersburg: Imperial Text and Cityscape* (2005); she is also the coeditor of several volumes on the cultural history of Russia.

Predrag Cicovacki is Professor of Philosophy at the College of the Holy Cross. He is the author of several books, including *Dostoevsky and the Affirmation of Life* (2012) and *God, Man, and Tolstoy* (2022). He is the coeditor of *Tolstoy and Spirituality* (with Heidi Grek, 2018) and editor of *The Human Soul* (2021).

Robert L. Holmes is Emeritus Professor of Philosophy, University of Rochester. He is the Past President of the Concerned Philosophers for Peace, editor of *Public Affairs Quarterly*, Senior Fulbright Lecturer at the Moscow State University, and Rajiv Gandhi Professor of Peace and Disarmament at the Jawaharlal Nehru University, New Delhi. He is the author of *On War and Morality* (1989; reprint 2014), *Basic Moral Philosophy* (2006), *Pacifism: A Philosophy of Nonviolence* (2016), and *Introduction to Applied Ethics* (2018). He is the coeditor (with Barry Gan) of *Nonviolence in Theory and Practice* (3rd edition, 2011).

Jeff Love is Research Professor of German and Russian at Clemson University. He is the author of *The Black Circle: A Life of Alexandre Kojève* (2018), *Tolstoy: A Guide for the Perplexed* (2008), and *The Overcoming of History in "War and Peace"* (2004). He has also published a translation of Alexandre Kojève's *Atheism* (2018), an annotated translation (with Johannes Schmidt) of F. W. J. Schelling's *Philosophical Investigations into the Essence of Human Freedom* (2006), a coedited volume, *Nietzsche and Dostoevsky: Philosophy, Morality, Tragedy* (2016), and an edited volume, *Heidegger in Russia and Eastern Europe* (2017). His most recent work is a translation of António Lobo Antunes's novel *Until Stones Become Lighter Than Water* (2019).

Gary Saul Morson is Lawrence B. Dumas Professor of the Arts and Humanities at Northwestern University and one of the leading literary critics of our time. He is the author of numerous books, including the following two on Tolstoy: *Hidden in Plain View: Narrative and Creative Potentials in "War and Peace"* (1987), and *"Anna Karenina" in Our Time: Seeing More Wisely* (2007). His comprehensive account of Russian literature and thought since 1855, *Wonder Confronts Certainty: How Russian Writers Asked the Ultimate Questions and Why Their Answers Matter*, was published by Harvard University Press in 2023.

Donna Tussing Orwin is Professor at the Department of Slavic Languages and Literatures at the University of Toronto. She is the author of *Tolstoy's Art and Thought, 1847–1880* (1993), *Consequences of Consciousness: Turgenev, Dostoevsky, and Tolstoy* (2010), *Simply Tolstoy* (2017), as well as many articles and several edited volumes on Tolstoy. She was editor of *Tolstoy Studies Journal* from 1997 to 2005. She is a member of the Royal Society of Canada and a recipient in 2008 of the Pushkin Medal for contribution "to the rapprochement and mutual enrichment of different people's cultures and the study and popularization of Russian language and culture."

Marie-Pierre Rey is Professor of Russian and Soviet History and Director of the Centre of Slavic Studies at the Sorbonne (University of Paris I). She is the author and editor of several books, including the much-acclaimed book *Alexandre Ier, le tsar qui vainquit Napoléon* (2009; English translation 2012).

Lina Steiner is Senior Lecturer in Philosophy at the University of Bonn and Research Associate at International Centre for Philosophy, North Rhein-Westphalia. Her books include *For Humanity's Sake: The Bildungsroman in Russian Culture* (2011), *Romanticism: Philosophy and Literature*, coedited with Michael N. Forster (2020), and *A Palgrave Handbook of Russian Thought*, coedited with Marina F. Bykova and Michael N. Forster (2021).

Translations and References

All passages from *War and Peace* in English translation are taken from the Pevear and Volokhonsky translation (New York: Alfred A. Knopf, 2007), followed by corresponding volume and page references to the Russian version in the Jubilee edition of Tolstoy's complete works: *L. N. Tolstoi. Polnoe sobranie sochinenii*, 90 vols. (Moscow: Gosudarstvennoe izdatel'stvo khudozhestvennoi literatury, 1928–58). For example, the reference to page 774 of the English translation of *War and Peace* is given after the quotation in the text of the included papers as (774; PSS 11:209). The references to all other works by Tolstoy are similarly given by citing the page number(s) in a recognized English translation, followed by the references to the volume and page number in the Russian edition of Tolstoy's completed works. A partial exception to this is the chapter by Donna Tussing Orwin: all of the translations of Tolstoy's works into English in her chapter are her own, and she gives the reference to the volume, part, and chapter of *War and Peace*. Like everyone else, she has in every case followed her translation by providing the reference to the Russian edition Tolstoy's completed works.

Introduction

Predrag Cicovacki

Literature deals with the intrusion of the extraordinary into the ordinary. This intrusion may begin in a work's very first sentence, as in Kafka's *The Trial*: "Somebody must have made a false accusation against Joseph K., for he was arrested one morning without having done anything wrong." Alternatively, it may be hinted at in the first sentences and more internally oriented, as in Dostoevsky's *Notes from the Underground*: "I am a sick man . . . I am a spiteful man. No, I am not a pleasant man at all. I believe there is something wrong with my liver. However, I don't know a damn thing about my liver; neither do I know whether there is anything really wrong with me."

Tolstoy avoids such dramatic openings and introduces the extraordinary into the ordinary by means of storytelling. Literature, he believes, tells us stories about experiences that take us, temporarily or permanently, out of our comfort zone, off well-trodden paths. The story can be simple or complex, funny or tragic, about a small incident or the shattering of one's world. Using an example from Tolstoy's own *What Is Art?*, the story could be about a boy who encounters a wolf in the forest yet manages to run back to the safety of his home to tell the story to his parents, or to anyone who is willing to listen. In *War and Peace*, the story is about a series of brutal wars that Russia fought against France between 1805 and 1812, in which the Russian troops were pushed to the brink of defeat but eventually managed to overpower Napoleon's invading army and re-establish peace.

Literary intrusions of the extraordinary into the ordinary provide rich soil for philosophical analysis. While literature is preoccupied with the details of the intrusion—how it happens, why, and with what consequences—philosophy is more directly interested in the structural aspects of things: What is ordinary and what is extraordinary? Do they operate on the same plane of existence, or is the extraordinary based on quite different and mutually irreducible metaphysical or moral principles? And if the ordinary and extraordinary are indeed based on such distinct principles, as facts and values seem to be, how can they interact with each other?

The extraordinary need not, but may be, otherworldly. What makes the wars that Tolstoy describes so extraordinary, besides the size of the armies involved and the ferociousness of their hostilities, is the alleged "divine mission" of the French emperor, Napoleon Bonaparte. Not only was he himself convinced of his own historical greatness and his divinely inspired goal of uniting Europe, so were many historians, even decades after the events took place that Tolstoy describes in *War and Peace*. Such outlooks were based not only on Napoleon's extraordinary military capabilities but also on traditional expectations with regard to the role of heroes and heroism in shaping the progress of civilization. But there was something else that was unique for the early nineteenth century and which is of great philosophical significance even today.

As Martin Buber explains, throughout the history of the human spirit, we can distinguish between epochs of *habitation* and epochs of *homelessness*. "In the former, man lives in the world as in a house, as in a home. In the latter, man lives in the world as in an open field and at times does not even have four pegs with which to set up a tent."[1] Expressed less metaphorically, in an epoch of homelessness, man feels an urgent need to recover both distinctiveness and a sense of belonging. He feels like an exile, hounded by a sense of loneliness and disorientation.

Buber argues that there were three epochs of habitation in the history of Western civilization: the first was inaugurated by

Aristotle, the second by Aquinas, and the third by Hegel. Each of these epochs was followed by challenges, doubts, and reversals. Aristotle viewed man as a rational animal living in a cosmologically unified and well-structured world. Augustine undermined this vision by arguing that man cannot be understood as part of the world, as a thing among things. He changed Aristotle's question "What is man?" into the more internally oriented "Who is man?" and postulated that man and the world each consist of two autonomous and mutually hostile kingdoms: one of light and one of darkness. Darkness, Augustine concluded, defines man's nature far more than the light bestowed by God and disrespected by man: man is a creature of guilt and sin.

A thousand years later, Aquinas combined some of the thoughts of Aristotle with the Christian credo, forming a grandiose new system that, due to its impregnability, resembled the greatest Gothic cathedrals. (Buber adds that Dante offered a poetic expression of this vision in his *Divine Comedy*.) Aquinas re-established the structure of the God-created and governed world, which secured an honored home for man. Just a few short centuries later, however, new scientific and geographic discoveries undermined that confidence. Bruno and Kepler, among others, discerned the twin infinities, that of the infinitely great and that of the infinitely small, which splintered Aquinas's view of the unified world and rendered man a refugee in the infinitely large and centerless universe.

Following the endeavors of his great modern predecessors, from Descartes to Kant, Hegel undertook to give man new security, to build a new house of the universe for man. Hegel's vision was oriented toward the temporal dimension of existence, rather than the spatial (as in Aristotle and Aquinas), and toward the immanent progress of humanity. Hegel believed that he had succeeded in bringing closure to modern philosophers' quest for epistemic certainty by methodologically demonstrating reason's undeflectable march through history, culminating in the completion of his own philosophical system.

Grand as it was, however, Hegel's intellectual image of a rationally structured and temporally determined universe was challenged almost immediately. His idea of reason's (*Geist*) self-knowing, providential presence in human life turned out not to be in fact historically discernible, and his sophisticated dialectical method was in some key points so detached from reality that it could induce him—and some of his followers—to believe in any kind of sophistry. In addition, it was also claimed that Hegel did not pay enough attention to the distinction between cosmological and anthropological times. Cosmological time, through which Hegel attempted to anchor absolute values, such as Truth, Goodness, and Beauty, is not humanly experienced time; rather, it is an abstraction that can be thought but not lived. Cosmological time left open the possibility that these idealities were nothing but the constructions of Hegel's great mind. Hegel's critics concluded that, if philosophy intends to offer genuine solutions to serious human problems, it should not proceed from the movement of thought toward things, as if it were descending from heaven. What drives us in our strivings is less our reason than our will, a mostly irrational force acting from the bottom of being, not from its top.

Once more, humanity found itself in an epoch of homelessness, which persisted throughout Tolstoy's lifetime and which dominates our age as well. Since this crisis affected Tolstoy's writing of *War and Peace*, as it impacts our reading of it, let us understand more fully what happen in reaction to Hegel's ambitious project.

Contrary to Hegel's convictions, an intellectual conception of the universe, which supposedly incorporates the goal of universal history, does not provide the desired sense of trust and certainty. The discrepancy between its confident claim to universality on the one hand, and the lack of its discernability in lived experience and history on the other, leads to a sense of disorientation; it leads to fear and impotence, as illustrated by the literary characters of the underground man and Joseph K. Nevertheless, Hegel succeeds in calling our attention to the relevance of time, temporality, and historicity for our lives, which had not been sufficiently understood or appreciated previously. One of the clearest testimonies to that is Heidegger's *Being and Time*, his most significant philosophical attempt to understand being not as simple and static but as becoming. Those following in the footsteps of Heidegger went even further. If being is wholly constituted and definable by its temporality, then we can hardly expect that there is any being with a capital B. All there is, and all that human life amounts to, is an endless procession of becoming, without any essence or true nature. Camus's *Stranger* indicates that there is hardly a story to tell since everything is contingent and prosaic—including not only the death of others but even our own; this work, together with the sense of lived experience that it articulates, delivers a powerful blow not only to Hegel's grand project but also to the conception of literature as the medium for beneficent intrusion of the extraordinary into the ordinary.[2]

If there is nothing extraordinary—no discernible presence of the eternal within lived experience—what is left for literature to do? Tim O'Brien suggests, in the narrative about his personal experience of the Vietnam War, that literature simply reflects reality as fragments that stand on their own, not united into any greater whole. In O'Brien's novel *The Things They Carried*, a randomly assembled group of soldiers rumbles from one assignment to another, without understanding either who issues their "assignments" or what role—if any—they may play in the overall theater of war. Instead of being about the grand goals of history and the warriors' heroism in the majestic battles of that war, O'Brien's "story" is about the things soldiers carried. In addition to their weapons,

> The things they carried were largely determined by necessity. Among the necessities or near-necessities were P-38 can openers, pocket knives, heat tabs, wristwatches, dog tags, mosquito repellent, chewing gum, candy, cigarettes, salt tablets, packets of Kool-Aid, lighters, matches, sewing kits, Military Payment Certificates, C rations, and two or three canteens of water. Together, these

items weighed between 12 and 18 pounds, depending upon a man's habit or rate of metabolism.[3]

We would never find such a list in Tolstoy—just as we are not going to come across it in Homer's *Iliad*—despite his also regularly describing the confusions of war and the randomness of its unfolding. But we come closer to Tolstoy's way of understanding war when we realize that all warriors, from those at Troy to those in Vietnam, also carry something that weighs more heavily upon them than any physical load: the lingering fear that their engagement is pointless. As poignantly expressed by the philosopher J. Glenn Gray, a veteran of World War II, beneath the hesitation regarding "What do we fight for?" lurks a pair of even more oppressive concerns: What do we die for? And what do we live for?

> The deepest fear of my war years, one still with me [several decades later], is that these happenings had no real purpose. Just as chance often appeared to rule my course then, so the more ordered paths of peace might well signify nothing or nothing much. This conclusion I am unwilling to accept without struggle; indeed, I cannot accept it at all except as a counsel of despair. How often I wrote in my war journals that unless that day had some positive significance for my future life, it could not possibly be worth the pain it cost.[4]

We must keep this point in mind when approaching Tolstoy's *War and Peace* as a philosophical text. The experience of temporality—felt as empty of Providence or any kind of ordering principle that might support a sense of being at home in the world—makes problematic any sort of recuperative contact with the extraordinary on the plausible assumption that such contact would have to be experienced in human time. The question of temporality and the question of the role of the extraordinary are not truly separate questions. We need to answer them together by thinking about how, if at all, any beneficent extraordinary is available within the modern temporal experience.

The issues concerning time, temporality, and ultimately historicism shape much of modern thinking, from Kant onward. Kant considers time, together with space, not as an independent dimension of reality but as a form of human intuition. All of our experiences have to be temporal and spatial, or else we cannot make any sense of them. Hegel takes temporality even more seriously than spatiality and connects it not so much with intuitions as with reasoning and goals of actions. Our actions in the course of time must have some goal, some aim. Hegel believes that such aims must ultimately be grounded in the dimension of the eternal: without the element of eternity, we cannot triumph over time and will always be its victims. The eternal can also provide an anchor for our human lives: it is against that eternal that human lives are measured and justified, or else life "could not possibly be worth the pain it cost."

The eternal, which Hegel holds to be the foundation for the entire edifice of human life in its historical realization, is precisely the greatest stone of contention in modern philosophy. As eternal, it is not in time; thus, it cannot be understood as either infinite time or as time everlasting. But if it is not in time and of time, how can we know that it even exists? What proof, what evidence, could we offer that would convince us that there is something nonquantifiable and unmeasurable, which we can call the eternal? And if there is no such proof and no sufficient evidence for it, should we not understand all we experience in time as contingent and transitory? Should we also not similarly treat human existence as wholly contained within the temporal dimension of reality? If so, temporality is all there is to our lives, whether or not it could "be worth the pain it cost."

In his book *Truth and Historicity*, Richard Campbell summarizes just how dominant this view, which he endorses, has become:

> The whole temper of our [i.e., twentieth] century is antimetaphysical; it sees no need for philosophical systems which

purport to describe the basic structure of what there is. The anti-metaphysical temper was expressed not only by the logical positivists, who declared all such attempts as meaningless. It is to be found also in Wittgenstein—who was not at all a positivist—and in such diverse continental European philosophers as Heidegger, Sartre, and the Frankfurt School. And in a more scientific form, it is manifested in the current fashion for "naturalistic" theories of knowledge. Underlying these different approaches is a new sensitivity to our own historicity, which requires us to take seriously the contingent character of what we ordinarily say and do. That calls into question any system which purports to present necessary truths concerning what there is.[5]

Despite this view being so widely endorsed, philosophers would not be philosophers if some of them did not disagree. Standing radically opposed to this mainstream view are, for example, philosophers as different as Nicolai Hartmann (with his theory of values as eternal and residing in the ideal world), Gabriel Marcel (with his insistence on permanence and presence, which includes the presence of the transcendent), Henry Bugbee (with his focus on believing in order to understand and act), Iris Murdoch (with her belief in the transcendent Good), Roger Scruton (with his view of the soul of the world and his insistence on the sacred), and Erazim Kohák (with his views that values are the function of eternity and that they ingress into the temporal dimension of reality). Kohák goes as far as to argue that "Historicism in all its forms has proved by far the most powerful opiate humankind has ever administered to itself—and the age devoid of a vision of eternity needs opiates badly."[6]

Kohák's thought is based on the realization that historicism always requires a posture of anticipation. Historicism associates later with better, and it assigns to any present merely instrumental value: as a means for the satisfaction of some later goal. We ignore the present—and the presence—insofar as we desire and focus on something that is not-yet. If that realization occurs, it sometimes brings disappointments since reality hardly ever lives up to our dreams and expectations. Even without such drawbacks, its realization leads to new expectations, thereby opening a chain of further delayed realizations and making us realize that historicism can offer no closure. The "vertigo of temporality," as Kohák calls it, can only beget a loss of confidence, in ourselves and in the world. This is where we stand now in our epoch of homelessness.[7]

Instead of relying so heavily on time and temporal metaphors, Kohák—together with Hartmann, Marcel, Bugbee, Murdoch, and Scruton—urges us not to return to the metaphor of spatiality (as Aristotle and Aquinas do) but to pay attention to the presence of the given. Their central task is to help us open ourselves to what the richness of the given can reveal to us. This is crucial for us to understand as we approach *War and Peace*, for Tolstoy is not only a master storyteller but also a masterful observer. When we read his descriptions, whether of battlefields or balls, of hunting or high-society salons, we have a feeling that we are present there, that it is as if we are experiencing it all firsthand. Tolstoy's power of observation and his sensitivity to countless details make his prose transparent and luminous.

Modern philosophers have dedicated an extraordinary amount of attention to the complexity of seeing: not only because we can be deceived by what we see but also because what we see is impacted by our subjective conditions. In his *Philosophical Investigations*, Wittgenstein makes a strong case that virtually all of our seeing is "seeing as": I do not simply see something in front of me; rather, I see this, here and now, as a red tulip. You, in turn, can see it as a plant in your garden that badly needs to be watered, or as a beautiful flower that you could give your wife as a present. "Seeing as" reflects our previous expectations and interests, as well as our conceptual structures and background knowledge.

Tolstoy's descriptions of persons and events are even more revelatory regarding the objects perceived. Instead of "seeing as," Tolstoy's way of perception and storytelling is better captured by Hartmann's distinction between "looking at something" and "looking through something." While the former refers to our ordinary cognitive approach to reality, which aims to identify what we see, the latter involves what Hartmann considers to be the perception of the second and higher order. Besides recognizing the physical characteristics of the landscape before us, we also recognize the landscape's mood: the calmness, or the tension before a battle about to begin. We can also sense the suffering or joy of a person standing in front of us. The arrangements of things in space and the small gestures of a person in front of us reveal a lot more than what is needed to identify them, and what they disclose is due not just to our background knowledge or our situational interests: the objects observed expose themselves to us. And they do so by revealing, among other things, the values interwoven with the objects we perceive and identify.[8]

Hartmann argues that such values can be of multiple kinds: vital (like health, strength), goods as values (wealth, good living conditions), cognitive (truth, justification), moral (goodness, truthfulness, justice), or aesthetic (beauty, sublimity). We can think of numerous scenes of *War and Peace* in which we recognize such values as appearing clearly in the faces, gestures, and acts of the characters, or in the events and landscapes that Tolstoy describes. In fact, values are so intimately intertwined with facts that it may be harder to find passages in Tolstoy's book that do not offer a picture of the "enchanted" world (as Max Weber called it) than to find passages that do—without offering us a fairy tale in which everything is magically beautiful and good. Tolstoy notes the evil as well and leaves it up to us to respond to what we see in his description.

One of the questions that make philosophers reluctant to accept what Hartmann describes as second-order perception and as the enchanted view of the world is this: If things we see reveal what they are as well as the values laden in them, how can two observers viewing the same thing have quite different experiences?

This question is important whether we are talking about our real-life experiences or about reading the same description in Tolstoy's novel. Hartmann does not think that such discrepancies expose the relativity of values. He explains the incongruences in what we perceive by calling our attention to the relativity of our feeling of values and the relativity of our judgment regarding values. The narrowness of an individual's awareness of values and sensibility toward them can vary to a significant degree: from one person to another, or from one stage in a person's life to another. An individual can be well attuned to a certain kind of value but oblivious to others. It is similar with the degree of sensitivity shown by one culture, or one age, as opposed to another.

Tolstoy would likely agree with Hartmann that the fact that such sensibilities change does not imply that values themselves change. Nor does it imply that all values are relative. If we find a reader who does not marvel at "Natasha's dance" or Prince Andrei's perception of the "lofty sky" as he lies wounded at Austerlitz, we would not think that values are relative but that there is something wrong with the value-feelings of the person untouched by these scenes. Just as the objective validity of any mathematical judgment does not mean that every person, or even every mathematically educated person, will grasp and approve of the judgment, we cannot expect universal acceptance of a given value judgment or our perception of reality. The door to the possibility of objectively valid values should not be closed. Nor should those doors that facilitate the experience of the eternal, the intimate interaction of facts and values, or the intrusion of the extraordinary into the ordinary—especially not if we can pay attention to the real and the present, rather than be carried away by our stream of consciousness and constant anticipation of what may come next.

Hartmann believes that perhaps the greatest problem of our age, and one of the key reasons for our sense of homelessness, is our blindness to values.[9] He maintains that such blindness is mainly due to our lack of ideals. In so many great works of art and philosophy, as well as in numerous religious scriptures, man is treated as a great mystery and his existence as a miracle. Nevertheless, we have no adequate philosophical anthropology and no clear idea of what it means to be a human being. Kant proclaims that "What is man?" is the ultimate philosophical question, but he himself does not offer any definitive answer to it.[10] Scheler makes an observation that may be representative of our entire epoch: "Man is more of a problem to himself at the present time than ever before in all recorded history."[11]

Contemporary philosophy struggles mightily with the issue of what it means to be and live like a human being. The dominant focus on temporality and the will directs our attention to action and what we want to accomplish, rather than to who we are. Instead of a rich and comprehensive conception of what it means to be a person, we have the concept of the individual and are obsessed with the questions: What do I want? What do I need to do? What is in my best interest? Like the underground man or Joseph K., the individual is understood as an isolated and anonymous individual, preoccupied with himself, and existing in a randomly assembled and indifferent world.

In his book *A Secular Age*, Charles Taylor makes an important observation that we should understand human beings as porous rather than as being sharply separated.[12] Although we are indeed complete strangers to the majority of other human beings, we are intimately related to some of them, and the impact those relations have on our lives should be neither overlooked nor underestimated. The lives of Tolstoy's characters are so deeply interwoven that, had he been a philosopher, he could have argued that speaking of persons in the singular is only grammatically and not philosophically correct. In our philosophical discourse, our focus should be on "persons" rather than "person,"[13] without shifting from the extreme of individualism toward the extreme of collectivism. As Buber puts it,

If individualism understands only a part of man, collectivism understands man only as a part: neither advances to the wholeness of man, to man as a whole. Individualism sees man only in relation to himself, but collectivism does not see *man* at all, it sees only "society." With the former man's face is distorted, with the latter it is masked.[14]

There is one further related issue that should be mentioned here. When we read *War and Peace*, we have a sense that the characters described have free will but that the "hand of destiny" is operative in their lives as well. To take these elements into account, perhaps we should say that, for Tolstoy, a person is someone who is understood not in terms of what is achieved *by* him but in terms of what is achieved *in* him. And what is achieved in him may in some cases deviate considerably from what that person might do and accomplish if he were merely living in his own world.

One illustration of this in *War and Peace* is offered through the character of Prince Andrei Bolkonsky. In the course of the narrative, this cold, detached, and strong-willed man transforms in front of the readers' eyes into someone who accepts the world with its limitations and imperfections. Dying in the arms of the person he has loved more than any other in his life, just when the obstacles to their happy life together seem removed, he comes to embrace his own mortality and finally finds inner peace. Natasha cannot heal him, nor even extend his life much longer, but her closeness and caring presence touch Prince Andrei's life and make a difference. Perhaps presence—more than the so-called essence, which philosophers of the old believed holds the key to our humanity and which contemporary philosophers so mightily oppose—may be what makes the difference. We cannot be masters of life or death, but we can care or not, touch or not, turn our encounters into a story and a song or not.

We struggle mightily with finding that elusive inner peace, just as we do with establishing international peace. They seem to be extraordinary, in comparison to our growing sense of inner restlessness and continuous social conflicts and warfare. One of the unanticipated messages of Tolstoy's novel may be that the ideal of man and the ideal of peace go together in a way that we have not yet adequately comprehended and that may open the door to a new epoch of habitation.

A great scholar of literature, Charles Allen Dinsmore, once remarked that "the poets have always believed that their office was to make men better. The highest human interests are Virtue and Truth."[15] Philosophers seem increasingly reluctant to admit both claims. Buber argues, I mentioned previously, that the first epoch of habitation was established by Aristotle, the second by Aquinas, and the third by Hegel. But this way of presenting things may be shortsighted. Before Aristotle, the great tragedians (such as Sophocles and Euripides) had done much to establish a conception of man that shaped the Greek way of understanding what makes life valuable. Before them, and even more important, were *The Iliad* and *The Odyssey*; for centuries to come, the Greeks measured themselves by Homer's heroic figures. Dante performed a similar service for the late medieval and Renaissance worlds, as Shakespeare did for the early modern world.

Tolstoy recognizes no great march of history, as Hegel does. Nor does he believe in great heroes or heroism, as Carlyle does; if anything, he sees "heroes" as the involuntary instruments of history. Moreover, Tolstoy presents no in-depth exploration of the dark labyrinths of the human soul, as Dostoevsky does. Yet it is unquestionable that Tolstoy's work also belongs with that of great poets who, in their desire to make men better and in their pursuit of Virtue and Truth, exert a significant influence on their age as well as on subsequent epochs. This collection aims to bring us closer to determining the impact of *War and Peace* on philosophical thought in our epoch.

Notes

1. Martin Buber, "What Is Man?" in Buber, *Between Man and Man*, trans. Ronald Gregor-Smith (New York: Routledge Classics, 2002), 150.
2. Hannah Arendt discusses the distinction between the sensory and the supersensory, which she believes dominates all of Western philosophy to the present age, and which seems analogous to the intrusion of the extraordinary into the ordinary in literature. The supersensory has traditionally been taken as "more real, more truthful, more meaningful than what appears." Following Nietzsche, Arendt claims that with the abandonment of this distinction, with the "death of God," we abolish not just the true world but the apparent one as well. Cf. Arendt, *The Life of the Mind* (New York: Harcourt Brace Jovanovich, 1978), 10–11.
3. Tim O'Brien, *The Things They Carried* (Boston: Houghton Mifflin Harcourt, 1990), 2.
4. J. Glenn Gray, *The Warriors: Reflections on Men in Battle* (Lincoln: University of Nebraska Press, 1970), 24.
5. Richard Campbell, *Truth and Historicity* (Oxford: Clarendon Press, 1992), 3. Campbell adds the schools of utilitarianism and pragmatism to this orientation as well.
6. Erazim Kohák, *The Embers and the Stars: A Philosophical Inquiry into the Moral Sense of Nature* (Chicago: University of Chicago Press, 1984), 170.
7. Richard Eldridge called my attention to the point that this need not be so, because many philosophers would subscribe to David Wiggins's idea that there are not one but two bootstrapping movements: we construct senses of point and value from reflection on our activities (which come first), but we also then use that conception to *find* value in them. As Wiggins puts it: "We need to be able to think in both directions, down from point [purpose or end] to the human activities which answer to it, and up from the activities to the forms of life in which [human beings] by nature can find their point." Wiggins, "Truth, Invention, and the Meaning of Life," *Proceedings of the British Academy* 62 (1976): 374–375.
8. Cf. Nicolai Hartmann, *Aesthetics*, trans. Eugene Kelly (Boston: de Gruyter, 2014), 42–82.
9. Nicolai Hartmann, *Moral Values*, trans. Stanton Coit (New Brunswick, NJ: Transaction Publishers, 2002), 44–45.
10. Immanuel Kant, *Lectures on Logic*, trans. J. M. Young (New York: Cambridge University Press, 1992), 538.

11. Max Scheler, *Man's Place in Nature*, trans. Hans Meyerhoff (New York: Noon Press, 1979), 4.
12. Cf. Charles Taylor, *A Secular Age* (Cambridge, MA: Harvard University Press, 2007), 37–38, where Taylor makes a distinction between the conception of the self as "buffered" and as "porous."
13. Robert Spaemann defends a similar view in his book *Persons: The Difference between "Someone" and "Something"*, trans. Oliver O'Donovan (Oxford: Oxford University Press, 2006).
14. Buber, "What Is Man?," 237. This need to balance individualism and communalism is a great theme in the work of Stanley Cavell. For a summary of his view, see Richard Eldridge, "Cavell on American Philosophy and the Idea of America," in *Stanley Cavell*, ed. Eldridge (Cambridge: Cambridge University Press, 2003), 172–189.
15. C. A. Dinsmore, *The Great Poets and the Meaning of Life* (Boston: Houghton Mifflin, 1937), 24.

Works Cited

Arendt, Hannah. *The Life of the Mind*. New York: Harcourt Brace Jovanovich, 1978.
Buber, Martin. "What Is Man?" Buber, *Between Man and Man*. Translated by Ronald Gregor-Smith, 140–244. New York: Routledge Classics, 2002.
Campbell, Richard. *Truth and Historicity*. Oxford: Clarendon Press, 1992.
Dinsmore, C. A. *The Great Poets and the Meaning of Life*. Boston: Houghton Mifflin, 1937.
Eldridge, Richard. "Cavell on American Philosophy and the Idea of America." *Stanley Cavell*. Edited Richard Eldridge, 172–189. Cambridge: Cambridge University Press, 2003.
Gray, J. Glenn. *The Warriors: Reflections on Men in Battle*. Lincoln: University of Nebraska Press, 1970.
Hartmann, Nicolai. *Aesthetics*. Translated by Eugene Kelly. Boston: de Gruyter, 2014.
Hartmann, Nicolai. *Moral Values*. Translated by Stanton Coit. New Brunswick, NJ: Transaction Publishers, 2002.
Kant, Immanuel. *Lectures on Logic*. Translated by J. M. Young. New York: Cambridge University Press, 1992.
Kohák, Erazim. *The Embers and the Stars: A Philosophical Inquiry into the Moral Sense of Nature*. Chicago: University of Chicago Press, 1984.
O'Brien, Tim. *The Things They Carried*. Boston: Houghton Mifflin Harcourt, 1990.

Scheler, Max. *Man's Place in Nature*. Translated by Hans Meyerhoff. New York: Noon Press, 1979.

Spaemann, Robert. *Persons: The Difference between "Someone" and "Something"*. Translated by Oliver O'Donovan. Oxford: Oxford University Press, 2006.

Taylor, Charles. *A Secular Age*. Cambridge, MA: Harvard University Press, 2007.

Wiggins, David. "Truth, Invention, and the Meaning of Life." *Proceedings of the British Academy* 62 (1976): 331–378.

1
Tolstoy on War

Robert L. Holmes

I. Introduction

Edith Hamilton writes that "[to] perceive an overwhelmingly important truth of which no one else sees a glimmer, is loneliness such as few even in the long history of the world can have had to suffer." In so doing she speaks of Euripides, a man, she says, who "saw with perfect clarity what war was, and wrote what he saw in a play of surpassing power."[1] That play was *The Trojan Women*. Tolstoy does the same with *War and Peace*. In so doing he encounters a thicket of philosophical problems ranging from the nature of history to the tension between freedom and necessity and the role of supposedly great men in history. More importantly for our purposes, he sets forth in a blend of fiction and philosophy the rudiments of a new understanding of war, one that emerges fully only in his later writing. More importantly still, Tolstoy distills from these reflections a conception of what makes life meaningful, which leads directly to his eventual commitment to pacifism and anarchism.

Hamilton calls *The Trojan Women* the greatest piece of antiwar literature there is. That it may be, if one does not consider *War and Peace* a piece of antiwar literature. The two are of such different scale and conception, however, as to make comparison difficult. The one is a Greek tragedy; the other is, according to Tolstoy, neither a novel nor an epic poem nor a historical chronicle. This makes it a unique blend of fiction, historical narrative, social and political commentary, psychological insight, and philosophical analysis. Discounting the Bible, it is possibly the best-known book in the Western world, one that everyone has heard of but few have read.

War and Peace is unquestionably a monumental intellectual achievement and a resource of provocative ideas on matters of transcendent importance, including war, the nature of love, and the meaning of life. In that respect it surpasses the *Iliad* and the *Odyssey* among works by a single author and rivals the Mahabharata among works by more than one author. It is, moreover, an essential part of a larger whole that is as fascinating as the book, and that is the life of Tolstoy himself, which evolved from gambling, dissipation, and military life to astonishing creativity and eventual nonviolent anarchism. According to critics, his creativity went off the rails in later life, and while his works of fiction are universally acclaimed, his later philosophical and religious writings are widely panned. Such critics do not show, however, where his later work fails or where there is discontinuity between that work and *War and Peace*. In what follows, I shall argue that Tolstoy's later views on war flow from views latent in *War and Peace* and that, seen in the context of his life as a whole and his understanding of the aim of creative writing, *War and Peace* is indeed an antiwar book.

The one certainty in all of this is that Tolstoy in his later years opposed war and did so absolutely and unconditionally. Why and how people can disagree about, but that fact is incontrovertible. For that reason we shall begin in Section 2 by summarizing his mature assessment of war. In Section 3 we shall examine two different conceptions of war found in *War and Peace* and Tolstoy's handling of the problem of free will and determinism. In Section 4 we shall identify the philosophical and literary elements in *War and Peace* that light the path to his later views.

II. Tolstoy's Pacifism and Anarchism

Whatever the causes of war, a topic that Tolstoy probes deeply in *War and Peace* and about which there is widespread disagreement, war is itself the cause of untold suffering, death, and destruction. That much can be agreed upon by pacifist and militarist alike. And it provides the centerpiece of Tolstoy's rejection of war, which has no more powerful statement than in the following passage from *What I Believe* in 1882:

> I pictured to myself that instead of these national enmities which are instilled into us under the guise of love of one's country, and instead of those applauded slaughters called war, which from childhood are represented to us as the most heroic deeds—I imagined that we are imbued with horror at and contempt for all those activities, political, diplomatic, and military, which promote the separation of peoples; and that it was suggested to us that . . . to go to war—that is to say, to kill people, people personally unknown to us, without any grounds—is the most horrible villainy, to which only a lost and perverted man, degraded to the level of a beast, can descend. I pictured to myself that all men believed this, and I asked: What would be the result?[2]

The answer to Tolstoy's question is provided by the whole of his analysis of the modern world and the spiritual perspective from which he viewed it. That understanding is rooted in the teachings of Jesus. He is not arguing from the standpoint of Christian religion, insofar as that is understood as the religion of the established church; in fact he denounces the church as having betrayed the teachings of Jesus. He is led rather to his own understanding of those teachings by his reflections on the meaning of life. If there is such a thing as *the* meaning of life, that meaning cannot be known, according to Tolstoy, because it would require near omniscience of a sort denied to humans. But *meaningful* lives do exist; they can be seen, described, and, he believes, understood. He finds them in the peasants of his day: hard-working, simple people who are in touch with nature and animal life and who accept the religion they are born into (as misguided as Tolstoy finds it to be). They exhibit a happiness denied to the privileged class of his day (which included himself), who Tolstoy thought tend to live self-centered lives divorced from nature and obsessed with salons, balls, operas, and wealth woven into the tapestry of aristocracy.

In *War and Peace* Platon Karataev represents a prototype of that sort of peasant. A middle-aged man who involuntarily became a soldier, he unexpectedly brings to Pierre's life a mix of innocence, insight, and spirituality. Reflecting the Taoist idea that the essential goodness of people becomes obscured by the accretions of counterproductive attitudes and practices, Tolstoy writes of Platon after he and Pierre meet as prisoners of the French:

> Having been taken prisoner and grown a beard, he had evidently thrown off everything assumed, alien, soldierly, and involuntarily returned to his former peasant, folkish ways.... Karataev had no attachments, friendships, or love, as Pierre understood them; but he loved and lived lovingly with everything that life brought his way, especially other people—not any specific people, but those who were there before his eyes.... Each of his words and each of his acts was the manifestation of an activity he knew nothing about, which was his life. But his life, as he looked at it, had no meaning as a separate life. It had meaning only as a part of the whole, which he constantly sensed. His words and acts poured out of him as evenly, necessarily, and immediately as fragrance comes from a flower. (973–974; PSS 12:49–51)

It is spiritual insight that Pierre takes away from knowing Platon. Pierre's life before knowing Platon represented the aimlessness of the lives of many of the wealthy class. Tolstoy writes of him before he meets Platon: "He now experienced a... sense of awareness that everything that constitutes people's happiness, the comforts of life, wealth, even life itself, is nonsense . . . in comparison with something. . . . With what, Pierre could not account for to himself" (753; PSS 11:184). After the two meet as prisoners of the French, Tolstoy writes of "the subtlest spiritual extract" that Pierre takes away from a conversation with Platon (1061; PSS 12:154). After Platon's death Pierre remembers an inspiring thought from him: "Life is everything. Life is God. . . . To love life is to love God. The hardest and most blissful thing is to love this life in one's suffering, in the guiltlessness of suffering" (1064; PSS 12:158).[3]

Tolstoy saw in peasants like Platon the elements that make life meaningful: simplicity, innocence, and endurance of pain and suffering that made them a part of nature, not something set against it. And having thrown off everything "assumed, alien and soldierly," Platon had, as Taoism teaches, stripped away those accretions that stand in the way of a good and happy life.

But Platon does not embody all of the elements of Tolstoy's later view; he is, after all, a soldier, and that entails a willingness to kill for the state. But, transcending the military life and its values, Tolstoy believes he has found in the life of peasants a key to understanding the teachings of Jesus. That key to that teaching is love. There is human love, which at one extreme is naive, shallow, and often short-lived, represented by the young Natasha, Sonya, and Nicolai, and that gives an almost soap-operatic feel to some of the subplots. In that form love can flare up suddenly, burn brightly, then flicker and die out almost as quickly as it began. It is often characterized somewhat dismissively as romantic love or, worse yet, puppy love, and distinguished from mature love, which has depth and stability and is capable of binding two people together happily for life through pain, suffering, and adversity. Pierre's love for Natasha is such a mature love. "The whole meaning of life," Tolstoy writes, "not only for him, but for all the world, seemed to him to consist only in his love and the possibility of her love for him" (1123; PSS

12:229). But beyond these aspects of human love there is yet another sense of love, what Tolstoy calls a divine love, that is deeper and more encompassing still. It is akin to the Christian sense of agape. It is love for all of humankind, strangers as well as neighbors, acquaintances as well as sweethearts, enemies as well as friends. This is represented in Prince Andrei's reflection as he lies mortally wounded:

> Compassion, love for our brothers, for those who love us, love for those who hate us, love for our enemies—yes, that love which God preached on earth, which Princess Marya taught me, and which I didn't understand; that's why I was sorry about life, that's what was still left for me, if I was to live. But now it's too late. I know it! (814; PSS 11:258)

And later, thinking of Anatole, who wronged him in his scheme to elope with Natasha and is now a pitiable amputee as the result of a war wound:

> "Yes, love" (he thought again with perfect clarity), "but not the love that loves for something, for some purpose, or for some reason, but the love I experienced for the first time when, as I lay dying, I saw my enemy and loved him all the same. I experienced the feeling of love, which is the very essence of the soul and which needs no object. . . . To love my neighbors, to love my enemies. To love everything—to love God in all His manifestations. You can love a person dear to you with a human love, but an enemy can only be loved with divine love. . . . Loving with a human love, one can pass from love to hatred, but divine love cannot change. Nothing, not even death, nothing can destroy it. It is the essence of the soul." (921; PSS 11:387)

And again:

> To love everything, everybody, always to sacrifice oneself for love, meant to love no one, meant not to live this earthly life. And the more imbued he was with this principle of love, the more he renounced life and the more completely he destroyed that dreadful barrier which, without love, stands between life and death. (982; PSS 12:61)

Natasha, through his death and her bonding with Marya, comes to recognize that love is the essence of life. In her, Tolstoy writes, "Love awoke, and life awoke" (1080; PSS 12:177).

Such love as Tolstoy understands it in his later writing entails a commitment to nonviolence, and a commitment to nonviolence entails renouncing war. It also, in his view, involves a renunciation of established religion with its distortion of the message of Jesus, as well as a renunciation of the institutions of control and oppression of people, including government, police, a judicial system, prisons, conscription, and a death penalty; in short, a renunciation of all the trappings of the modern nation-state. A commitment to love entails both pacifism and nonviolent anarchism.

Tolstoy does not draw these conclusions from a prior acceptance of a God who has commanded them; it is not from obedience that he would have us act. It is because the teachings of Jesus are true, he believes, that we should accept them; and it is because they are true that we should accept his divinity. Their truth is borne out by reason and verified in experience.

III. Two Conceptions of War in *War and Peace*

The nature of war is one thing; its assessment is another. Although Tolstoy came to be certain about his final assessment of war (and, as we shall see, is closer to that assessment in *War and Peace* than one might suppose), he was not of one mind about the nature of war in

War and Peace. The philosophical essays that contain much of his account read like drafts of philosophical works in progress rather than finished pieces. Much the same is true of what he writes about freedom and necessity. If one contextualizes *War and Peace* in the whole of Tolstoy's life and thought—including his conviction about the proper function of literature (verbal art as he calls it)—it can be seen to be part of an evolving process that eventuates in his later views. *War and Peace* is arguably an antiwar piece of literature because of its role in that process. It contains virtually all of the seeds that germinate into his later pacifism and anarchism.

Let us begin by noting the rudiments of two different philosophies of war in literature and history insofar as they help to clarify two different conceptions of war in the book. The Trojan War (as mythologized) was fought over Helen, who left her husband Menelaus, the king of Sparta, for Paris, a prince of Troy, an event that Tolstoy alludes to in *War and Peace*.[4] To avenge that betrayal, the Greeks sailed a thousand ships across the Aegean Sea to attack Troy. What is important for our purposes is that this was not the action of a single state. It was the action of a collection of city-states brought together to avenge a wrong to a single individual. For several centuries thereafter, war in the Western world was fought mostly by the private or professional armies of emperors, kings, or nobles and for a multitude of reasons, eventually including religion. Not until the emergence of nation-states did modern war come into existence. With the benefit of widespread conscription, it was war carried on by hundreds of thousands—and eventually millions—of men and fueled by patriotism for a larger sociopolitical collectivity, the nation-state. The Napoleonic Wars were modern wars in this sense.

Napoleon's armies swept to victory over Austria in 1805, Prussia in 1806, and Russia in 1807. The army with which he launched a second war with Russia in 1812 was the largest in recorded history to that time. That war, which proved disastrous for Napoleon, is the centerpiece of *War and Peace*. A nationalistic spirit was at work on both sides. On the French side it was expressed in the systematic rule-governed science of war that Tolstoy disparages. On the Russian side, it seemed only in retrospect to have been guided by rational choice. It was in fact expressed in mysterious ways, most notably through the judgments of Kutuzov—baffling to his advisers—who rather than acting decisively according to military theory let patience and time work their ways. And thus the outmanned Russian army overcame the French, combined with the spontaneous actions of partisans and Cossacks, and aided by mother nature and the onset of the unforgiving Russian winter.

Those modern wars exemplify in their character a political philosophy of war.[5] As epitomized by Clausewitz, who appears briefly in *War and Peace* (774; PSS 11:209), war is a continuation of politics by other means.[6] Although that is the most oft-cited claim of Clausewitz's, it is not his definition of war, which is that war is "an act of violence intended to compel our opponent to fulfill our will."[7] The emphasis is upon violence and the imposition of one's will. *Our* will, whoever "we" are. That is, it is viewed for the most part from the perspective of one side only, whatever that side might be.[8] And with the emphasis upon that side's national interest, that perspective downgrades morality in favor of personal pride, honor, retribution, national pride, or other essentially nonmoral considerations. Leaving aside the relatively recent academic interest in the just war theory, this has come to typify the understanding of war in the contemporary world.

The political philosophy of war, again, typically views war as *us* (whoever we are) against *them* (whoever they are). This is of the first importance, because war viewed from the point of view of one side only is not the whole of war. It is but one aspect. World War II is often said to have been a just war, but when people say that they do not mean that the whole of the war was just—that is, the entirety of the fighting by both sides, which makes no sense. They mean the fighting on one side only. *Our* side. The other side (*them*, from our point of view) was unjust. Tolstoy, like Euripides, in his indictment of war is talking about whole war, not merely war from the perspective of one side only.[9] This is his perspective in *What I Believe* and *The Kingdom of God Is within You*. It is also at times his perspective in *War and Peace*, although he does not adhere consistently to it and at other times writes as a Russian viewing the war with Napoleon from a Russian perspective.

Though he does not identify it as such, Tolstoy rejects the political philosophy of war in *War and Peace* and its corollary that there can be a rule-governed science of war. On the French side, the case is clear. Napoleon thinks of himself as a great man and is under the delusion that he can control events. On the Russian side, most of Kutuzov's advisers reflect permutations of the idea of a rule-governed science of war as epitomized by Ernst von Pfuel, the Prussian general in Kutuzov's council of war (634; PSS 11:39–44). But Kutuzov, the commander of the Russian army, ignores their various theories. Inexplicably to them, he chooses, as Tolstoy repeatedly says, to let time and patience work their way. Patience and time, Tolstoy says, are his motto (1086; PSS 12:185). Remarkably for a general, Kutuzov's powers are directed "not at killing and destroying people, but at sparing and pitying them" (1087; PSS 12:185). Sparing and pitying people is a nonviolent end. He is a Lao-tzu to their Clausewitz.

At other times, however, Tolstoy represents war differently. He sees it as an event that happens to people rather than something they choose. This way of thinking suggests a cataclysmic philosophy of war,[10] in which war is seen as more akin to natural disasters like earthquakes, tornadoes, and floods than to rationally chosen undertakings. Once it has begun, however, in Tolstoy's view, it runs its course fatalistically and, as Tolstoy sometimes represents it, mechanically:

> As in the mechanism of a clock, so also in the mechanism of military action, the movement once given is just as irrepressible until the final results, and just as indifferently motionless are the

parts of the mechanism not yet involved in the action even a moment before movement is transmitted to them.... As in a clock the result of the complex movement of numberless wheels and pulleys is merely the slow and measured movement of the hands pointing to the time, so also the result of all the complex human movements of these hundred and sixty thousand Russians and French—all the passions, desires, regrets, humiliations, sufferings, bursts of pride, fear, rapture—was merely the loss of the battle of Austerlitz, the so-called battle of the three emperors, that is, a slow movement of the world-historical hand on the clockface of human history. (258; PSS 9:315)

In the cataclysmic conception, war lies outside of human design or control, and once it has begun, its workings are largely unfathomable to historians as well as to its participants. Carried to its logical conclusion, this approach leaves virtually no room for freedom of choice. Fatalism seems to prevail.

It is unclear whether Tolstoy is literally endorsing fatalism when he speaks this way or is simply overstating the case to make a point. He says, for example, "Fatalism in history is inevitable for the explanation of senseless phenomena (that is, those whose sense we do not understand). The more we try to explain sensibly these phenomena of history, the more senseless and incomprehensible they become for us" (605; PSS 11:6). Here he seems to be saying that when we find that we do not understand historic events, we turn to the language of fatalism; not because there are no causes for such events but because we cannot discern what they are. The language of fatalism, in other words, is a convenient explanation. And this fatalistic way of thinking undoes the science of war. There cannot be rules for rationally designing the course of war if war is a cataclysmic event, seemingly impervious to human design and control and whose causes are unknown. And as Tolstoy says of Prince Andrei as he listens to Kutuzov's military advisers:

Prince Andrei was simply amazed at what they all said. The thoughts he often used to have long ago, during the time of his military activity, that there was not and could not be any military science, and therefore there could not be any so-called military genius, now acquired for him the perfect evidence of truth. (643; PSS 11:52)

Because of its immensity and complexity, war cannot fully be comprehended, least of all by those in the midst of it. As Siegfried Sassoon was to write later of his experience in a World War I trench, "I felt a great longing to be liberated from these few hundred yards of ant-like activity—to travel all the way along the Western Front—to learn through my eyes and with my heart the organism of this monstrous drama which my mind had not the power to envision as a whole." And paradoxically, as Sassoon experienced despair lying wounded in a hospital, he thought to himself: "Why hadn't I stayed in France where I could at least escape from the War by being in it?"[11] For the same reason that we cannot understand the causes and full nature of war, there cannot be a science of war, which consists of rules for navigating supposed causes.

Tolstoy at times extends the fatalistic way of thinking to individual choices as well. He does so, for example, when he says of Pierre:

How horrified he would have been if, seven years ago, when he had just come from abroad, someone had told him that there was no need to seek or invent anything, that his rut had long been carved out for him and determined from all eternity, and that, however he twisted and turned, he would be that which everybody was in his position. (536; PSS 10:296–297)

And later, after his marriage to Natasha: "He felt that his way of life was now defined once and for all, till death, that to change it was not in his power" (1162; PSS 12:275). But *War and Peace* abounds with decisions that bear all the marks of free choices, from Anna Pavlovna's manipulation of people at her salon in the opening passages, to Petya's determination to enter the military, Anatole's scheme to marry Natasha, and Pierre's decision to save a child from the Moscow fires, to mention only a few. This of course is paradoxical. If everything is determined and the outcomes of acts are fated,[12] then there is little to do other than just sit back and watch it all happen. Personal decisions and the anguish that often goes into making them (in the mistaken belief that they are free) are of little more consequence than daily changes in the weather, since neither they (or for that matter an author's depiction of them) could have been otherwise.

This bears directly upon Tolstoy's disparagement of so-called great men in history, which is not merely a personal bias on his part but central to the view he projects in *War and Peace*.[13] As he says, "In historical events the so-called great men are labels that give the event a name, which, just as with labels, has the least connection of all with the event itself" (606; PSS 11:7). And he presents and defends his thinking on that view. It is reflected in his dealing with the tension between freedom and necessity, the understanding of which has caused consternation among those trying to understand *War and Peace* as a whole. So let us examine that problem, which has bedeviled philosophers almost from the beginning.

IV. Freedom and Necessity

There are endless permutations of the problem, but put simply it holds: if every event has a cause and human actions are events, then they too will be caused, and therefore (so a common argument goes) determined. Hence necessity will prevail. But if whenever one chooses one could have chosen otherwise, then human actions appear to be free. What is important for our purposes is that this problem surfaces in *War and Peace*. For if both individual acts and historical events (including wars) are determined by fate, as Tolstoy at times implies, then how can one understand the seemingly free choices of individuals that abound in the book? And what point is there to denouncing war, as he does in his later writings, if such horrific events are fated? One might as well denounce storms of wind and hail. This is a problem not only for showing the continuity of *War and Peace* with Tolstoy's later works but also in making sense of *War and Peace* on its own.

In one form or another, this has been a perennial problem in literature and history. Some approaches to world events in literature and history leave little or no room for freedom. The Greek tragedians played upon this, representing the gods as ultimately in control of man's fate. And in early Christianity, Augustine writes of the killing that one does in war that it is necessity and not your hand that does the killing.[14] In the same spirit, Pierre thinks to himself as he contemplates assassinating Napoleon, "It is not I but the hand of Providence that punishes you, I'll say" (900; PSS 11:361).

In practice, we sometimes view determinism as prevailing, at other times freedom. In assessing the interaction of chemicals in a test tube we adhere strictly to the causal hypothesis, a bedrock of science. But in trying to establish mens rea for an alleged crime in a court of law we assume free choice and look for motives and intentions. Sometimes, that is, we view determinism as prevailing, at other times, freedom. Is that a problem? Theoretically, of course it is. In practice, not so often. We shift back and forth depending upon the problematic situation. In any event, the problem is not unique to ethics. Light sometimes behaves as if it were a particle and sometimes as if it were a wave, and there is no definitive showing that it is always one or the other. Science lives with that, as does much of quantum physics with the view that Schrödinger's cat is both dead and alive until observed to be one or the other. There are, in other words, unresolved—and possibly unresolvable—dilemmas in the realm of rational thought. Tolstoy, over the five years of writing *War and Peace*, struggled with one of these and embraced conflicting views of freedom and necessity at different times during those years.

But thirty years later Tolstoy settled the matter decisively in favor of freedom, as is clear in his advice to a Hessian conscript in an 1899 letter:

> It is not only Christians but all just people who must refuse to become soldiers—that is, to be ready on another's command (for this is what a soldier's duty actually consists of) to kill all those one is ordered to kill.... For a man who knows its significance, the call to the army is perhaps the only opportunity for him to behave as a morally free creature and fulfill the highest requirement of his life.[15]

In speaking of the opportunity to behave "as a morally free creature," Tolstoy is now endorsing the radical freedom of twentieth-century existentialists like Jean-Paul Sartre, who, in a passage particularly relevant to the problem of war, wrote years later:

> If I am mobilized in a war, this war is my war; it is in my image and I deserve it. I deserve it first because I could always get out of it by suicide or by desertion; these ultimate possibles are those which must always be present for us when there is a question of envisaging a situation. For lack of getting out of it, I have *chosen* it.... This choice will be repeated later on again and again without a break until the end of the war.[16]

Sartre, of course, does not say that one's free choice ought to be the one Tolstoy urges for the draftee; he is no pacifist. But a choice is forced, and the choice is a free one. Pleading necessity as an excuse to go along with the obedient majority, he would say along with Tolstoy, is the rationalization of those who are in denial about human freedom. We are, as Sartre puts it rather dramatically, condemned to be free.

It is one thing, however, to opt for freedom, as Tolstoy and Sartre do; it is another to make sense of that choice, for there remains the countervailing evidence of seemingly ineluctable determinism. The first part of the problem is to make conceptual sense of the dilemma; the second is to provide a justification for choosing to believe in freedom, a belief that Tolstoy thinks is infused in our consciousness.

A way of making sense of the first part of the problem was presented by Immanuel Kant, who held that there is no freedom of the will so long as we view things from a purely phenomenal perspective. But if the will belongs to a noumenal realm separate from the phenomenal realm (in which cause and effect reign supreme), the will can be seen to be unconstrained by physical causes and to be free. Although morality presupposes freedom and is possible only if there is a noumenal realm, the existence of such a realm cannot be proven. It must be postulated. That is why freedom for Kant is what he calls a "Postulate of Practical Reason."[17]

The Kantian perspective represents a useful way of conceptualizing the problem, but it does not justify choosing freedom in the dilemma of freedom and determinism other than from a wish to preserve morality. Such a justification was proposed by William James, a contemporary of Tolstoy. He argued that there are certain situations in which we are confronted with a genuine option that cannot be settled on intellectual (that is, rational) grounds. An option is genuine, he says, when it is live, momentous, and forced; that is, when it is one that a person is predisposed to take seriously, whose implications are of significant consequence, and which is confronted in circumstances in which even not to make a choice is, for all practical purposes, to make a choice (as Sartre seems to regard the choice to participate in a war). Belief in God represents for some people such an option, and if those conditions are satisfied, they have a right to believe in God even though God's existence cannot be proven. But the choice between free will and determinism also represents such an option for some, and for those for whom it does, the choice to believe in freedom is justified.[18] That is a justification that Tolstoy did not use in his letter to the conscript, but if James's argument is sound—which we cannot undertake to assess here—it was one that was available to be made. And it would have been consistent with what Tolstoy says about the limitations of reason in *A Confession* and *What I Believe*, where he put faith in reason as the best guide to truth as far as it can take us but recognized limits to how far it can do so when dealing with questions about the meaning of life. Philosophers such as Zeno, Parmenides, and Kant had explored the limits of reason and come up with different answers to how best to adjust to those limits.

V. The Morality of War

Political philosophy typically represents war as governed by national interest and its associated notions of patriotism, honor, and pride. But national interest is egoism writ large and is as distinct from morality at the collective level as at the individual level. Under the banner of political realism in contemporary thought, political philosophy holds that morality either has no place in war or at best a secondary place as embroidery to the claims of national interest. The cataclysmic conception lifts war altogether out of the realm of morality. Earthquakes and tornadoes can be judged bad but not to have acted wrongly in the death and destruction they cause. War, if it is a fated calamity that befalls humankind, is also immune to moral assessment.

But the wrongness of war is a foundational conviction of Tolstoy's later writings, and he repeatedly introduces negative moral judgments about war into *War and Peace*. Upon viewing the wounded and dead at Austerlitz, for example, Tsar Alexander exclaims: "What a terrible thing war is, what a terrible thing!" (255;

PSS 9:312). And Tolstoy writes of the initiation of Napoleon's invasion of Russia, in terms laden with moral judgments:

> On the twelfth of June [1812], the forces of western Europe crossed the borders of Russia, and war began—that is, an event took place contrary to human reason and to the whole of human nature. Millions of people committed against each other such a countless number of villainies, deceptions, betrayals, thefts, forgeries and distributions of false banknotes, robberies, arsons, and murders as the annals of all the law courts in the world could not assemble in whole centuries, and which, at that period of time, the people who committed them did not look upon as crimes. (603; PSS 11:3)

Later, reflecting upon the battle of Borodino, he writes:

> Exhausted men on both sides, without food and rest, began alike to doubt whether they had to go on exterminating each other, hesitation was seen on all faces, and in every soul alike the question arose: "Why, for whom, should I kill and be killed? You kill whomever you like, do whatever you like, but I don't want any more of it!" (818; PSS 11:263–264)

Reflecting his ambivalence about the nature of war and human freedom, Tolstoy continues the passage by alluding once again to a fatalistic, cataclysmic conception:

> But though by the end of the battle the men felt all the horror of their actions, though they would have been glad to stop, some incomprehensible, mysterious power still went on governing them.... and the terrible thing continued to be accomplished, which was accomplished not by the will of men, but by the will of Him who governed people and worlds. (818; PSS 11:264)

But Prince Andrei reflects:

> War isn't courtesy, it's the vilest thing in the world, and we must understand that and not play at war. We must take this terrible necessity sternly and seriously. That's the whole point: to cast off the lie, and if it's war it's war, and not a game.... The aim of war is killing, the instruments of war are espionage, treason and the encouragement of it, the ruin of the inhabitants, robbing them or stealing to supply the army, deception and lying are called military stratagems; the morals of the military estate are absence of freedom, that is, discipline, idleness, ignorance, cruelty, depravity, and drunkenness. (775–776; PSS 11:211)

And Tolstoy, in describing Count Rastopchin after the killing of Vereshchagin, writes: "As long as the world has existed and people have been killing each other, no one man has ever committed a crime upon his own kind without calming himself with this same thought. This thought was *le bien publique*, the supposed good of other people" (891; PSS 11:350).

Not only does Tolstoy express his own moral judgments about war and represent moral judgments in the words and thoughts of characters, he depicts various characters denouncing killing in general. Pierre, for example, as he arrives for his duel with Dolokhov, thinks to himself: "Why this duel, this murder?" (314; PSS 10:24); later reflecting on the duel in conversation with Prince Andrei, he says: "The one thing I thank God for is that I didn't kill the man." To Prince Andrei's expression of a different opinion about killing, he adds: "No, to kill a man is bad, it's wrong" (383; PSS 10:110).

The negative views of war and killing seem to have gone unnoticed by many commentators, but they are essential connections with Tolstoy's later pacifism, just as his account of Platon foreshadows his view of peasants in his later thought and their centrality to his exploration of the question of what makes life meaningful. A third element, however, is Tolstoy's emphasis upon love, noted earlier. He takes love to be the heart of the teachings of Jesus (and it is a theological virtue in traditional Christianity), and, as we have noted, he takes the truth of those teachings to be borne out by experience.

These three elements, the importance of understanding the lives of peasants, the nature of war, and the nature of love, are all essential to Tolstoy's later views. *War and Peace* sets forth all of them, not in a systematic way, but scattered through dialogue and philosophical disquisition. In this sense, *War and Peace* is an antiwar book in that it is part of a larger whole—the evolution of Tolstoy's thought itself—that culminates in pacifism, nonviolence, and anarchism. It may be objected that the views that are cast in the words or thoughts of various characters are not necessarily those of Tolstoy. This is a fair point, and critics may justifiably cross swords over how to interpret him in this regard. But the fact remains that these thoughts, even if in embryonic form, were in Tolstoy's mind in the years he was writing *War and Peace*, whether he took direct ownership of them in the philosophical essays or put them into the words of various characters. And it is those thoughts that unmistakably appear in full-blown form in his later writings.

VI. Conclusion

The political and cataclysmic philosophies of war represent different ways of thinking about the nature of war. The moral and nonmoral points of view represent different perspectives for evaluating war. The distinction between whole war and partial war represents the scope of concern when evaluating war, whether from a moral or a nonmoral point of view.

Tolstoy does not declare that war is wrong in *War and Peace*. But neither do Euripides or Socrates or Jesus in their views that arguably entail a repudiation of war. But he dismantles the standard conception of war as a rationally chosen, rule-governed action by political leaders and supposedly "great men." And that is necessary to clearing the way for fresh thinking about war, which one finds in his later works. For that reason *War and Peace* constitutes a central piece in the final moral, philosophical, and religious edifice that is the legacy of his life; a life, one is tempted to say as a counterexample to his own teaching, that exemplifies the qualities of a great man. One misses its significance if it is viewed as a finished product in isolation from the rest of that life. Perhaps more than all but a few major figures in history, Tolstoy's life is an organic whole, evolving right to the end. The earlier stages flow into the later stages. This is particularly true of *War and Peace*. His thinking was evolving even during the years of writing it, no doubt accounting for some of the inconsistencies it contains, and continued evolving, most significantly after the crisis recounted in *A Confession*. There emerged from that life a conception of a summum bonum. The renunciation of war was part of that end. But the end is not negative, anti-this or anti-that. It is positive, emphasizing happiness and, even more than happiness, the moral well-being of humankind. The message is contained in the title of his 1894 book, *The Kingdom of God Is within You*. He has a different conception of the highest good than Plato, but like Plato he sees love as the key to advancing its realization.[19] Plato characterizes love as the desire for the everlasting possession of the good. For Tolstoy, that is also true, but with a different understanding of the good. For Plato it is something fully attainable only after the soul sheds the mortal body and is capable of fully apprehending the Good. For Tolstoy it is attainable in this life by shedding, not the physical body, but the destructive attitudes epitomized by the commitment to war, killing, cruelty, greed, oppression, and alienation from nature that, contrary to reason and human nature, has taken hold of humankind. It also arguably undermines the standard moral justification of war, namely the just war theory, which, in effect, substitutes moral rules for the "scientific" rules of the standard conception and proceeds to try to assess war rationally as a case of *us* against *them*. Perhaps most important,

War and Peace both in the philosophical essays and scattered throughout in the words of various characters lays the foundation for Tolstoy's later pacifism. In keeping with his commitment to the rudiments of a process philosophy of historical change, Tolstoy's approach to war in *War and Peace* flows into his later philosophical and religious views. It is not *an* antiwar book in the way in which *The Trojan Women* is an antiwar play or *All Quiet on the Western Front* is an antiwar book, because there is so much more in it than its antiwar element, namely the depiction of the lives of its central characters. But it is antiwar nonetheless, in the sense of sowing in fictionalized form, buttressed by the scaffolding of philosophical argument, the seeds that are later nurtured into a full-blown pacifism. In a world that was and remains unready for what he perceived as the truth about war, Tolstoy was in the end enveloped in a loneliness of the sort Hamilton ascribes to Euripides.[20]

Notes

1. Edith Hamilton, "A Pacifist in Periclean Athens," in *War: An Anthology*, ed. Edward and Elizabeth Huberman (New York: Washington Square Press, 1969), 100–101.
2. Leo Tolstoy, *What I Believe*, in *A Confession, The Gospel in Brief, and What I Believe* (London: Oxford, 1961), 403 (PSS 23:369–370).
3. When asked by Natasha after years of marriage whether Platon would approve of him now, Pierre, after reflection, says no, but that he would approve of their family life (1176; PSS 12:292–293).
4. Cf. 211; PSS 9:258. Pierre's wife, who in the beauty imputed to her might remind some of Helen, and who presumably was unfaithful to her husband, as Helen of Troy was to hers, is interestingly named Hélène. In some accounts, it should be noted, Helen of Troy was abducted by Paris and did not leave voluntarily.
5. In the account of philosophies of war, I am largely following Anatol Rapoport in his introduction to *Clausewitz on War*, ed. Anatol Rapoport (Baltimore, MD: Penguin Books, 1968).

6. Tolstoy writes "All historians agree that the external activity of states and nations, in their conflicts among themselves, is expressed in wars; that the political power of states and nations increases or decreases owing directly to their greater or lesser military successes" (1031; PSS 12:118).
7. Clausewitz, *On War* (Baltimore: Penguin, 1968), chap. 1, 2, Definition.
8. Clausewitz is not consistent in this and sometimes views war in the broader context of two or more sides.
9. Tolstoy is not consistent, however, in his rejection of the point of view of partial war. Sprinkled throughout *War and Peace* are references to *our* grandparents (3; PSS 9:4), *our army* (364; PSS 10:86), *our* fathers (1032; PSS 12:119), *our* government (1035; PSS 12:123), and *our* vanguard (1069; PSS 12:163) in which he is evidently speaking as a Russian to other Russians and identifying with the collectivity that is the Russian people.
10. I borrow this term from Anatol Rapoport's introduction to *Clausewitz on War* and adapt it to Tolstoy's account in *War and Peace*.
11. Siegfried Sassoon, *Sherston's Progress* (London: Folio Society, 1974), 153 and 169.
12. Tolstoy does not distinguish determinism from fate (nor either of these from predestination), as one should in a thorough philosophical analysis of these issues.
13. Thomas Carlyle epitomizes this view when he writes: "Universal History, the history of what man has accomplished in this world, is at bottom the History of the Great Men who have worked here. They were . . . the modellers, patterns, and in a wide sense creators, of whatsoever the general mass of men contrived to do or to attain"; Carlyle, *Heroes and Hero Worship* (New York: Home Book Company, n.d.), 5–6.
14. Augustine, Letter CLXXXIX to Boniface, *Nicene and Post-Nicene Fathers*, in *A Select Library of the Christian Church*, vol. 1 (Peabody, MA: Hendrickson, 1994), 552–555.
15. Leo Tolstoy, "Advice to a Draftee," in Huberman and Huberman, *War*, 280, 282–283. The Hessians were noted for maintaining mercenary armies (sometimes called auxiliaries) that were contracted out by their leaders to be used in other country's conflicts. The French army that invaded Russia in 1812 was about half French and reportedly contained Hessians as well as Poles, Austrians, Germans, Swiss, Portuguese, and Croatians, among others.
16. Jean-Paul Sartre, *Being and Nothingness*, trans. Hazel E. Barnes (New York: Philosophical Library, 1956), 554–555.

17. See Immanuel Kant, "Foundations of the Metaphysics of Morals," Third Section, in *Kant Selections*, ed. Lewis White Beck (New York: Macmillan, 1988), 285–299.
18. See William James, "The Will to Believe" and "The Dilemma of Determinism," in *The Will to Believe and Other Essays on Popular Philosophy* (New York: Dover Publications, 1956), 145–184.
19. See Tolstoy, *What is Art?* (New York: Penguin, 1995), especially sections 18–20 for an understanding of his conception of the end of artistic activity, including the writing of literature. For Plato on love as the desire for the everlasting possession of the good, see his *Symposium*, Steph. 205–206.
20. Appreciation to Veronica S. Holmes for helpful comments on an earlier draft of this essay.

Works Cited

Augustine. Letter CLXXXIX to Bonaface. *Nicene and Post-Nicene Fathers: A Select Library of the Christian Church*. Vol. 1. Peabody, MA: Hendrickson, 1994.

Carlyle, Thomas. *Heroes and Hero Worship*. New York: Home Book Company, n.d.

Clausewitz, Carl von. *On War*. Translated by J. J. Graham. Baltimore: Penguin, 1968.

Euripides. *The Trojan Women*. *The Complete Greek Drama*. Edited by Whitney J. Oates and Eugene O'Neill Jr. Vol. 2. New York: Random House, 1938.

Hamilton, Edith. "A Pacifist in Periclean Athens." *War: An Anthology*. Edited by Edward Huberman and Elizabeth Huberman, 100–108. New York: Washington Square Press, 1969.

James, William. *The Will to Believe and Other Essays*. New York. Dover, 1956.

Kant, Immanuel. "Foundations of the Metaphysics of Morals." *Kant Selections*. Translated and edited by Lewis White Beck, 244–299. New York: Macmillan, 1988.

Plato. *Symposium*. *The Collected Dialogues*. Edited by Edith Hamilton and Huntington Cairns, 528–575. Princeton, NJ: University Press, 1961.

Rapoport, Anatol. *Clausewitz on War*. Baltimore, MD: Penguin, 1968.

Sartre, Jean-Paul. *Being and Nothingness*. Translated by Hazel E. Barnes. New York: Philosophical Library, 1956.

Sassoon, Siegfried. *Sherston's Progress*. London: Folio Society, 1974.

Tolstoy, Leo. "Advice to a Draftee." *War: An Anthology*. Edited by Edward and Elizabeth Huberman, 280–284. New York: Washington Square Press, 1969.

Tolstoy, Leo. *The Kingdom of God Is within You.* Translated by Constance Garnett. New York: Noonday, 1961.

Tolstoy, Leo. "What I Believe." *A Confession, the Gospel in Brief and What I Believe.* Translated by Aylmer Maude, 303–539. London: Oxford, 1961.

Tolstoy, Leo. *What Is Art?* Translated by Richard Pevear and Larissa Volokhonsky. New York: Penguin, 1995.

2
Overcoming System and "Science" in *War and Peace*

Gary Saul Morson

I. A Hard Social Science?

If by "science" we mean a discipline resembling physics, are there any social sciences? If not, will we have them soon—or ever? Are there reasons to suppose that a social science is impossible? Contrary to almost everyone else, and especially to the Russian intelligentsia of his day, Tolstoy denied that there either was or ever could be a hard social science.[1] He dedicated *War and Peace*, often thought of as the world's greatest novel, to justifying this denial. Since the sort of thinking Tolstoy critiqued is still very much with us, *War and Peace* speaks to us today with all the more force.

Some intellectual historical observations might help situate the issues. Since the seventeenth century, Western thinkers have dreamed that what Newton did for astronomy, other thinkers could do for society. The human sciences could be just that—hard sciences like physics—and soon would be. Newton managed to explain the amazingly complex movements of the planets in terms of four equations, simple enough for a beginning algebra student to understand. Why should there not be a Newton of psychology, society, ethics, or history? Time and again, such putative Newtons have arisen and attracted followers. The many failures to sustain a claim to scientific status has not discouraged new claimants.

It seemed so obvious: since people are natural objects, they must be governed by natural laws no less than stones. Whatever those laws turn out to be, they must be reducible to physics and therefore must be no less certain. Also like physical laws, these human ones must be entirely deterministic. It follows that we call chance or choice whatever we have not yet explained scientifically.

The great accomplishment of seventeenth-century rationalists and the "moral Newtonians"[2] who followed was to convince philosophers that only scientific knowledge was worth the name and that disciplines are valuable to the extent they resemble mathematics or physics. Prior to that, Aristotle's insights seemed plausible, and thinkers like Montaigne and Erasmus took them for granted. Aristotle held that we need not one but two models of knowledge. Theoretical disciplines, like mathematics, promise certainty; practical disciplines give us insights that are true "on the whole and for the most part" (one of Aristotle's favorite phrases). Practical wisdom offers us not laws but rules of thumb, and its recommendations are always tentative and revisable in light of future developments. This is the view that Tolstoy defends in *War and Peace* and *Anna Karenina*.

One reason that no social science will ever be able to predict events is that in the human world genuine contingency reigns. At any given moment more than one thing can happen. Some believe that "there are no real alternatives, but that all that is or takes place is the outcome of necessity,"[3] Aristotle explains, but that view is mistaken:

> For we see that deliberation and action are causative with regard to the future, and that, to speak more generally... there is a potentiality in either direction. Such things may either be or not be; events also therefore may either take place or not take place....
> It is therefore plain that it is not of necessity that everything takes place; but in some instances there are real alternatives.[4]

Determinists notwithstanding, contingent events—defined as those that can "either be or not be"—exist. For Leibniz and other the seventeenth-century rationalists, and for their social scientific heirs, such a view made no sense. How could something happen that a cause had not specified? Leibniz insisted that there must be a "sufficient reason" for all events ensuring why that event, and only that event, could have taken place. Modern determinism has borrowed Leibniz's concept in fact, if not in name.

The eighteenth-century mathematician and astronomer Pierre-Simon Laplace famously suggested that if some "calculating demon" could know all natural laws and the position of each particle in the universe, he could predict everything that would ever happen or, looking to the past, retrodict everything thing that had happened. In Laplace's view, time is a solid block, with each moment compatible with one and only one totality. There is no loose play. If by "suspense" we have in mind the possibility of multiple outcomes, then suspense is an illusion created by our ignorance. Laplace, who made major contributions to probability theory, maintained that the concept of probability is, strictly speaking, inapplicable to events, which are absolutely certain. It is not events that are probable but our guesses about them. Probability measures the accuracy of those guesses about events that are themselves absolutely certain.

Time and again, moral Newtonian prophets have arisen. Each claims to have established, at last, a hard social science. Bentham, Marx, Freud, Skinner, and, in our time, Jared Diamond have all advanced such a claim. Before Auguste Comte decided to call his new discipline "sociology," he planned to call it "social physics." Planetary astronomy also provided a model for the formulators of modern economics: the stability of the solar system suggested economic equilibrium. Most economists today still believe they possess a real science.[5]

In the same spirit, Bronislaw Malinowski, the founder of modern anthropology, asserted that his new science would show that "adventitious and fortuitous happenings" do not exist and would soon generate "prediction of the future."[6] His successor Claude Lévi-Strauss was enthused about the ability of social scientists to formulate a table of human possibilities "that would be comparable to the table of elements which Mendeleieff introduced into modern chemistry" and that by looking at such a table these scientists would "discover the place of languages that have disappeared or are unknown own, or yet to come or simply possible."[7] If anthropology never actually achieved scientific status, the solution was soon at hand. Gary Becker won a Nobel Prize in Economics for showing that other social disciplines could be made scientific by adopting an economic model.[8]

These prophets of science often held out utopian promises. If we knew the laws governing human behavior, they argued, we could use them to design the perfect society. Social engineering must work as well as electrical engineering—which is why the term "social engineering" is ideologically loaded. Since it would be intellectuals who would do the engineering—for who else would have mastered complex scientific disciplines?—it has taken little effort to persuade them that a social science really exists and that, if only people would give up this foolish democracy of the unlettered and leave matters to their intellectual betters, things would go swimmingly.

As Tolstoy writes in the epilogue to *War and Peace*, "it is natural and agreeable" for learned people "to think that the activity of their estate is the basis for the movement of all mankind" (1185; PSS 12:304), just as it is natural and agreeable for merchants, agriculturalists, and shoemakers to think that humanity depends on them; and if we have theories arguing for power to be given to intellectuals, but no theories arguing it should be given to shoemakers, that is only because shoemakers do not construct theories.

In our time, city planners—a utopian discipline deriving from seventeenth-century rationalism—wound up producing the monstrous projects that blighted our cities and caused misery for the unfortunate people supposedly helped.[9] For Russians, Petersburg—a legendarily inhospitable city founded on a swamp by Peter the Great's fiat—became, as the first city actually built according to utopian city-planning principles, a symbol of intellectual hubris and disastrous social planning.

On a still grander scale, Lenin and his followers were certain that when scientific economic planning replaced "the chaos of the market," great wonders could be achieved. The very nature of human life would be fundamentally transformed. People would no longer be controlled by nature, but would for the first time control it, a development that Engels, in his significantly titled essay "Socialism: Utopian and Scientific," referred to as the leap from the kingdom of necessity to the kingdom of freedom:

> Anarchy in social production is replaced by systematic, definite organization.... The whole sphere of the conditions of life which environ man, and which have hitherto ruled man, now comes under the dominion and control of man.... Man's own social organization, hitherto confronting him as a necessity imposed by nature and history, now becomes the result of his own free action. The extraneous objective forces that have hitherto governed history pass under the control of man himself.... It is the ascent of man from the kingdom of necessity to the kingdom of freedom.[10]

Life will be perfected when it is controlled by "scientific" (as opposed to merely "utopian") socialism. The *collective* human freedom of which Engels speaks arises only when people surrender their freedom as individuals so that enlightened thinkers can exert total power according to their scientific principles.

If *War and Peace* teaches anything, it is the folly of all such thinking. Whenever leaders, like Moscow mayor Rostopchin, try to direct historical events, they find that countless unsystematic decisions by individuals thwart their plans. After the fact, of course, historians pretend that what actually happened was what the leaders had ordered and select evidence supporting that conclusion while ignoring the rest. No matter what people wind up doing, someone will have advocated something like it, so the conclusion can always be fallaciously justified.

But real efficacy derives not from plans but from "swarm life," the actions of countless individuals acting on their own initiative with no thought of grand strategy. Historians argue about who had the brilliant idea of burning Moscow to the ground and depriving the French of a place to winter, but, according to Tolstoy, no one had such an idea. Individual people just left Moscow so as not to be under French control. A city built of wood, where fires constantly break out, is bound to burn down when foreign soldiers light campfires and the inhabitants have left. Or as Tolstoy writes, "Moscow was burned by its inhabitants, true; but, not by the inhabitants who stayed in it, but by those who left it" (898; PSS 11:358). Tolstoy memorably phrases the point later in the book: "In historical events what is most obvious is the prohibition against eating the fruit of the tree of knowledge. Only unconscious activity bears fruit, and a man who plays a role in a historical event never understands its significance. If he attempts to understand it, he is struck with fruitlessness" (944; PSS 12:14).[11]

By the same token, those who imagine they can plan an economy leap from the kingdom of productivity to the kingdom of penury. When Lenin put Marxist "scientific" principles into practice by abolishing money, seizing property, outlawing the market, and introducing a comprehensive economic plan, the result was a famine costing millions of lives. It seemed so simple, with the results scientifically guaranteed. As Trotsky recalled in 1924,

> In Lenin's "Theses on the Peace," written in early 1918, it says that "the triumph of socialism in Russia [required] a certain interval of time, *no less than a few months*" . . . this was not a slip of the pen. . . . I recall very clearly that in the first period . . . Lenin

invariably repeated that we shall have socialism in half a year and become the mightiest state.¹²

Every pseudoscience claims to be a science. All such claims should be rejected until a record of prediction, replication, and expanding knowledge comparable to those of acknowledged sciences is established.

If Russian history shows anything, it is that nothing causes more misery than the promise to abolish misery altogether. And nothing more frequently justifies the actions causing this misery, or more thoroughly distorts real understanding, than the false claim of "social science."

Tolstoy was certain that no such science could ever exist. Experience has repeatedly endorsed his view.

II. The Intelligentsia

When Tolstoy was publishing *War and Peace* (1865–69), a group to become famous as "the intelligentsia" had just formed. We get the word "intelligentsia" from Russian, where it was coined about 1860, but its Russian meaning was quite different from the way the term is usually used in English (or Russian) today. It emphatically did not mean educated people. It was possible for a barely literate person to be an *intelligent* (member of the intelligentsia) if he or she had the right opinions. If by "intellectual" we mean a person who thinks for himself or herself, instead of just accepting received opinion, then *intelligent* was close to its opposite. An *intelligent* accepted without question a set of prescribed, progressive—indeed, revolutionary—opinions.

In the narrow sense of the term, the intelligentsia was marked by three defining characteristics. First, an *intelligent* identified primarily *as* an intelligent, rather than, let us say, by social class, ethnic group, or profession. The *intelligent* owed his highest loyalty to the (revolutionary) intelligentsia, which is why in Dostoevsky's novel *Demons* (or *The Possessed*) a character asks whether it is wise to hire an engineer who, as an *intelligent*, believes in universal destruction. Because Tolstoy remained proud of his aristocratic forebears, and used his title "count," no one would have considered him a member of the intelligentsia.

Second, and most important, the *intelligentsia* shared a set of beliefs. These beliefs varied over time, but they always included a commitment to atheism, materialism, revolution, and some form of socialism or anarchism. Not only was Tolstoy no revolutionary, he even believed in God, so, again, no one would have considered him an *intelligent*; indeed, he would have been insulted by the mere suggestion.

Finally, an *intelligent* adopted a special way of living, which included sexual license (of a strictly regulated sort), dress codes, topics of conversation, occupation, habits, hygiene, and (bad) manners. To be sure, not any bad manners would do; they had to resemble those of the person the intelligentsia regarded as a sort of patron saint, the writer and critic Nikolai Chernyshevsky, whom Tolstoy dismissed as "that gentleman who smells of bedbugs."[13] Journals with Chernyshevsky's essays were read to tatters and treated as sacred texts, and his "novel" *What Is to Be Done?*—it is more accurately described as a piece of utopian fiction—established itself as the most widely read book of pre-revolutionary Russia.[14] Lenin adored it, and would allow no criticism of it. In the Soviet period, it was revered and taken as a model for socialist realism.

Chernyshevsky believed that a hard science of human behavior had been achieved. He was less clear on what that science was than on the fact of its existence, but its key tenets were clear enough. It was at root an extreme form of utilitarianism—Russians prided themselves on taking everything to extremes—presuming that there was only one motive for all human actions (the pursuit of pleasure), that those actions were necessary and absolutely predictable, and that mastery of the laws of social science would—within years, not decades—lead to a perfect utopia, to be established by a revolution.

Since everything happens by necessity, Chernyshevsky reasoned, "one ought not to blame people for anything at any cost."[15] "It is now clear to us," he continued, "that everything depends exclusively on circumstances. . . . Before you accuse someone, perceive first whether he is guilty of what you accuse him or whether circumstances and social customs are responsible."[16] They always are.

Chernyshevsky expressed utter contempt for the realist novel, the genre that Tolstoy valued above all else, because novels presume that human nature is complex and that each individual is unlike all others. On the contrary, Chernyshevsky explained, "you have practically reached the limits of human wisdom when you become convinced of the simple truth that every person is exactly like every other one."[17] The differences novelists discern either do not exist or are too trivial to matter.

> Only try to begin to look at people in order to verify whether a man who at first glance seems different from others really differs in anything important . . . every man is like every other and . . . each is made up precisely like the other. . . . The differences seem important only because they appear on the surface and strike your eye, but beneath the visible, apparent differences is hidden a total identity.
>
> And indeed, why should a person really prove to be a contradiction of all nature's laws? In nature cedars and hyssops feed and bloom, elephants and mice move and eat, are angry and glad according to the same laws. . . . If we take two healthy people of the same age and same temperament, the pulse of one will naturally

beat a little faster and a little stronger than the other's. But is that difference great?[18]

Gary Becker would have no trouble with this picture of uniformity. What irritated Tolstoy was not only the denial of human complexity, but especially the smug certainty with which Chernyshevsky, and other *intelligents*, uttered "the simple truth" they held to be "the summit of human wisdom."

When Pierre, one of the heroes of *War and Peace*, delivers his speech to the Freemasons, he discovers a truth the exact opposite of the spurious one Chernyshevsky thought so obvious. Pierre wants his audience not only to agree with him but also to understand his points exactly as he does. Pierre is a utopian, and like all utopians, he seeks a truth as an unambiguous as mathematics, for how could one create a world perfect for all people if they cannot even understand the simplest ideas the same way? And so Pierre is most distressed not by those who disagree with him but by those who agree.

> Pierre was struck for the first time at this meeting by the infinite variety of human minds, which makes it so that no truth presents itself to two people in the same way. Even those members who seemed to be on his side understood him in their own fashion, with limitations and alterations which Pierre could not agree to, since his main need consisted precisely in conveying his thought to others exactly as he understood it himself. (436; PSS 10:175)

When, at the end of novel, Pierre at last attains wisdom, the "endless variety" that so dismayed him now delights him. He recognizes "the impossibility of changing a person's opinion with words" and acknowledges "the possibility for every person thinking, feeling, and looking at things in his own way. . . . This legitimate individuality of each person, which formerly had troubled and irritated Pierre, now constituted the basis of the sympathy and interest he took in people" (1107; PSS 12:209).

III. Discarding the Telescope

Throughout the novel Pierre has sought an indubitable system capable of thoroughly explaining the world: the equivalent of the social sciences of Tolstoy's own time. Assuming that knowledge to be valuable must be absolutely certain, like mathematics or physics, he alternates between confidence that he has discovered such knowledge and despair that it cannot be attained. There is no middle ground. It never occurs to Pierre that there might be such a thing as wisdom, based on experience sensitively considered, which does not promise certainty. At one point Masonic numerology persuades him that he is the person destined from all eternity to kill Napoleon, and he stays in French-occupied Moscow to accomplish this destiny. If this numerology seems ridiculous to the reader, Tolstoy suggests, it is at bottom no less so than other putatively certain explanatory systems. They are just numerologies we take for sciences.

As the novel ends, Pierre attains the wisdom that had eluded him. He appreciates particular moments and people, not grand systems. Previously he had seen in everything near and comprehensible

> only the limited, the petty, the humdrum, the meaningless. He had armed himself with a mental telescope and gazed into the distance where the petty and the humdrum, disappearing in the distant mists, had seemed to him great and infinite, only because it was not clearly visible.... Now he had learned to see the great... in everything, and therefore... naturally abandoned the telescope he had been looking through until then over people's heads, and joyfully contemplated the ever-changing, ever-great, unfathomable, and infinite life around him. (1104; PSS 12:205–206)

Wisdom consists not in seeing the world as fundamentally simple and comprehensible, the way the intelligentsia did, but as infinite and ultimately, though not totally, unfathomable. It requires not the application of supposedly infallible systems but a proper orientation to a world of radical contingency. The wisest general in the novel, Kutuzov, has acquired such wisdom, and the novel's other hero, Prince Andrei, gradually learns it.

IV. Appreciating Contingency

Andrei begins the novel holding two appealing beliefs that prove mistaken. Like his friend Pierre, he presumes that what really matters in life is not the ordinary and prosaic but the extraordinary and dramatic. Like other young men, he is therefore fascinated with Napoleon, a grand figure supposedly illustrating what can be achieved by willpower, courage, strength of character, and intelligence. Andrei possesses all these qualities to a supreme degree, and so imagines that he can be the Napoleon to conquer Napoleon. With that goal in mind, and to escape the petty society life to which his charming but limited wife is addicted, he enlists.

Andrei also believes, as do almost all the generals he encounters, in a science of warfare. Tolstoy means this putative science to stand for any possible social science. The reasoning the generals use to justify it, and to explain away disconfirmations, characterizes all social sciences.

On the face of it, it would seem that of all human activities, battle would make the worst material for a science. After all, would it not make a difference if a stray bullet killed Napoleon or some other prominent general? Or if some chance event induced panic in a key platoon at an important moment? Before Tolstoy, all descriptions of battle took the form of neat narratives—the left flank advanced, the third column marched—like a description of a chess game (a common comparison). Tolstoy shocked his readers by describing battle as sheer chaos where nobody knows what is going on.[19]

When Andrei attends the council of war before the battle of Austerlitz, he listens to generals present conflicting plans, all derived from a supposed science of warfare. Although they cannot agree on what that infallible science prescribes, they are all sure that they can "foresee all contingencies" (a phrase repeated in *War and Peace*). Even if the enemy did something we have not specified, one general smugly maintains, "he was only saving us a great deal of trouble, and all orders, to the smallest detail, remain the same" (263; PSS 9:322). One must have enormous confidence in a plan to be sure not the "minutest detail" could be changed!

The wise commander in chief Kutuzov presides over such nonsense only because the emperor, too, believes in the generals' "science." Kutuzov dozes off. At last he calls a halt to the proceedings:

> "Gentlemen, the disposition for tomorrow, for today even (because it's already past twelve), cannot be changed now," he said. "You have heard it, and we will all do our duty. And there's nothing more important before a battle . . ." (he paused) "than a good night's sleep." (263–264; PSS 9:322)

If there were a science of battle, and if success were a matter of implementing the right plan, then it would pay to stay up late to get the plan right. But in a world of radical uncertainty, where unforeseeable dangers and opportunities constantly present themselves, what matters most is reacting appropriately on the instant, a capacity that depends on alertness. That is why Kutuzov recommends a good night's sleep.

Tolstoy presents us with two radically different worldviews. One sees life as fundamentally simple, predictable, and plannable. This is the worldview of social science and social planners generally. From planning a battle to planning an economy is but a step. The other worldview appreciates the radical contingency of things. Some loose principles obtain, "on the whole and for the most part," and we may arrive at a few guiding but not infallible rules of thumb.[20]

But we must be humble about what we know. It is unwise to commit ourselves unreservedly to any unchangeable plan. We must be able to adjust to the unforeseen and unforeseeable. We need wisdom as well as knowledge and alertness as well as preparation.

In one remarkable scene, Tolstoy shows us the sort of thinking and action that actually makes a difference. Another of the novel's heroes, the line officer Nikolai Rostov, observes approaching French dragoons climbing a hill. He realizes—though he could not say how he knows—that the position they are in makes the French momentarily vulnerable to an attack. Rostov "sensed intuitively that if he were to strike the French dragoons with his hussars now, they would not hold out; but if he were to strike, it would have to be now, at this moment, otherwise it would be too late" (652–653; PSS 11:63). He obeys his instinct, charges, and the result is what he had anticipated. "Rostov did not know himself how and why he was doing it. He did it all as he did at the hunt, not thinking, not reflecting. He saw that the dragoons . . . would not hold, and he knew there was only one moment, which would not return if he missed it" (653; PSS 11:64).

No advance plan could anticipate such a moment, and no general in central command would be in a position to notice such a localized, fleeting opportunity. Moments like this decide a battle. In such circumstances, generals matter less than trained line officers, who, if they are alert, can take advantage of opportunities invisible to the central command. The best generals, like Kutuzov or Bagration, recognize the importance of good line officers and do everything they can to enable and encourage them.

Something similar explains why the Soviet economy failed. Managers, the economic counterpart to line officers, could not adjust the plan they were given without permission from Moscow, which could take years, and so valuable opportunities were missed and countless unforeseen obstacles could not be sidestepped.

The late Russian émigré economist Aron Katsenelinboigen (1927–2005), who had served on the Soviet Union's central economic planning committee before concluding that central plans could not work, liked to pose a question: evolution has designed many remarkable structures—think of the liver—but has never built a quadruped with wheels. Anyone contemplating a trip to California knows the advantage that wheels have over legs, so why did evolution let such an opportunity slip? Wheels, after all, are a lot simpler than livers!

The answer is that the world is not paved. Imagine a wheeled antelope escaping a predator and encountering a log that wheels cannot get over. Wheels are more efficient in restricted, predictable environments, like carefully maintained highways, but, precisely because of their specialization, they are much less flexible. They are less capable of negotiating unforeseen obstacles. The fact that quadrupeds all have legs instead of wheels therefore testifies to the inescapable uncertainty of things. If the world were simple and predictable, Katsenelinboigen liked to say, antelopes would have wheels and central planning would work. He liked to cite passages in *War and Peace* to illustrate this point.[21]

Andrei comes to recognize the correctness of Kutuzov's view. Experience has taught him that contingency reigns and experience matters. In battle, in social affairs, and in life generally, one requires not abstract systematic theory but practical wisdom. No social science is possible. At his last council of war, before the battle of Borodino, Andrei reflects: "What science can there be in a matter in which, as in any practical matter, nothing can be determined and everything depends on countless circumstances, the significance of which is determined at a certain moment, and no one knows when that moment will come?" (643–644; PSS 11:53).

As in any practical matter: Tolstoy means this insight to apply not just to a science of battle but to any conceivable social science that might ever be proposed.

The night before Borodino, Pierre visits Andrei on the battlefield and repeats the conventional view that a good general can "foresee all contingencies." He is surprised to hear Andrei call such an opinion nonsense. Chance, contingency, and choice are all real and cannot be subsumed by any science or plan. "What faces us tomorrow?" Andrei asks. "A hundred million diverse chances, which will be decided on the instant by whether we run or they run, whether this man or that man is killed" (773; PSS 11:208). *This man or that* man: obviously no plan could foresee the path of countless bullets. *On the instant*: for those who believe a deterministic science of events is possible, each moment is exhaustively determined by preceding moments. Nothing is left to "the instant." But Andrei sees a world in which presentness matters. Each moment has more than one possible outcome. Suspense is real. Events can either be or not be. Play the tape over, and the same circumstances will end differently. The greater the uncertainty, the more a vision allowing for the unexpected is needed. We need not an impossible science, but wisdom.

Tolstoy expressed contempt for intellectual elites and their tendency to credit themselves with knowledge that nobody can have. In the epilogue to *War and Peace*, Tolstoy describes how historians of the Napoleonic Wars—much like historians and journalists of our own day—love to pass judgment on people of the past. They loved to condemn those who made up what they called "the reaction," a pejorative word for those who did not see the world as do the historians who judge them. "All the well-known people of that time, from Aleksander and Napoleon to Mme de Staël, Photius, Schelling, Fichte, Chateaubriand, and others, pass before their severe judgment and are either acquitted or condemned, depending on whether they contributed to *progress* or *the reaction*" (1129; PSS 12:235).

These historians imagine that, unlike the historical figures they examine, their judgments do not reflect their own time and prejudices but are objective, like a science. In this they are mistaken. All that their high-handed judgments really mean is that Alexander and his contemporaries "did not have those views of the good of humanity now possessed by a professor who from his youth has been taken up with learning, that is, with reading books, attending lectures, and copying things from these books and lectures into a notebook" (1130; PSS 12:236). Their own habits and occupations—the conditions of an academic—shape their opinions as much as the conditions in which battles are fought shape generals' opinions or the conditions in which trade is conducted shape those of merchants.

Intellectuals readily accept pseudosciences conferring importance on themselves. If anything, they do so more readily today than ever before, much as intellectuals assign still greater privilege to present opinions. Shakespeare and George Washington pass before the stern tribunal of associate professors and National Public Radio anchors. But real thinkers know that, far from assuming the correctness of present opinions, or the views of one's social group or profession, one should be especially skeptical of them precisely because it is so "natural and agreeable" to see what makes us feel morally and intellectually superior.

The more our beliefs flatter us, the more likely we are deceiving ourselves. The real thinker is the one who turns his skepticism on himself and on the groups with which he identifies. That is what it means to think like Kutuzov or Tolstoy.

Notes

1. On the Russian intelligentsia's insistence on a hard social science, as certain and capable of prediction as physics and astronomy, see Gary Saul Morson, *Wonder Confronts Certainty: Russian Writers on the Timeless Questions and Why Their Answers Matter* (Cambridge, MA: Harvard University Press, 2023). On the idea of a hard social science in Western thought since Newton, see Gary Saul Morson, *Prosaics and Other Provocations: Empathy, Open Time, and the Novel* (Boston: Academic Studies Press, 2013), 58–67. For a critique of the pretensions of modern economics to scientific status, see Gary Saul Morson and Morton Schapiro, *Cents and Sensibility: What*

Economics Can Learn from the Humanities (Princeton, NJ: Princeton University Press, 2017).

2. The term "moral Newtonians" belongs to the great intellectual historian Élie Halévy, *The Growth of Philosophical Radicalism*, trans. Mary Morris (Boston: Beacon Press, 1955), 6.
3. Aristotle, "On Interpretation," in *The Basic Works of Aristotle*, ed. Richard McKeon (New York: Random House, 1941), 48–49.
4. Aristotle, "On Interpretation," 47–48.
5. See Stephen Toulmin, *Cosmopolis: The Hidden Agenda of Modernity* (New York: Free Press, 1990), and Toulmin, *Return to Reason* (Cambridge, MA: Harvard University Press, 2001).
6. Bronislaw Malinowski, *A Scientific Theory of Culture and Other Essays* (Chapel Hill: University of North Carolina Press, 1944), 8.
7. Claude Lévi-Strauss, *Structural Anthropology*, trans. Claire Jacobson and Brooke Grundfest Schoepf (New York: Basic Books, 1963), 58.
8. See Gary S. Becker, *The Economic Approach to Human Behavior* (Chicago: University of Chicago Press, 1976).
9. For the classic critique of city-planning utopianism and its effects, see Jane Jacobs, *The Death and Life of Great American Cities* (New York: Modern Library, 1993).
10. Friedrich Engels, "Socialism: Utopian and Scientific," in Karl Marx and Friedrich Engels, *Basic Writings on Politics and Philosophy*, ed. Lewis S. Feuer (New York: Anchor Books, 1959), 109.
11. For a recent account of what happened during the Napoleonic Wars and the burning of Moscow, see Alexander Mikaberidze, *Kutuzov: A Life in War and Peace* (New York: Oxford University Press, 2022).
12. Richard Pipes, *The Russian Revolution* (New York: Knopf, 1990), 675. In Pipes's chapter "War Communism" (671–713), he notes that after the experiment failed so disastrously, Lenin started calling it "war communism" as if it had been intended as a temporary measure, but this piece of hindsight contradicts the facts, as Lenin and Trotsky well knew.
13. Or "stinking bug"; see Evgenii Lampert, *Sons against Fathers: Studies in Russian Radicalism and Revolution* (Oxford: Clarendon Press, 1965), 114.
14. On the enormous influence of Chernyshevsky's book on morals, life, and manners of the intelligentsia, see Irina Paperno, *Chernyshevsky and the Age of Realism: A Study in the Semiotics of Behavior* (Stanford, CA: Stanford University Press, 1988).

15. Nikolai G. Chernyshevsky, "The Russian at the Rendez-vous," in *Belinsky, Chernyshevsky and Dobrolyubov: Selected Criticism*, ed. Ralph E. Matlaw (New York: Dutton, 1962), 115.
16. Chernyshevsky, "The Russian at the Rendez-vous," 119.
17. Chernyshevsky, "The Russian at the Rendez-vous," 118.
18. Chernyshevsky, "The Russian at the Rendez-vous," 117.
19. Historians have since come to describe battle as Tolstoy did. See the classic by John Keegan, *The Face of Battle* (New York: Penguin, 1978). In Stendhal's *The Charterhouse of Parma*, Waterloo is described as chaotic, but only because it is perceived from the perspective of the naive observer, Fabrizio. For Tolstoy, Fabrizio was perceiving things as they really are.
20. That was the argument of Karl von Clausewitz's classic *On War*. Clausewitz briefly appears as a character in *War and Peace*.
21. I heard this parable directly from Katsenelinboigen when we were colleagues at the University of Pennsylvania in the late 1970s and early 1980s.

Works Cited

Aristotle. *The Basic Works of Aristotle*. Edited by Richard McKeon. New York: Random House, 1941.

Becker, Gary S. *The Economic Approach to Human Behavior*. Chicago: University of Chicago Press, 1976.

Chernyshevsky, Nikolai G. "The Russian at the Rendez-vous." *Belinsky, Chernyshevsky, and Dobrolyubov: Selected Criticism*. Edited by Ralph E. Matlaw, 95–129. New York: Dutton, 1962.

Clausewitz, Carl von. *On War*. Translated by J. J. Graham. New York: Barnes & Noble, 1966.

Engels, Friedrich. "Socialism: Utopian and Scientific." Karl Marx and Friedrich Engels, *Basic Writings on Politics and Philosophy*. Edited by Lewis S. Feuer, 68–110. New York: Anchor Books, 1959.

Halévy, Élie. *The Growth of Philosophical Radicalism*. Translated by Mary Morris. Boston: Beacon Press, 1955.

Jacobs, Jane. *The Death and Life of Great American Cities*. New York: Modern Library, 1993.

Keegan, John. *The Face of Battle*. New York: Penguin, 1978.

Lampert, Evgeniĭ. *Sons against Fathers: Studies in Russian Radicalism and Revolution*. Oxford: Clarendon Press, 1965.

Lévi-Strauss, Claude. *Structural Anthropology*. Translated by Claire Jacobson and Brooke Grundfest Schoepf. New York: Basic Books, 1963.

Malinowski, Bronislaw. *A Scientific Theory of Culture and Other Essays*. Chapel Hill: University of North Carolina Press, 1944.

Mikaberidze, Alexander. *Kutuzov: A Life in War and Peace*. New York: Oxford University Press, 2022.

Morson, Gary Saul. *Prosaics and Other Provocations: Empathy, Open Time, and the Novel*. Boston: Academic Studies Press, 2013.

Morson, Gary Saul. *Wonder Confronts Certainty: Russian Writers on the Timeless Questions and Why Their Answers Matter*. Cambridge, MA: Harvard University Press, 2023.

Morson, Gary Saul, and Morton Schapiro. *Cents and Sensibility: What Economics Can Learn from the Humanities*. Princeton, NJ: Princeton University Press, 2017.

Paperno, Irina. *Chernyshevsky and the Age of Realism: A Study in the Semiotics of Behavior*. Stanford, CA: Stanford University Press, 1988.

Pipes, Richard. *The Russian Revolution*. New York: Knopf, 1990.

Toulmin, Stephen. *Cosmopolis: The Hidden Agenda of Modernity*. New York: Free Press, 1990.

Toulmin, Stephen. *Return to Reason*. Cambridge, MA: Harvard University Press, 2001.

3
War and Peace as a Historical Novel

Marie-Pierre Rey

As much a literary monument as a memorial monument, *War and Peace* (published between 1867 and 1869, initially in the form of chapters in the *Russian Messenger*) belongs among those works that are extremely rare in the history of literature: works that can federate a whole people, serving as a primordial if not absolute reference lasting for decades and even centuries, but also constituting a major and universal frame of reference for many other readers who are foreign to this nation. Due to the spiritual speculations that run through the text, the atemporal character of the sentiments, internal conflicts, and psychological states of the multitude of its characters, and the fundamental questions it raises about good and evil, violence, morality, and passion, *War and Peace* touches human life in general, both individual and social, at its most essential.

The novel, of rarely matched density, is teeming with the interwoven destinies of more than five hundred characters; it traces in this fresco, spanning ten years from 1805 to 1815, the fate of Russia as a whole, from the first advances against Napoleon in 1805 through to the throes of 1812, encompassing the years of peace brought about by the Treaty of Tilsit that lasted from 1807 to 1812. Soon after its publication, the novel echoed the crucial historical process that in 1812 gave birth to Russian national consciousness, thanks as much to its outstanding literary qualities as to its subject: the resistance of Russia to the invader. It did not take long for the novel to become the object of a cult and of a myth that was as much literary as national. Generations upon generations of

Russians in the tsarist empire, then in the USSR, and nowadays in post-Soviet Russia, grew up reading the novel, studied it carefully in school, and finally acquired their "knowledge" of 1812 through Tolstoy's narrative and approach.

At first sight, this finding does not seem to give rise to reservations. As soon as one starts reading *War and Peace*, various signs indicate the omnipresence of historical references and documentation in the novel. The work contains a chronology that is both broad and precise; it mixes fictional characters and real ones (like Kutuzov, Tsar Alexander, Barclay de Tolly, Michaud, etc.); it realistically and plausibly describes a number of military episodes, ranging from the great battles of 1812 to lesser "affairs." But does this realism, this claim to the reality and materiality of historical facts, make *War and Peace* a "trustworthy" work from a historical viewpoint? In a word, did Tolstoy act as a historian, or should we be cautious about his historical discourse and assertions?

To answer these questions, this chapter is divided into three sections. The first goes back to the origins of the work and the sources that Tolstoy used to write his novel. The second analyzes Tolstoy's historical methodology and examines how and why the novel might be considered a reliable source for historians. And the third section balances this view by shedding light on historical distortions and exaggerations that attest to a subjective, passionate, and committed writing about 1812.

Let us start by going back to the origins of the book, its context, and the sources that Tolstoy employed.

I. Origins, Context, and Sources

In 1862, Tolstoy had a plan to write a vast opus on the Decembrists of 1825, of which "War and Peace" would have been the first part. The novel bears the traces of this initial project: the epilogue that takes place in 1820 serves, in effect, as a transition and bridge to what would have been the story of the Decembrists, presumably featuring the children of the main protagonists of *War and Peace*. But this plan was gradually abandoned as the novel assumed greater breadth.

In preparing to write the novel, Tolstoy conducted documentary research in libraries as well as in the archives of the Russian state. He also had recourse to some private archives owned by the great aristocratic families, starting with his own family's records. Born in August 1828, Lev Tolstoy was the son of Countess Maria Sergeevna Volkonskaya, herself the daughter of Field Marshal Nikolai Sergeevich Volkonsky (1753–1821), who was promoted to Kutuzov's aide-de-camp in 1805, then, after 1812, became part of the retinue of Emperor Alexander I; Volkonsky would be depicted in the novel as Prince Nikolai Bolkonsky. Moreover, the writer's mother was the wife of Count Nikolai Ilyich Tolstoy, himself a veteran of the Russian campaign. Two other family members took part, directly or remotely, in the Napoleonic Wars. Foremost was Count Piotr Alexandrovich Tolstoy (1761–1844) who, having served under Suvorov in the wars against Poland and the Ottoman Empire, was made general in 1797, would be sent to Paris as ambassador in 1807 (after the Peace of Tilsit), and would later become the governor of St. Petersburg and of Kronstadt, from 1828 until his death in 1844. And finally, there was Alexander Ivanovich Tolstoy (1772–1857), who, though from a more distant branch of the family, would inherit titles, the property, and the name of his uncle Ivan Andreyev Osterman (1725–1811), last in the Osterman line. Osterman-Tolstoy, who became illustrious at the young age of eighteen in the battle of Izmail, where he served under Kutuzov, later distinguished himself while facing the Napoleonic troops at Charnova in 1807. A brilliant general, he was decorated for bravery at the battles of Pułtusk (December 1806) and Eylau (February 1807) and fought in 1812, under the command of Barclay de Tolly, in the battles of Ostrovno (in July) and of Moscow (in September), then in 1813 in the battles of Bautzen (May) and of Kulm (August), where he lost his left arm. All these officers had left correspondences and private documents from which Tolstoy drew generously.

Unable to cite all the sources that Tolstoy utilized, I offer merely a few examples to illustrate the varied and heterogeneous nature of his documentation. A lot of materials directly come from the Russian state archives. This is the case, for example, of the letter sent by Alexander I to Kutuzov after the battle of Tarutino, in which the emperor reproaches the field marshal for the loss of Moscow and the threat that now hovers over St. Petersburg (992–993; PSS 12:72–73). From the military archives of the Russian state, Tolstoy also obtained French documents, such as the proclamations that were written by Napoleon in Moscow and addressed either to Muscovites or else to peasants in the surrounding areas (1003–1005; PSS 12:85–88), or the long letter from Berthier to Napoleon written on November 9 and intercepted by Russian spies, which attests to the sufferings of the Grande Armée's stampeding retreat (1067; PSS 12:161). Moreover, Tolstoy did not just resort to very well-known military sources; he also consulted other kinds of documents less commonly drawn from that I myself used while preparing my own book on the Russian campaign.[1] We can mention here a police report written by a district "commissar" assigned by Napoleon to maintain law and order in the holy city that had been deserted by the Russians. While I found the last name of this commissar that figures at the bottom of the document, Tolstoy does not mention him, merely asserting: "Here is what the army officers reported:[2] . . . 'Nothing new, except that the soldiers allow themselves to steal and loot. 9 October'" (1007; PSS 12:90).[3]

In the novel, the archival sources are often cited in their original language. Thus, at the very beginning of the third volume dedicated to the premises of the conflict and its beginnings, the novelist cites extensively—and in French—the letter sent by Alexander I to Napoleon on the morning of June 26, 1812.[4] The letter asks Napoleon to withdraw his troops so that, as Alexander writes, "I will regard what has occurred as canceled, and an agreement between us will be possible" (613; PSS 11:15).[5] Documentary sources are sometimes integrated in the form of extracts that are mingled with fiction: this is the case with the conversations, well known to historians, that took place between Napoleon and Balashov, who was charged with bringing to the French emperor a final letter from the tsar. Reading it, Napoleon complained in French about Alexander's "duplicity" and missed opportunities: "All that he would have owed to my friendship.... Ah, what a fine reign, what a fine reign! What a fine reign the reign of the emperor Alexander might have been!" (621–622; PS 11:26).[6]

The novel also presents extracts from sources found in private holdings. For example, there is a verbatim record of the conversation between Alexander I and General Michaud, (derived from the latter's memoirs), where he brought the news of the uncertain outcome of the battle of Borodino; in Tolstoy, the text (in French) is mixed with subjective notations (in Russian)—a stylistic device that is frequently used in the novel:

> "But if ever it were written in the decrees of divine Providence,"[7] he said, raising to heaven his beautiful, meek eyes, shining with emotion,[8] "that my dynasty must cease to reign on the throne of my ancestors, then, after exhausting all the means in my power, I will let my beard grow to here"[9] (the sovereign put his hand to the middle of his chest)[10] "and I will go to eat potatoes with the least of my peasants rather than put my signature to the shame of my country and of my people, whose sacrifices I know how to appreciate!"[11] (942–943; PSS 12:12)

The extracts also include French sources; for example, the *Memorial of St. Helena* (whose first edition dates from 1823) is quoted in the second part of volume 3 (chap. 28), where Napoleon looks back on the Russian campaign and mourns the failure of the European dream, which he thought was stolen from him. Some primary sources are also covered in an indirect way; sometimes they are barely mentioned but instead integrated into the narrator's thought, as when Tolstoy alludes to the Berezina: "It was senseless to wish to take prisoner the emperor, the kings, the dukes—people whose capture would have hampered the actions of the Russians in the highest degree, as was recognized by the most skillful diplomats of that time (Joseph de Maistre and others)" (1072; PSS 12:167).

The novel also relies on quotations extracted from French memoir writers and historians. Several times the writings of Baron Fain are mobilized. Thiers is also invoked, but in this case it is usually to contradict the author of *L'Histoire du consulat et de l'Empire*. For example, we read from Tolstoy's pen:

> In the military respect, the brilliant plan of campaign, of which Thiers says that his genius had never imagined anything more profound, more skillful and more admirable[12] and concerning which Thiers, getting into polemics with M. Fain, proves that the drawing up of this brilliant plan should be dated not to the fourth but to the fifteenth of October,—this plan never was and never could have been carried out, because nothing in it is close to reality. (1005–1006; PSS 12:88)

Similarly, he does not hesitate to argue with witnesses who had become historians of the campaign, for example criticizing the work of Alexander Mihailovsky-Danilevsky.[13]

Finally, even at the heart of his fiction, documentary sources and echoes of historic incidents find a place: Natasha attends a mass in which the Metropolitan pronounces a homily that he actually gave.

Thus, *War and Peace* appears as well and truly founded on a solid scientific substrate, and this solid and varied base underpinned the writing of what seems a chronicle of historical scope.

II. A Reliable Chronicle of Historical Scope

To support this assertion, the prime evidence concerns the unfolding of events, many of which are precisely dated and presented as a professional historian might do: "On the 29th of May, Napoleon left Dresden, where he had spent three weeks surrounded by a court of princes, dukes, kings and even one emperor" (607; PSS 11:8).

Similarly, we read, "On the same day which Napoleon gave orders to cross the Niemen . . . Alexander spent the evening at Bennigsen's house at the ball given by his adjutant generals" (610; PSS 11:12). Discussing the mission entrusted by Napoleon to his faithful Balashov—charged with going to the French emperor for a final round of negotiations—Tolstoy mentions precisely that he left "on the fourteenth of June, at two o'clock in the morning" (613; PSS 11:15).

We also note Tolstoy's desire to explain, in the manner of a professional historian, one detail or another that might escape his reader, not using footnotes but narrative asides. Last, to support his claims, he relies on cartographic documents; he even includes a map of the battle of Borodino that he himself drew after visiting the site.

To give more depth to his text, and to "incarnate" the novel, Tolstoy draws a lot of morals and portraits that are faithful to the available sources. In Vilnius, when Napoleon had just crossed the Niemen and is getting ready to receive Balashov, he is described in line with the painting and engravings that have come down to us:

> He was in a dark blue uniform, open over a white waistcoat which went down over his round stomach, white buckskins stretched tight over the fat haunches of his short legs, and jackboots. His short hair had obviously just been brushed, but one strand hung loose over the middle of his wide forehead. His plump white neck stood out sharply against the black collar of his uniform; he smelled of cologne. (619: PSS 11:22)

Regarding Kutuzov, on the eve of the battle of Borodino, he is portrayed "in a long coat on an immensely fat body, with a somewhat rounded back, an uncovered white head, a blinded white eye in a puffy face" (764; PSS 11:197). However, the portraits are not limited to the most famous characters of the Napoleonic Wars. Tolstoy gives a striking portrait of General Ludwig Pfuel: "Pfuel was of small stature, very thin, but broad-boned, of course, robust build, with broad lips and sharp shoulder blades. His face was very wrinkled, his eyes deep-set" (639; PSS 11:47).

These deftly sketched portraits enable us to visualize the men of 1812. Generally speaking, they resemble the John Dawe's paintings that were exhibited in St. Petersburg in the war gallery of the Hermitage: undoubtedly these works inspired the novelist.

Historical facts—known and quite real, from the most anodyne to the most important—are meticulously narrated in order to seem to be the "truth."

Describing Napoleon on the morning of June 11 (June 24 in the Gregorian calendar), when the Grande Armée was preparing to cross the Niemen, Tolstoy says that he "changed into a Polish uniform" (607; PSS 11:8), and a few pages later, he alludes to the forged assignats that Napoleon ordered fabricated and distributed clandestinely in the all-Russian empire. However, the descriptions of places, battles, and military operations stand out in the novel's narrative history. It is not that these descriptions are always very long, nor are they foregrounded: the battle of Smolensk that raged on the fourth and fifth of August (sixteenth and seventeenth in the Gregorian calendar), entailing the death and disappearance of almost twelve thousand combatants on the Russian side and ten thousand from the Grande Armée—to which should be added hundreds of dead civilians—is barely mentioned. By contrast, the battle of Borodino is at the forefront of the novel. Appearing several times, it assumes crucial importance: one of the key characters, Prince Andrei, is severely wounded at Borodino and a few weeks later dies from his wounds. But while the description of his behavior during the military operations is reminiscent of Stendhal's account of Fabrice del Dongo in *The Charter-House of Parma* (which is being echoed by the admiring Tolstoy), the battle itself is the subject of a precise and almost clinical description, which again might have been written by a historian:

> The main action of the battle of Borodino took place over a stretch of seven thousand feet between Borodino and Bagration's *flèches*. (Outside that stretch, on one side, there was a show of Uvarov's cavalry in the middle of the day, and on the other side, beyond Utitsa, there was a clash between Poniatowski and Tuchkov; but these were separate and weak actions compared with what was happening in the middle of the battlefield.) On the field between Borodino and the *flèches*, by the woods, on a stretch open and visible from both sides, the main action of the battle took place in the most simple, artless way. (798; PSS 11:239)

Apart from military operations properly speaking, Tolstoy includes a good number of the key episodes of the 1812 war: he describes, quite credibly and respecting the sources, the council held at Fili that decided to abandon Moscow; he highlights the extent of pilfering and looting that undermines the coherence of the army; he salutes the birth of the partisan movement; he pays particular attention to the mood of the troops; he refers to the bad blood between Kutuzov and Bennigsen, and he emphasizes the asymmetric nature of the conflict.

In order to solidly anchor his text in the reality of the year of 1812 and better express it, Tolstoy largely resorts to the language of Molière. It has been estimated that about 2.5 percent of the whole text is in French in the novel,[14] echoing the fact that at that time French was dominant among the aristocratic elites.[15] This was no longer the case when Tolstoy was writing his novel, which complicates the understanding of the text and gives it a foreign if not exotic air; but for the writer, this bias was voluntary and unavoidable.

In the novel, French is, first and foremost, the language of oral communication between Russian and French military men and diplomats and the official language of the French-Russian and Russian-French written correspondences.[16] It is also the chosen language of the highest aristocratic elites, and its mastery is directly correlated to the social position of the individual who speaks it. The very pure, "irreproachable" French,[17] as "spoken by Voltaire," emanates from the representatives of the highest social strata, embodied by Kutuzov or Prince Bolkonsky, while the small provincial nobility or the modest military nobility speak it with mistakes.[18] This is, for example, the funny French language spoken by General Miloradovich:

> "God be with you, General," said the sovereign.
> "By my faith, Sire, we will do that what which will be within our possibility, Sire!"[19] he replied merrily, nevertheless calling up mocking smiles among the gentlemen of the suite with his bad French. (277; PSS 9:340)

From this point of view, Tolstoy reminds us that in the first quarter of the nineteenth century, French was clearly used to distinguish oneself as much as to identify oneself within a group.

Finally, as a professional historian, Tolstoy does not hesitate to take a position on polemical issues, rejecting certain historical interpretations in favor of iconoclastic positions. According to him, for example to use the Imperial Guard or not (a question still disputed until today among historians!) would have changed nothing at Borodino; and here, he is quite sarcastic about the French emperor: "Napoleon enters Moscow after the brilliant victory *de la Moskowa*; there can be no doubt of the victory, since the battlefield remains with the French" (1001; PSS 12:82).[20]

This ironic remark is no exception in the novel. There are many others, which combined with historical exaggerations and distortions, form part of a subjective, passionate, and committed representation of 1812.

III. A Subjective, Passionate, and Committed Writing

Among Tolstoy's historical exaggerations and distortions, some of them were very early spotted and vigorously criticized by the writer's contemporaries.

While *War and Peace* quickly enjoyed major success, several veterans of 1812 took it to task,[21] among them Prince Pyotr Andreevich Viazemsky (1792–1878),[22] Avraam Sergeevich Norov (1795–1869), a philologist, historian, and member of the State Council who as a young man fought at Borodino and lost a leg there, and Parmen Semionovich Demenkov, the author of *Zametki veterana 1812 goda*. The three men's objections are relevant; for them the text does not pay tribute to the courage of combatants, does not do justice to the obstinacy of the soldiers, and invents, exaggerates, or even caricaturizes various anecdotes. Norov felt particularly insulted by the episode in which Tolstoy's Kutuzov, while assuming supreme command of the Russian army at Tsarevo-Zaimishche, is engrossed in reading a cheap French novel by Madame de Genlis. According to Norov, this was "a totally improbable and inappropriate detail," as the veteran testified:

> Before and after Borodino, all of us, from Kutuzov down to the last artillery lieutenant, like myself, burned with the same lofty and sacred fire of patriotism; we regarded our calling as some kind of religious rite; I do not know how comrades-in-arms would treat someone who would have among his belongings a book for light-reading, especially a French one, such as a novel by Madame de Genlis.[23]

For his part, while Viazemsky accepted along with Tolstoy that at Borodino, from the ground, nobody saw or understood very much, and that the battle had nothing heroic about it, he was totally revulsed by Tolstoy's tale of the arrival of Alexander in Moscow in July 1812. The novelist wrote:

> The dinner was already over, the sovereign stood up and, finishing a biscuit, went out to the balcony. The people, with Petya among them, rushed to the balcony.
> "Angel! Father! Hurrah! Dearest!" cried the people and Petya. . . . A rather large piece of the biscuit that the sovereign was holding broke off, fell onto the railing of the balcony, and from there to the ground. A cabby in a jerkin, who was standing closest of all, rushed to this piece of biscuit and snatched it up. Some people in the crowd rushed to the cabby. Noticing that, the sovereign asked for a plate of biscuits to be brought and began tossing biscuits from the balcony. Petya's eyes became bloodshot, the danger of being crushed aroused him still more, he rushed for the biscuits. He did not know why, but it was necessary to take a biscuit from the tsar's hands and necessary not to give it up. (675; PSS 11:90–91)

There follows a description of the poor onlookers being stampeded by the crowd, a story harshly rejected by Viazemsky as nonsense and an insult to the memory of Emperor Alexander:

> This account betrays a total lack of knowledge of Alexander I's personality. He was so measured, so careful in all his actions and slightest moves; he was so apprehensive of anything that could seem ridiculous or awkward; he was so deliberate, so proper, so imposing, so cautious and scrupulous up to the smallest detail that he would have rather jumped into the water than appear before the people munching a biscuit, especially on such a solemn and remarkable day. Moreover, he amuses himself by throwing

biscuits into the crowd from the balcony of the Kremlin Palace as if he were some sort of a backwoods squire pitching gingerbread in order to provoke a fight among village boys on a holiday! This is again a caricature, which by all means is absolutely out of place and is out of keeping with the truth.[24]

In fact, it is hard to imagine Emperor Alexander being guilty of such irresponsibility and cruelty, or to suppose that violence of this kind could occur at the moment when the sacred union between the people and their sovereign was to be sealed. And indeed, it would have been in total contradiction with all we know about Alexander's personality and character.[25]

This criticism is part of a wider critique formulated by Konstantin Leontiev in his 1890 book titled *Analiz, stil' i veianie: o novelkh gr Tolstogo*.[26] For Leontiev, the freedom of the tone and even the psychologic introspection attributed to characters, real or fictional, in *War and Peace* are all anachronistic:

> At the times of Austerlitz and Berezina one did not delve too deeply into the souls of others . . . if one noticed somebody's pimple, one probably did not consider it his civic duty to become immersed in its contemplation; one had not read Gogol yet; and Gogol himself would have been writing not "The Overcoat" and "Dead Souls," but rather odes about some "volcanoes erupting with entire nations."[27]

Later on, other literary critiques and writers—including the Symbolist Dmitry Merezhkovsky—would in their turn attack the "anachronisms of atmosphere" in *War and Peace*:

> As one reads *War and Peace* it is very difficult to get rid of the . . . impression that all the events depicted . . . take place in our own days. The air we breathe in *War and Peace* and *Anna Karenina* is one and the same; the historical scent in both epics is

one and the same; both here and there, we have a similar atmosphere of the second half of the nineteenth century, which is so familiar to us.[28]

On top of these anachronisms and exaggerations are the ironic and sarcastic commentaries that are biased and not always historically documented. We can here refer to Tolstoy's severe judgment of the elites of St. Petersburg. He describes them as selfish and indifferent to the fate of the people and of the country:

> But the calm, luxurious life of Petersburg, concerned only with phantoms, with reflections of life, went on as of old; and beyond this course of life it took great effort to realize the danger and the difficult situation of the Russian people. There were the same levees and balls, the same French theater, the same interests of the courts, the same interests of the service and intrigues. (935; PSS 12:3)

The upper aristocracy is also implicitly criticized by its excessive use of the French language, which contributed to its being cut off from the people, its isolation and its maintaining, artificially and completely illegitimately, a feeling of superiority. In Tolstoy's mind, it also contributed to its lack of national consciousness. In the text, the use of the French language aims to recreate the actual atmosphere at the start of the century, but this choice is not neutral. It also intends to discredit the most "Westernized" and "de-Russified" characters as the most selfish, pretentious, and immoral people of the novel. Indeed, in a sort of perfect symmetry, the fictional characters who are most at ease in French are also those who are most egotistical, lacking any true patriotism. As B. Gorelov relevantly writes in analyzing the character of Pierre Bezukhov:

> At the start of the novel, he is a young admirer of the ideas of the French Revolution and of Napoleon who arrives from Paris

to St. Petersburg and he even experiences difficulty in thinking and expressing himself in Russian. He is looking for his path and wonders what to do in life.

But at the end of the novel, he has understood that what counts is to be good, natural and to observe the laws of morality. To make himself understood, he no longer has need of French, the recondite and artificial language of a privileged caste. Like Tolstoy at the end of his life, it is only in Russian that he can express himself.[29]

This ideological stance with respect to the aristocratic elites also leads the writer to harshness about Rostopchin, the governor general of Moscow. He blames him for the balderdash found in his posters and his rants; he denies him any responsibility for the burning of Moscow and the consequent salvation of Russia, considering that "a city made of wood abandoned by its inhabitants ought to necessarily burn," and he reproaches him for the execution of the unfortunate Vereshchagin, sacrificed to the populace as a scapegoat. By contrast, Kutuzov is given a halo in the narrative. Certainly, Tolstoy does not hide any of the faults of the man whose unbridled sexual inclinations and his courtier's *veulerie* he condemns. But he also describes him as a good and just commander, determined to spare his men and those close to them (1029; PSS 12:117).

Tolstoy salutes the wisdom of Kutuzov, which is "not of great men, not of the *grands hommes* whom the Russian mind does not recognize, but of those rare, always solitary men who, discerning the will of Providence, submit their personal will to it" (1084–1085; PSS 12:183). As we already mentioned, some of Tolstoy's opinions are deliberately outrageous, but when it comes to Kutuzov, they are generally full of praise, in order to better distinguish the "sincere" Russian general from the false hero, the so-called idol incarnated by Napoleon. The various vitriolic portraits throughout the novel are part of an endeavor of demystification. For the writer, the "heroes" to whom courage is ascribed—and, in the case of Napoleon, intelligence and drive and organizational genius—all suffer from a total illusion regarding their own power. In Tolstoy's eyes, not only do these pseudo-heroes have no real impact on events, but they are the playthings of these events, unlike wise men like Kutuzov. Denouncing Napoleon's arrogance and pretention, Tolstoy again strikes back, underlining Kutuzov's modesty: "Kutuzov never spoke of forty centuries looking down from the pyramids, of the sacrifices he was making for the fatherland, of what he intended to accomplish or had accomplished: he generally said nothing about himself" (1085; PSS 12:183).

A little later, "this temporizer Kutuzov, whose motto is 'patience and time,'" is described as a discreet and modest man who, "alone against all," was able to incarnate Russianness and Russian "national sentiment" (1086; PSS 12:185) because he was precisely the opposite of the "false" European hero (1087; PSS 12:185–186).

This last point is crucial. Page after page, Tolstoy's vision of Kutuzov has nothing more to do with the true Kutuzov. The latter became a sacred figure, courageously leading the struggle against the invader on the one hand and accepting his fate with serenity on the other, in unison with the Russian people, the true victor over Napoleon, but within the limits of his own margin of maneuvering. For Tolstoy,

> The drawing of Napoleon into the depths of the country occurred not according to someone's plan (no one even believed in such a possibility), but occurred as the result of the most complex interplay of intrigues, aims, and desires of the people participating in the war, who did not perceive what was to happen and what would be the only salvation of Russia. It all occurs by chance. (684; PSS 11:102)

While exalting the nationalist feeling incarnated in Kutuzov and denouncing the illusion of power symbolized by Napoleon, Tolstoy nevertheless asserts that no one—no historical actor and no historian—is in a position to impose a single will upon others and that nobody has the capacity to influence other people's destinies. According to Tolstoy's skeptical view, the multiplicity and almost infinite number of small happenings that intervene at the same time in all human events make any outcome all the more uncertain and unpredictable because these events succeed each other in a totally contingent, however seemingly inevitable, manner.

Such views make Tolstoy's *War and Peace* appear not only a magnificent novelistic fresco and a well-documented historical chronicle, but also a work committed to an uncompromising rejection of some widely accepted historical illusions. The reader is, nevertheless, left wondering: In debunking some historical illusions, has not Tolstoy promoted some of his own?

Notes

1. See Marie-Pierre Rey, *L'effroyable tragédie, une nouvelle histoire de la campagne de Russie* (Paris: Flammarion, 2012).
2. Moreover, this is an approximation since this report involved not military but civilian authorities, to which Napoleonic power had devolved police functions.
3. The extract is quoted in French by Tolstoy.
4. That is, on June 14, in the Russian Julian calendar; all the dates given by Tolstoy are based on the Julian calendar.
5. In French in the text: "Je regarderai ce qui s'est passé comme non avenu, et un accommodement entre nous sera possible."
6. In French in the text: "Tout cela il 'aurait dû à mon amitié. . . . Ah, quel beau règne, quel beau règne! Quel beau règne aurait pu être celui de l'empereur Alexandre!"
7. In French in the text: "Mais si jamais il fut écrit dans les décrets de la divine providence."
8. This textual aside is in Russian.
9. In French in the text: "que ma dynastie dût cesser de régner sur le trône de mes ancêtres, alors, après avoir épuisé tous les moyens qui sont en mon pouvoir, je me laisserai croître la barbe jusqu'ici."
10. This textual aside is in Russian.

11. In French in the text: "Et j'irai manger des pommes de terre avec le dernier de mes paysans plutôt que de signer la honte de ma patrie et de ma chère nation, dont je sais apprécier les sacrifices."
12. In French in the novel.
13. Alexandre Mikhailovski-Danilevski, *Description de la première guerre de l'empereur Alexandre 1er contre Napoléon, Description de la deuxième guerre de l'empereur Alexandre 1er contre Napoléon, Description de la Grande Guerre patriotique de 1812*. The first edition was published in French.
14. See R. F. Christian, *Tolstoy's "War and Peace": A Study* (Oxford: Clarendon Press, 1962), 158.
15. See Derek Offord, Vladislav Rjeoutski, and Gesine Argent, *The French Language in Russia: A Social, Political, Cultural and Literary History* (Amsterdam: Amsterdam University Press, 2018), 699.
16. See Lioudmila Vedenina, "La langue française dans le roman Guerre et Paix de L. N. Tolstoï," *La Linguistique* 58, no. 1 (2022): 181–195.
17. See B. Goreloff, "La signification de l'emploi du français par la haute aristocratie russe dans Guerre et Paix de Tolstoy," in *Etudes slaves et est européennes* 20–21 (1975–1976): 74.
18. Vedenina, "La langue française," 187–188.
19. In French: "Ma foi, sire, nous ferons ce que qui sera dans notre possibilité, Sire!"
20. In French in the text. Remember that the French spoke and still speak of the battle of Moscow (because it was supposed to open to them the road to Moscow), whereas Russians mention the battle of Borodino, from the name of the village where it took place.
21. See Dan Ungurianu, "Visions and Versions of History: Veterans of 1812 on Tolstoy's *War and Peace*," *Slavic and East European Journal* 44, no. 1 (2000): 48–63.
22. In *Vospominania o 1812 gode*.
23. Ungurianu, "Visions and Versions," 48–63.
24. Ungurianu, "Visions and Versions," 52.
25. Cf. Marie-Pierre Rey, *Alexander I, the Tsar Who Defeated Napoleon* (Dekalb: Northern Illinois University Press, 2012).
26. *Analysis, Style, and Drift: On the Novels of Count L. N. Tolstoy.*
27. Quoted in Ungurianu, "Visions and Versions," 53.
28. Quoted in Ungurianu, "Visions and Versions," 53.
29. Goreloff, "La signification," 78.

Works Cited

Christian, R. F. *Tolstoy's "War and Peace": A Study*. Oxford: Clarendon Press, 1962.

Goreloff, B. "La signification de l'emploi du français par la haute aristocratie russe dans Guerre et Paix de Tolstoï." *Etudes slaves et est européennes* 20–21 (1975–76): 74–78.

Leontiev, Konstantin. *Analiz, stil' i veianie. O romanakh gr. L. N. Tolstogo*. Providence: Brown University Press, 1965.

Mikhailovski-Danilevski, Alexandre I. *Opisanie otechestvennoj vojny 1812 goda*. 4 vols. Saint Petersburg, 1839.

Offord, Derek, Vladislav Rjeoutski, and Gesine Argent. *The French Language in Russia: A Social, Political, Cultural and Literary History*. Amsterdam: Amsterdam University Press, 2018.

Rey, Marie-Pierre. *Alexander I, the Tsar Who Defeated Napoleon*. Translated by Susan Emanuel. Dekalb: Northern Illinois University Press, 2012.

Rey, Marie-Pierre. *L'effroyable tragédie, une nouvelle histoire de la campagne de Russie*. Paris: Flammarion, 2012.

Ungurianu, Dan. "Visions and Versions of History: Veterans of 1812 on Tolstoy's *War and Peace*." *Slavic and East European Journal* 44, no. 1 (2000): 48–63.

Vedenina, Lioudmila. "La langue française dans le roman Guerre et Paix de L. N. Tolstoï." *La Linguistique* 58, no. 1 (2022): 181–195.

4
Denis Davydov's Truth in *War and Peace*

Donna Tussing Orwin

This chapter discusses the contribution of Denis Vasil'evich Davydov (1784–1839) to Leo Tolstoy's *War and Peace*.[1] Davydov was a career soldier who fought proudly in eight wars and was known internationally as the "Black Captain" for his exploits in the guerrilla movement he initiated in 1812 against Napoleon's invading army.[2] He was also famous as both a poet and an author of memoirs and studies of the wars between Russia and Napoleonic France. In a note to a list of sources compiled while he was writing the novel, Tolstoy characterized Davydov's influence on writing about the Napoleonic Wars period as follows: "Davydov was the first to set a truthful tone" (PSS 15:240).[3] I begin by analyzing this cryptic formulation. I then discuss similarities between Tolstoy and Davydov as these emerge from *War and Peace* before turning to their disagreements. These last are significant, especially as regards the great man theory of history and the related problem of freedom and necessity in it. Nonetheless, Tolstoy expresses his differences with Davydov only indirectly. I will conclude by exploring reasons for his reticence.

I. A Truthful Tone

Both today and in Tolstoy's time, the Russian word *ton* (tone) refers first of all to sound, mostly musical but also vocal. The lead definition of *ton* in Vladimir Dal's famous dictionary (*Tolkovyi slovar'*), first published 1863–66 (when Tolstoy was writing *War and Peace*), includes "voice" (*golos*) at the end of a list of kinds of "tones": "any sound (*zvuk*), ringing (*zvon*), rumble (*gul*), voice (*golos*)." In English "tone" has approximately the same meaning; the long entry for it in the Oxford English Dictionary begins with "a musical or vocal sound considered with reference to its quality, as acute or grave, sweet or harsh, loud or soft, clear or dull." In English as in Russian, tone of voice expresses emotion. Definition 5 (out of eleven) in the OED associates it with "affirmation, interrogation, hesitation, decision, or some feeling or emotion." In writing, according to J. A. Cuddon's classic *Dictionary of Literary Terms and Literary Theory*, "tone" can be "the reflection of a writer's attitude (especially toward his readers), manner, mood and moral outlook in his work" or "the counterpart of tone of voice in speech."[4] In other words, tone expresses the "voice" or point of view of an author or his characters. Since point of view is crucial in the construction of any Tolstoy text, so is tone.

"Truth" (*pravda*) is something that the young Tolstoy valued and practiced in his war writing. The narrator in his second Sevastopol sketch, *Sevastopol in May*, which reveals the corrosive effects of vanity in wartime, declares that the only "hero" of his tale is *pravda* itself, which debunks the rhetoric of war to get to the bottom of what really happens in it. "Sevastopol in May" appeared, distorted by censorship but still a bombshell, in September 1855 in the St. Petersburg journal *The Contemporary*. In late November its author himself, an artillery lieutenant, arrived in the capital from Crimea. It was during his first months in St. Petersburg that Tolstoy wrote and published "Two Hussars" ("Dva gusara") with an epigraph from a poem by Davydov. The most extensive review of "Two Hussars" and a very positive one was by Aleksandr Vasil'evich Druzhinin (1824–1864), one of the Petersburg literati who welcomed Tolstoy as a war hero and rising literary star.[5] Druzhinin, whom he met the day after his arrival, became a close friend and mentor whose opinion and approval he sought. They shared a love of truth and hatred of what they called *frazy*, that is, empty or hypocritical bombast.[6] Four years later Druzhinin favorably reviewed the 1860 edition of Davydov's works,[7] writing that "all those who value truth (*pravda*) must respect Denis Davydov as the destroyer and opponent of our old military literature with its boastful and official blandness."[8] According to Druzhinin, Davydov's memoirs in this edition are outstanding for their truthfulness. He reveals weaknesses even in commanders he admires, like his relative and friend General of the Artillery A. P. Ermolov (1777–1861) and General Prince P. I. Bagration (1765–1812), under whom he served. Eschewing the black and white categories of Russian military odes, he generously praises the enemy where deserved. All of this differs astonishingly from the "tone" (*ton*) of other literature on the war of 1812, whose models have been "on the one hand, the saccharine panegyric of *a bard in the camp of the Russian warriors*, and on the other, unscrupulous books whose praise no one believed or wanted to believe."[9] Druzhinin then complains that boastful panegyrists have deprived Russians of much of the heritage of 1812.

> Military historians and military anecdotists have sketched us a series of Chinese pictures without shadows, and now, when a new age has dawned in which everyone recognizes that a picture without shadows is no picture, it is too late to do it over again. Documents have disappeared and the last witnesses of that glorious time are leaving the stage. Among the panegyrists and insipid war writers, Denis Davydov stands alone, a man totally alive. He did not bury his talent, he did not subordinate it to the whims of captious personages, and every one of his writings was a rebuke to the insipid war writing of the old days.[10]

In Cuddon's terms, Druzhinin is analyzing "tone" understood as the voice of the author. Druzhinin's representation of Davydov as a truth-teller in fact and especially in tone links it to his assessment of Tolstoy in 1856.[11] The same 1860 edition of Davydov's works reviewed by Druzhinin sat on Tolstoy's desk as he wrote *War and Peace*.[12] "Davydov was the first to set a truthful tone": this statement sums up Druzhinin's praise of Davydov so neatly as to confirm that Tolstoy had read it or at least discussed Davydov with his friend.

Finally, by using the expression *ton pravdy* rather than simply saying that Davydov spoke the truth about the wars, Tolstoy emphasizes Davydov's sincerity. The phrase can indicate sincerity even when the *pravda* itself might be unpalatable or unacceptable. So, in a very nasty review of the 1860 Davydov edition that appeared a month after Druzhinin's, radical critic M. L. Mikhailov (1829–1865) criticizes Davydov for his—as he sees it—Asiatic vulgarity, expressed in his poetry with a *ton pravdy* that makes it impossible not to believe in its sincerity.[13] As we shall see, Tolstoy admires Davydov's honesty and his ability to express his point of view as virtues in and of themselves.

II. Davydov's Voice

In "Meeting with Field Marshall Count Kamensky" ("Vstrecha s Fel'dmarshalom grafom Kamenskim") (1834), Davydov himself draws attention to his quarrel with other writers over their tone.

> On the same field a picture of a different sort shook my soul. We had stepped out, as I said, onto the plain of the battle of Mohrungen. "Already," as one of our melodious prose writers puts it, "the field had groaned itself out, already the blood had cooled. Thousands lay in the snow. Tumbled-over corpses with open, dimmed eyes seemed still to stare at the sky, but they no longer saw either earth or sky. They lay collapsed, tossed about, like vessels of a precious drink broken by a hostile hand. The gloomy winter day imparted a kind of bluish paleness to these

fresh ruins of humankind in which two days earlier passions had raged, hopes had played, and fresh desires had bubbled as do the years of fresh youth."

Out of curiosity I inspected the whole battlefield. First I observed our position, and then that of the enemy. It was obvious where firepower and fighting had been concentrated from the number of bodies lying in those places. The artillery of our advance guard had been commanded by the already well known Aleksei Petrovich Ermolov, and its action was in every sense of the word ruinous for the infantry columns and lines of the enemy cavalry, because whole crowds of the former and the first rows of the latter lay in the village of Pfarrersfeldchen, struck down by cannon balls and grapeshot in the same order in which they had advanced or stood during the battle.

In the beginning, this plain of death, trampled upon by our men who were rushing toward a similar fate, those faces and bodies mutilated and deformed by firearms and hand weapons, made no particular impression on me. But the more I gave in to my imagination, I must confess with shame, the more I became disturbed about *my own self*, or, to put it simply, I felt such timidity that, having arrived in Mohrungen, I did not sleep a wink the entire night, fearing just such a mutilation.[14]

The poetic abstractions of the "melodious writer" shield readers from what they purport to convey. Davydov's own description by contrast is without *frazy*. It contains only one powerful metaphor— the plain of death (*ravnina smerti*)—which the rest of it fully realizes. Whereas the (anonymous and perhaps fictional) "melodious author" conjures up a romantic painting, Davydov's report makes us visualize the actual battle. Very much like one of Tolstoy's eyewitnesses or narrators, Davydov tours the battlefield explaining exactly where, why, and how the dead lie. The "melodious" author does not identify with the dead, who are aestheticized as broken vessels. He and his readers stand safely back and cluck with the tumultuous living conjured up at the end of his tableau. In Davydov's rendering, Ermolov's artillery has mowed down many of the fallen, but "we"—Russian troops? The living?—have also damaged the bodies as "we" rushed over them toward our own deaths. The narrator, exposed to the horrors of war for the first time, imagines himself as one of the mutilated dead, and he is afraid.

III. The Psychology of War: Similarities

The description of the battlefield at Mohungren is Tolstoyan in its debunking of overwrought prose, but also in its psychological realism. We know that Tolstoy read it while he was writing *War and Peace*, because, as we shall see, he borrowed from the memoir in which it appears. For him, certain aspects of reality are accessible only through individual consciousness and feeling. He therefore used Davydov's poetry and its poetic persona to access the warlike spirit of Russia's wars with Napoleon.[15] Military readers of Davydov recognized their own experience of war and army life in his poetry, just as they did in Tolstoy's war stories, and Tolstoy would have appreciated Davydov as his predecessor in this regard.

This takes us to that second meaning of Davydov's "tone" that Tolstoy may have had in mind, namely, the communication of inner truths through the voices of individual characters. I have counted ninety-five instances in *War and Peace* where the word is used in this way.[16] (There are also innumerable instances in the text where a "tone" of voice or opinion is described without using the word itself.) At times, the meaning of "tone" expands to indicate the mood of a character expressed not only through speech but also gesture and expression; occasionally it can indicate the general mood of a gathering or group, and this last can be generated by an individual or the particular circumstances. In one such case—at the Christmas celebrations at Otradnoe—the narrator employs the very same expression that Tolstoy had applied to Davydov: Natasha "first set the tone of Christmas merriment" (II.2.x; PSS 10:281).[17] Here Natasha's "tone" infects others, as it can do in life and literature.

As others have observed, Davydov's "truthful tone" or voice in this sense is expressed in *War and Peace* first and foremost in hussar officer and partisan Vaska (Vasilii) Denisov. Tolstoy foregrounds the connection to Davydov by including both his first name (Denis) and his patronymic (Vasilievich) in Denisov's name. Furthermore, Denisov appears first in the early part of the novel, which is indebted to Davydov's memoirs of the campaigns of 1806 and 1807, and then plays a major role in the part that borrows from Davydov's memoirs of the partisan war. In crucial respects, Denisov's career parallels that of Davydov. Like Denisov, Davydov was a hussar and a partisan in the war of 1812. Like him, Davydov was a loyal servant of tsar and nation who got in trouble with the authorities.[18] Davydov himself revealed how he narrowly avoided court-martial during the campaigns of 1813–14 for acting without orders.[19] Tolstoy would have had Davydov's independent spirit in mind in presenting Denisov as seizing supplies from another unit to feed his starving men (II.2.xvi; PSS 10:128–132).[20] Denisov looks like Davydov—short with dark eyes and dark curly hair—in portraits from the period. He even writes poetry. The romantic imagery and meter (iambic pentameter) of the love song he composes for Natasha (II.1.xv; PSS 10:57) imitate Davydov's poetic style. Denisov's courtship of the fifteen-year-old Natasha reproduces a theme in some of Davydov's love poetry, namely, the love of an older man for a younger woman.[21]

At the same time, Denisov and Davydov are no more the same than Davydov the author and his warrior persona. It is this persona that Denisov mostly represents. As if to make this point, Davydov even figures in *War and Peace* as a character related to but different from Denisov.[22] Denisov more resembles the early warrior, the "hussar poet," from whom Davydov later partially distanced himself, than he does Davydov.[23] He dresses like Davydov's hussar poet in a cloak, pleated trousers, and a rumpled "hussar cap," and he smokes a pipe (I.2.iv; PSS 9:156). All these except the trousers occur in "Song of an Old Hussar" ("Pesnia starogo gusara," 1817), from which Tolstoy took the epigraph for "Two Hussars."[24] Like Davydov's hussar, Denisov gambles. (In his first appearance in the text, he has returned from a card game in which he has lost heavily.) Complaining about the absence of women and saying that there is nothing to do but drink, he longs for battle. Later (chap. 8), when he gets his wish, he is in his element. He swaggers as if drunk (his face "was the same as always, especially toward evening, after downing a couple of bottles" [I.2.viii; PSS 9:175]), and at one moment, his commanding officer reprimands him for unnecessarily "flaunting his bravery" (I.2.viii; PSS 9:178).

Like Davydov's hussar persona, Denisov epitomizes the spirited Russian soldier. In his first appearance in the published drafts of the novel, just as in the final text, he bursts onto the page. "Vaska Denisov, when he learned what Telianov [an earlier version of Telianin] had done, flew into a rage" (PSS 13:301). He is spontaneous, lively, cheerful, prone to anger, and courageous. Tolstoy then develops these distinctive qualities in a related draft.

> Vaska Denisov, *always in some kind of a frenzy*, would quarrel with the squadron commander about regimental training, arguing that they weren't doing it in the regiment the way they should. . . . He *sprang up* on his short, bowed cavalry legs. . . . Officers regarded him as a duelist and told terrifying stories about him, but Rostov didn't find any such duels, but saw in him only *infinite indestructible merriment*, good nature, amiability with everyone and most of all with his own kind, naiveté, and childlike ignorance and indifference to everything not hussar. (PSS 13:307–308; emphasis added)

Unlike the Davydov of the later poems and prose writings, Denisov is not reflective, although he can be crafty. In his final text, Tolstoy keeps Denisov within boundaries consistent with his limited persona. In one draft, for instance, Petya Rostov worships Denisov as his "Napoleon," and Denisov enjoys this adulation and also the role of a Napoleon and leader. The final text excludes this hubris as not consistent with Denisov's impulsiveness.

While Tolstoy used materials from Davydov's life and poetry to construct the type of the model hussar, he also incorporated some of Davydov's youthful experiences, as reported in the memoirs, into the lives of his more psychologically complex characters. Two of Davydov's memoirs stand out especially in this regard: "A Meeting with Field Marshal Count Kamensky (1806)," already discussed above, and "A Lesson for a Rascal (1807)" ("Urok sorvantsu," 1836). Both describe the enthusiasm, fearlessness, and glory-seeking of a young officer. "A Lesson for a Rascal" is dedicated to Davydov's five sons as a warning but also an example of youthful nobility. Written from the nostalgic perspective of a veteran, the essays may have inspired the element of childishness in Tolstoy's first extended characterization of Denisov in the drafts quoted above. This childishness is absent from Denisov's character in the final text of *War and Peace*. There, however, the theme of the young warrior, present in earlier Tolstoy war stories, is further developed with the aid of Davydov's memoirs. Like the young Davydov in "Meeting with Kamensky" when he goes abroad for the first time on the way to Liebstadt, Rostov's high spirits spill over into an embrace of everything German.[25] Like Davydov in his baptism of fire in "Lesson," Nikolai Rostov rides eagerly into his first battle (Schöngraben, 1805); like Davydov he finds himself unhorsed in a field with enemies pursuing him; and like Davydov he is saved by the chance appearance of friendly forces.[26] Nikolai is not as reckless as Davydov depicts himself in "Lesson," but Petya Rostov will be (IV.3.xi; PSS 12:150).

IV. Differences in War Psychology and Morality

Davydov's voice therefore is present in *War and Peace* beyond its partial incarnation in Denisov. It is the way Tolstoy incorporates material from the memoirs that reveals a difference between him and Davydov. While they both regard the escapades of the youthful warrior indulgently, they disagree on the lessons to be drawn from them. Nikolai Rostov is chastened by his near capture or death, and his brother Petya will die. In "Lesson," by contrast, Davydov's actions earn him a medal: "The Prince [General Bagration] chewed me out mildly for my recklessness, and, so far as I could tell, with an approving smile, and ordered that I be given his cloak to replace the one that had been torn off me. He even very soon nominated me for a medal."[27]

There are other divergences. For instance, the lesson that Davydov draws from his view of the field of Mohrungen is not a Tolstoyan one.

> If my reason had taken any part at all in my imagination, I would have easily seen that such a death is not only not terrible, but enviable, because the more fatal the wound, the shorter the suffering, and what do I care if after death I will frighten living people with a mutilation that I myself don't feel?
>
> Thank God, with dawn came mental healing, and, having returned to my earlier state, I laughed at myself. In the course of my long service I have never fallen again into a similar paroxysm of diseased imagination.[28]

Tolstoy would not deny that battle hardens soldiers, and he demonstrates this in *War and Peace* just as in the early war stories. He chooses, however, to highlight different consequences of this universal experience. What Davydov dubs "diseased" imagination, Tolstoy considers a healthy mechanism for quenching excessive love of war; he wants the horrors of war to tame warlike impulses. Nikolai Rostov eventually loses his taste for the hussar life, and once settled at Bald Hills with his family, he will go to war only when necessary. By contrast, nowhere in Davydov's oeuvre, whether in poetry or prose, does he present himself as tired of war. Though embittered in his later years by the enemies who sabotaged his career and denied him the recognition he thought he deserved, and though happy in his family life, he continues to celebrate battle as the peak human experience. Even in the poem "Half a Soldier" ("Polusoldat") (1826), in which, having mostly left his hussar persona behind, he confesses (and laments) that he now prefers the family hearth to the campfire, he still claims to love battle itself. In "The Field of Borodino" ("Borodinskoe pole") (1829), he implores the heroes of the most important battle in which he fought to return him to that glorious day.

> But where are you? I listen. No response! From the fields
> The smoke of battle has whirled away, no clang of swords is heard,
> And I, your nursling, bowing my head over a plow,
> I envy the bones of a comrade in arms or friend.
> —"The Field of Borodino: An Elegy"[29]

Here Davydov takes the view of the warrior who prefers death in battle to ignominious old age. His Borodino elegy celebrates glory "and the noise of firearms and steel, and battle!" Tolstoy mostly does not present the career officer as reflective about death. When he is, as in the case of Tushin at Schöngraben and Prince Andrei at Borodino, he focuses on duty over the thrill of battle. Tolstoy's thoughtful professional officer is more like Homer's Sarpedon, who reasons that since we will all die eventually, we might as well die honorably in battle when it is necessary.[30]

Tolstoy and Davydov also disagree about heroes. In his essay on the great general Alexander Vasil'evich Suvorov (1730–1800),

Davydov describes his feelings on meeting him as a nine-year-old child in 1793.

> I recall how my skipped a beat, just the way it would fall later when I met a beloved woman. I was all eyes and attention, all curiosity and joy, and as if it were now I see the crowd of four colonels, adjutants, and orderlies from the staff of the corps, and before this crowd—Suvorov.[31]

Along with the desire for glory and self-sacrifice in war, worship of older warriors and ancient models is an attribute of noble youth in *War and Peace*.[32] Just as the desire for glory is associated in *War and Peace* with Davydov's memoirs, so is this hero worship. In particular Nikolai's love for the tsar is compared to that of a lover for his beloved in a passage (I.3.xviii; PSS 9:349) that brings to mind Davydov's account of his love for Suvorov.

Nikolai, however, outgrows his adoration of Tsar Alexander just as he does his love of glory; in particular his hero disappoints him at Tilsit by refusing to pardon Denisov as well as by agreeing to a humiliating treaty with Napoleon (III.1.xx–xxi; PSS 10:146, 149–150). Davydov, by contrast, deeply admired certain contemporaries, who, while he occasionally criticized them, remained on the pedestal where he had placed them.

Unlike Tolstoy, Davydov affirmed the importance of heroes in shaping war and history. In "The Field of Borodino" and elsewhere, he evinced the highest respect for Generals N. N. Raevsky (1771–1829), Ermolov, and Bagration and the roles they had played in victory at Borodino.[33] Tolstoy has nothing good to say about the first two in *War and Peace*, and he debunks purported heroic deeds for which Davydov praises them.[34] Bagration plays a more positive role in the novel. His intrigues against General M. A. Barclay de Tolly (1761–1818) do not undercut his heroism in Tolstoy's presentation any more than they do in Davydov's.[35]

The two authors present his heroism somewhat differently, however, and this comes out in the way that Tolstoy adapts Davydov's portrait of Bagration. Tolstoy relies heavily on the following passages from Davydov's memoirs.

> In my five-year service under Prince Bagration as his adjutant, during military operations I never saw him other than fully dressed night and day. His sleep was always extremely short—three or at the most four hours, and that with interruptions: anyone who came from the outposts was to wake him if the news he brought warranted it. He loved to live in luxury: everything around him was in abundance, but for others, not for himself. He himself was satisfied with very little, and he was extremely abstemious; I never saw him drink vodka or wine, except for two shots of Madeira at dinner. During that time, his clothing was the following: a military uniform with the Star of St. George of the Second Class, a felt cloak, a sword that he had carried with him in Italy under Suvorov, a lambskin hat, and in his hand a Cossack whip.[36]
>
> Prince Pyotr Ivanovich Bagration, so famous for his astonishing valor, his elevated disinterestedness, his decisiveness and drive, unfortunately received no education.... His great native abilities, his valor, his drive, and his incomparable vigilance—all these qualities in place of knowledge—drew the attention of the great Suvorov.... From that immortal war [i.e., Suvorov's Italian campaign] he learned that quickness in operations, that art of maneuver, that suddenness in attacks, that concentration in applied force which earned him the complete trust, boundless love, and deep respect of the entire army.... His brilliant qualities, an open character, and kind treatment of everyone won the hearts of all his subordinates, among whom, inspired by his example, even the weak and the timid became heroes.... The magnificent stride and the bearing of the prince, as well as his eagle gaze, captivated everyone.[37]

For his depiction of Bagration at Schöngraben, Tolstoy borrowed an episode from Davydov's account of the battle of Preussisch-Eylau. In Davydov's text, the Russian army under L. A. Bennigsen was retreating toward Eylau with Napoleon in pursuit and Bagration commanding the rear guard. Bagration had orders to engage the enemy if necessary. During a sleepless night, he coolly directed operations. Several other generals approached him to commiserate, "Yet the prince not only seemed unperturbed, but joked more than usual, as he always did in moments of the greatest danger." In the morning the resumed retreat went well as "the prince, standing on the main road and showered with cannon balls and grapeshot, gave orders with the greatest sangfroid. . . . In a word, all the regiments that comprised the rear guard, inspired by the example of the fearless Prince Bagration, competed with one another in zeal and valor." The French then occupied Eylau, and Bennigsen ordered Bagration to expel them.

> The prince, dismounting, stood at the head of the column. With his characteristic magnificent sangfroid, he started to walk toward the city. The troops followed him quietly and in silence, but as they entered the streets, shouting "Hurrah!" they assaulted the enemy with bayonets and took the city.[38]

In the published drafts of *War and Peace*, Bagration first appears in preliminary notes for the depiction of the battle of Schöngraben that ends part 2 ("War") of *1805*.

> P[rince] Bagration in his lambskin hat, his Suvorov sword—they are reminiscent of Suvorov. A powerful brown face with lackluster, dead eyes. P[rince] Andrei ponders and doesn't know what to make of these eyes. A Cossack is killed. P[rince] Bagrat[ion] glances back to see what nonsense is going on. He rides to the right side. A moment of indecisiveness. He silently dismounts, and walks, stretches his legs out for walking. Everyone is

watching him, and he starts walking and the whole column starts walking (irresistible motion). Hurrah! They outstrip one another. Everything is running, but it is growing in size like a ball down the rampart. D[olokhov]. He has been running in the attack. Dolokhov is fighting all covered in blood behind the rampart. I won't give in to the Frenchmen (in a frenzy). Bagration. In the evening he pauses by the cannons, resting, and again rides on to where the shooting is.

N[ikolai] is frightened in the attack just like the first time.

On the l[eft] [flank] there is no leadership.

T[ushin] is fighting in the hollow, not seeing what effect his action is having on the French; they are coming close.

That evening in Guntersdorf everyone rides there and a [captured] flag.[39] (PSS 13:29–30)

The Bagration at Schöngraben of the final text is already completely imagined here. On the one hand, Tolstoy takes many concrete details about him from the passages from Davydov summarized and quoted above; on the other, just as he creates Denisov from Davydov, he has already crafted a Tolstoyan type of the warrior leader out of the historical figure. He captures the ferocity and charisma of Davydov's portrait. Gone are any references to Bagration's "open character" and "kind treatment" of his subordinates.[40] He is pitiless toward the wounded, whose cries might unman their comrades, and whose treatment takes the healthy away from the fight. Even though this particular detail does not appear in the final text, there are hints there of Bagration's ruthlessness. At Austerlitz he does not hesitate to send the eager Rostov in search of General Kutuzov even though he knows he is likely to be killed (I.3.xvii; PSS 9:344). Tolstoy's Bagration is all war, with an "eagle gaze" (from Davydov) that remains deceptively "lackluster"—a detail added by Tolstoy and perhaps conjured up from Bagration's sleeplessness as reported by Davydov—until his eyes light up in battle. Here he is in the final text of the novel as viewed by Prince Andrei at Schöngraben.

> His face expressed that concentrated and happy resoluteness a person feels as he readies himself on a hot day to plunge into the water and is running toward it. No more sleep-deprived lackluster eyes, no more feigned look of profundity; the round, firm, hawk eyes joyfully and a bit disdainfully were looking ahead, obviously not fixed on anything in particular, while the previous slowness and measure remained in his movements. (I.2.xviii; PSS 9:223–224)

In *War and Peace* Bagration appears not as a classical hero—Davydov compares him to Achilles in battle[41]—but as a great bird of prey. This is expressed not only in his eagle gaze, but also in the way that he "straightens his legs" (I.2.xviii; PSS 9:225) after he has dismounted: the verb—*raspravit'*—translated as "straighten" usually refers to the action of a bird unfolding its wings. He is like an eagle warrior in an eighteenth-century ode. Within the iconography of the novel, he is part of the natural world of predators in which, already in the quotation above from the earliest drafts, Dolokhov, "covered in blood," feels at home in combat, while Nicholas Rostov is "frightened." Unlike in Davydov's portrait, where Bagration is comfortable in high society—dining "as usual" at the home of the tsar's mistress M. A. Naryshkina[42]—in *War and Peace* at the banquet in Moscow in his honor his sangfroid deserts him, and he moves tentatively like a great beast transported from the jungle to civilization (II.1.iii; PSS 10:17–18).

For both Davydov and Tolstoy, Bagration is at home in war. For both, he leads by example. He is fearless, and that state of mind communicates itself to his army. It is this moral, emotional element, in Tolstoy's opinion, that constitutes leadership in battle; the hero responds to events but does not control them in any way. Tolstoy's

Bagration (unlike Davydov's) only pretends to give orders. Absent from Tolstoy's portrait are references, frequent in Davydov, to Bagration's tactical skills.

If Tolstoy and Davydov both admire Bagration, they disagree about Napoleon. Davydov fought against Napoleon from 1806 to 1814 and saw him once in person, at the signing of the Treaty of Tilsit in 1807. He frequently equates him with his hero Suvorov. He describes him as "this unique mental phenomenon for the ages and the universe, this blinding meteor, invested with the charm of the most elevated poetry."[43] Poetry—by which Davydov means charisma and tactical genius—is necessary because he (like Tolstoy) believes that chance can be decisive in battle. The general must therefore follow the ebb and flow of forces on the battlefield and take advantage of chance occurrences; only warrior poets with their instinct, intensity, and courage can do this. This is the thesis of the "Memoir of the Battle of Preussisch-Eylau," which Davydov considered his definitive statement about the military leader as inspired poet.[44] Since one can never be certain of mastering chance, losing a battle or even a war while striving for greatness does not constitute a failure to achieve it. Hence in the poem "A Song on the Present Day" ("Sovremennaia pesnia," 1836) Davydov praises rather than damns Napoleon as "a squanderer for glory" who had risked everything for fame.[45]

Tolstoy, though he approves of aggressiveness in front-line troops—the "frenzy" that he admired in Denisov—criticizes it in senior officers. For one thing, he associates it with overweening ambition. For another, commanders in chief need to pay attention to deep trends and allow them to unfold. Kutuzov's motto, pronounced to Andrei on the eve of Borodino, is therefore "patience and time" (III.2.xvi; PSS 11:173).

Davydov's Napoleon has the charisma, fearlessness, and tactical skill of a Bagration, but he is also a masterful strategist, a "unique mental phenomenon for the ages and the universe." Davydov emphasizes repeatedly that Napoleon dominated his time. Tolstoy does not deny this, but he reduces Napoleon's achievements to smoke and mirrors. He subjects him to a debunking psychological analysis that turns his strategies, his heroic deeds, and his demeanor into mere show prompted by cheap vanity.[46] Tolstoy's Napoleon (unlike his Bagration) thinks, but only to advance his own interests and especially to increase his power, which he overestimates. Both Kutuzov and Napoleon take part in a historical drama that neither controls. The difference is that Tolstoy's Kutuzov seems to understand the limitations of his role, and his Napoleon does not.

V. Davydov Pro and Contra

In their differing attitudes to Napoleon and what he represents, we reach the point of greatest divergence between Tolstoy's and Davydov's truths. Although Tolstoy could not have created certain parts of *War and Peace* without Davydov, the two do not see eye to eye on war or the role of great men in it. Why does he not engage in open polemics with Davydov, especially, as Leighton points out, in the war scenes after the fall of Moscow that owe so much to Davydov's historical account? Why does he not fault Davydov for his celebration of war, warriors, and heroes? Leighton explains this as partly a tribute to Davydov, whom Tolstoy greatly admired, and partly a necessity because Tolstoy cannot undercut a source that has contributed so much to the novel.[47] Both may be the case, but there are other reasons for Tolstoy's uncharacteristic silence.

First of all, as we have seen, Tolstoy does correct Davydov's unabashed love of glory and his hero worship. Characters like Denisov and Bagration, though descended from Davydov's writings, are shaped to reflect Tolstoy's perspective. He does not allow them to speak for themselves in explaining their actions, perhaps because no senior officer could see himself as the way Tolstoy presents these two.[48] As we have seen, however, Davydov's own voice is integrated into the world of the novel. Tolstoy trusts Davydov to speak the truth as he perceives it, or, where this is not politically possible, to hint at it. This truth includes an honest account of not only external, but internal, psychological reality. Davydov's point of view, *even where Tolstoy, or his narrator, disagrees with it,* therefore becomes an entryway into the world that he seeks to recreate. He does not deny its sincerity or its charm for energetic ambitious young men even as he tries to cure them of their attraction to it. When Davydov reports what he felt as a young officer, Tolstoy accepts this as true. When Davydov reports what others did, Tolstoy accepts that as true also, especially if Davydov witnessed the deed himself. When Davydov analyzes the behavior of others or expresses an opinion about it, Tolstoy accepts that as his sincere belief, but feels free to think otherwise. Furthermore, belief in the decisive role of heroes and heroism represents eternal and recurring attitudes toward war. This is why the war experience of officers like Nikolai and Petya Rostov and Prince Andrei does not simply negate the warrior's belief in his own freedom and dignity. As the novel ends, in a new round of an epic cycle, Andrei's son Nikolenka is dreaming of taking up arms to fight for truth and glory.

Pierre Bezukhov also has grand ambitions as the novel ends, and this represents an even greater concession by Tolstoy to Davydov's truth. Not a youthful naif like Nikolenka, Pierre should have been thoroughly disabused by personal experience and the teachings of Platon Karataev of the possibility of an individual's influence on history. Yet in the first epilogue he is already involved in the beginnings of what would become known as the Decembrist Uprising. We readers know that this uprising will fail, so it stands as yet another proof of Tolstoy's thesis about the futility of politics and war. Pierre's behavior teaches us something else, however. Honorable human beings want to participate in public life, and in order to do this, they must believe in their freedom, and therefore their responsibility for it. Even Kutuzov, who according to Tolstoy's narrator always operates reactively and therefore wisely within circumstances he cannot control, does so. On the single occasion within the novel when we eavesdrop on his inner thoughts, he takes personal responsibility for allowing Napoleon to seize Moscow.

> One terrible question preoccupied him. And he heard no answer to this question from anyone. For him the question now consisted only in this: "*Can it be that I allowed Napoleon to get as far as Moscow? And when, then, did I do it? When was it decided?* Was it yesterday, when I sent Platov the order to retreat, or was it the evening before, when I dozed off and told Bennigsen to give the orders? Or still earlier? . . . But when, when was this terrible matter decided? Moscow must be abandoned. The troops must retreat, and the order has to be given."[49]

Kutuzov bows to necessity here, but he assumes that he took part in creating it. *War and Peace* therefore contains two truths, the contemplative one of the philosopher-narrator, and the practical one of the man of action, like Davydov, whose sense of honor and duty does not allow him to stand on the sidelines of great public events. As Tolstoy implicitly acknowledges in the passage just quoted, even the most experienced and thoughtful leaders must believe in their freedom to shape events, at least to some extent.

VI. Conclusion

Though not definitive, Davydov's truth adds something essential to the debate in *War and Peace* about freedom and necessity in history. Tolstoy's statement about Davydov's "truthful tone" appears in a list of sources for *War and Peace* among which Davydov is the only one who is not a historian. Davydov is mentioned after Lt. General M. I. Bogdanovich (1805–1882), author of the three-volume *History of the 1812 War of the Fatherland* (*Istoriia otechestvennoi voiny 1812 g., po dostovernym istochnikam*; 1859–60). It won the prestigious Demidov Prize, but both it and Bogdanovich's subsequent histories of the period were harshly criticized by surviving veterans because they relied mostly on official documents rather than memoirs, which he considered unreliable.[50] Tolstoy compares the two: "On Bogdanovich there's nothing to say; there's nothing original.[51] Davydov was the first to set a truthful tone" (PPS 15:240).

Tolstoy is not claiming that Bogdanovich gets his facts wrong. He relies on him for these—there is a copy of the 1812 history in the Iasnaia Poliana library with many marks and comments in Tolstoy's hand—but he criticizes him for his methodology.[52] In his view, Bogdanovich's history is completely derivative, while Davydov brought something unique to the history of the war, namely, eyewitness accounts that faithfully and fearlessly conveyed the truth as Davydov perceived it. The list of sources begins a draft that the Jubilee editors associate with the novel's epilogue, but that is as likely related to Tolstoy's 1868 article "A Few Words about the Book *War and Peace*."[53] On the all-important question of the existence of freedom in human life and history, as Tolstoy argues in both "A Few Words" and the second epilogue, objective (external) and subjective (inner) truths may not always agree, but both help construct historical reality, which cannot be explained without both. Davydov's voice, his "truthful tone," helps to save the novel from the two-dimensionality of the strictly objective point of view of an outside rational outsider like Tolstoy's narrator, but also from partisan excesses such as those criticized by both Davydov and Tolstoy. Tolstoy and his readers get to have things both ways. So far as reason and experience can discern, Tolstoy's narrator is right in his digressions about the limits of human agency in public life, but his truth does not generate and cannot govern the world of action portrayed in Tolstoy's narrative. There Denis Davydov's alternate truth about glory, greatness, and freedom flourishes if it does not ultimately rule; there notes sounded by thousands, even millions, of actors combine to create great impersonal chords of natural and historical dynamics. Among these are the heroes and leaders who must believe in their freedom in order to play their crucial roles.

Davydov's point of view—his truthful tone—helps us understand why such people make war and history even if objectively speaking they do not control them.

Notes

1. For previous excellent work on the subject, see K. Pokrovskii, "Istochniki romana *Voina i mir*," in *Voina i mir. Sbornik*, ed. V. P. Obninskii and T. I. Polner (Moscow: Zadruga, 1912), 118; N. N. Apostolov, *Lev Tolstoi nad stranitsami istorii* (Moscow: Komissiia po oznamenovaniiu stoletiia so dnia rozhdeniia L. N. Tolstogo, 1928); and Lauren Leighton, "Denis Davydov and *War and Peace*," in *Studies in Honor of Xenia Gasiorowska*, ed. Lauren Leighton (Columbus, OH: Slavica, 1983), 21–36.
2. For an especially detailed account of Davydov's life, see N. N. Sovetov, "D. V. Davydov," in *Sbornik biografii kavalergardov, 1801–1826*, vol. 3 (St. Petersburg: Ekspeditsiia zagotovleniia gosudarstvennykh bumag, 1906), 28–45. See reprint, Moscow: Tri veka istorii, 2001. Richard Peace provides a good summary in English of Davydov's life and works. See https://ratnik.tv/articles/heroes/pevets-gusar-denis-davydov/.
3. The exact phrase in Russian is "a tone of truth": *Davydov pervyi dal ton pravdy*. Since this is awkward in English, I will translate it as "a truthful tone," but going forward it is important to keep in mind that Tolstoy uses two nouns—tone and truth—rather than an adjective and a noun, and both nouns are equally important.
4. J. A. Cuddon, *Dictionary of Literary Terms and Literary Theory*, 4th ed., revised by C. E. Preston (New York: Penguin Books, 1999).
5. The review, which also discusses Tolstoy's story "Metel" (The Snowstorm), appeared in *Biblioteka dlia chteniia* 9 (1856): Kritika, 1–30. See Druzhinin, *Sobranie sochinenii A. V. Druzhinina* [hereafter SS], 7 vols. (St. Petersburg: Tipografiia Imperatorskoi akademii nauk, 1865–67), 7.1:168–189. See also http://az.lib.ru/d/druzhinin_a_w/text_0140.shtml. The two most thorough accounts of the friendship of Druzhinin and Tolstoy are K. Chukovskii, "Druzhinin i Lev Tolstoi," in *Kornei Chukovskii. Liudi i knigi*, 2nd ed. (Moscow: Gosudarstvennoe izdatel'stvo khudozhestvennoi literatury, 1960), 44–97; and A. M. Brojde, *A. V. Druzhinin. Zhizn' i tvorchestvo* (Copenhagen: Rosenkilde & Bagger, 1986), 432–462. See also Donna Tussing Orwin, "Aleksandr Druzhinin v roli posrednika mezhdu

L'vom Tolstym i Denisom Davydovym," in *Lev Tolstoj v Ierusaleme* (Moscow: Novoe literaturnoe obozrenie, 2013), 191–201.

6. On their use of the word *frazy*, see Orwin, "Aleksandr Druzhinin," 195–196.
7. Druzhinin, "'Sochineniia D. V. Davydova' Tri toma. Moskva, 1860," *Biblioteka dlia chteniia* 5 (1860): Literaturnaia letopis', 1–16. See Druzhinin, SS 7.2:639–649. The full reference to the 1860 edition is *Sochineniia Denisa Vasil'evicha Davydova*, Izdanie chetvertoe, ispravlennoe i dopolnennoe po rukopisiam avtora, 3 vols. (Moscow: V tipografii Bakhmetova, 1860). The 1860 Davydov edition often differs from later ones, and for this reason I cite it when referring to what Tolstoy would have known about the prose. Please note that sections in the first volume of this edition are numbered individually. The most complete edition of Davydov is *Sochineniia Denisa Vasil'evicha Davydova*, ed. A. Kruglyi, 3 vols. (St. Petersburg: Izdanie knigoprodavtsa Ia. Sokolova, 1895); it was first published in 1893 as a free supplement to the journal *Sever*. The 1940 edition corrects glaring inaccuracies in the 1860 and 1895 editions. For a general description of these inaccuracies, see *Denis Davydov. Voennye zapiski*, ed. Vl. Orlov (Moscow: Gosudarstvennoe izdatel'stvo "Khudozhestvennaia literatura," 1940), 429–431. Information about the publication of Davydov's individual works is taken from the 1940 edition.
8. Druzhinin, SS 7.2:648.
9. Druzhinin, SS 7.2:647–648. The phrase emphasized by me is the title of a well-known poem by V. A. Zhukovskii.
10. Druzhinin, SS 7.2:648.
11. In this regard, see also Druzhinin's 1856 review of Tolstoy's collection of war stories ("Voennye rasskazy"), Druzhinin, SS 7.1:242–257. It originally appeared in *Biblioteka dlia chteniia* 11 (1856): Literaturniaia letopis', 29–46. For further discussion see Orwin, "Aleksandr Druzhinin."
12. The library at Iasnaia Poliana still contains the 1860 edition with several pages marked by turned-down corners in the prose volumes (1 and 2), as well as an 1825 polemic by Davydov on Napoleon's memoirs (Davydov Denis, *Razbor trekh statei, pomeshchennykh v "Zapiskakh Napoleona"*, Moscow, 1825). See *Biblioteka L'va Nikolaevicha Tolstogo v Iasnoi Poliane, Knigi na russkom iazyke*, pt. 1 (Moscow: Izdatel'stvo Sovetskoi Rossii, 1958), 216. (The 1825 polemic is also included in the 1860 edition [II:45].)
13. *Russkoe slovo* 6, no. 2 (1860): 72–88, 84.
14. Davydov, "Vstrecha s Fel'dmarshalom grafom Kamenskim," 1860, II:45.

15. On this subject, see Boris Eikhenbaum, "Ot voennoi ody k 'gusarskoi pesne,'" in Eikhenbaum, *O poezii* (Leningrad: Sovetskii pisatel', 1969), 148–168; see especially 166–167.
16. By contrast, I found only one case where "tone" referred specifically to something not human, namely, bullets (I.3.xiii; PSS 9:328). Where appropriate, volume, part, and chapter of *War and Peace* will be provided in the following form: I.3.xiii. Unless otherwise stated, all translations in this chapter are my own.
17. *Natasha pervaia dala ton sviatochnogo vesel'ia* (I.1.i).
18. On Davydov's politics, see Lauren Leighton, "Denis Davydov's Hussar Style," *Slavic and East European Journal* 7, no. 4 (1963): 349–360; Lotman, "Dekabrist v povsednevnoi zhizni," in Lotman, *Besedy o russkoi kul'ture. Byt i traditsii russkogo dvorianstva (XVIII—nachalo XIX veka)* (St. Petersburg: "Iskusstvo-SPB," 1994), 356–366 and passim; V. L. Orlov, "Denis Davydov," in Orlov, *Puti i sud'by* (Moskva-Leningrad: Sovetskii pisatel', 1963), 61–101, 72, 77; and V. E. Vatsuro, "Denis Davydov—Poet," in Denis Davydov, *Stikhotvoreniia*, Biblioteka poeta (Leningrad: Sovetskii pisatel', 1984), 5–48, 23–24. Orlov and Vatsuro provide references to other Soviet scholars of Davydov's politics.
19. See his memoir "Zaniatie Drezdena 1813 g. 10 marta" (1836) in 1860, II:36; 1895, II:155–183.
20. For the most thorough account of these borrowings, see Apostolov, *Lev Tolstoi nad stranitsami istorii*, 186–189.
21. See, for instance, Elegiia IX (1817). See the entry on Davydov in *Russkie pisateli, 1800–1917*, vol. 2 (Moscow: Nauchnoe izdatel'stvo "Bol'shaia Rossiiskaia Entsiklopediia," 1992), 69.
22. Apostolov, *Lev Tolstoi nad stranitsami istorii*, 148–150.
23. For Davydov's own awareness of this distinction, see *Russkie pisateli*, II:71. On various aspects of Davydov's self-conscious relation to his poetic persona, see Orlov, "Denis Davydov," 85–86; G. A. Gukovskii, *Pushkin i russkie romantiki* (Moscow: Izdatel'stvo "Khudozhestvennaia literatura," 1965), 147–162; and Vatsuro, "Denis Davydov—Poet," 38–45 and passim. On the cultural symbol of the hussar that Davydov's poetry created, see V. A. Koshelov, "Gusar—znak i simvol russkoi kul'tury," in *Znak i symbol*, ed. Olga Glówko and N. I. Ishchuk-Fadeeva (Łódź, Tver': Uniw. Łódźki; Tver. Gos. Un-t., 2010), 50–60.
24. On Tolstoy's debt to Davydov in "Two Hussars" and, through it, in *War and Peace*, see E. M. Zhiliakova, "Denis Davydov i povest' L. N. Tolstogo 'Dva

gusara,'" in *Russkaia povest' kak forma vremeni*, ed. A. S. Ianushkevich (Tomsk: Izd. Tomskogo un-ta, 2002), 216–226.
25. Compare 1860, II:42–44; 1895, I:118–119 to *War and Peace* I.2.ixv (PSS 9:155), where the episode is transferred from 1807 to 1805 and from Saxony to Braunau am Inn in Austria. As K. Pokrovskii notes ("Istochniki romana *Voina i mir*," 118), this scene is also inspired by one in the second volume ("1813-yi god. Voina v Germanii") of Il'ia Radozhitskii's four-volume *Pokhodnye zapiski artillerista, s 1812 po 1816 god artillerii podpolkovnika I... R...* (Moscow: V tipografii Lazarevykh Instituta vostochnykh iazykov, 1835), 2:163–164.
26. Compare "Lesson" 1860, II:185–91; 1895, I:249–254 to *War and Peace* I.2.ixx (PSS 9:227–229). Tolstoy also borrows from a scene in Stendhal's *The Charterhouse of Parma* in these scenes. See Apostolov, *Lev Tolstoi nad stranitsami istorii*, 94–96.
27. "Lesson," 1860, II:191; 1895, I:255. The lack of clarity in the Russian of the first sentence in this translation reflects its somewhat garbled nature in the 1860 text. Orlov revises the sentence in 1940 (82). This is but one example of the many differences between the two editions.
28. 1860, II:45–46; 1895, I:121.
29. No gde Vy? Slushaiu... Net otzyva! S polei
Umchalsia brani dym, ne slyshen stuk mechei,
I ia, pitomets vash, sklonias' glavoi u pluga,
Zaviduiu kostiam soratnika il druga.

—Borodinskoe pole. Elegiia

30. See Book 12 (ll. 310–328) of *The Iliad* in the Gnedich translation that Tolstoy read. Jasper Griffin, using this example, points out that the necessity to face mortality makes human beings superior to the gods. See *Homer on Life and Death* (Oxford: Oxford University Press, 1980), 93.
31. "Vstrecha s Velikim Suvorovym" (Meeting with the Great Suvorov), 1860, II:20; 1895, I:97. On the place of Suvorov in *War and Peace*, see Orwin, Suvorov v "Voine i mire," *Tolstoi i mirovaia literatura*, papers from conference at Iasnaia Poliana, August 2012 (Tula: Izdatel'skii dom "Iasnaia Poliana," 2014), 5–21.
32. Examples include Denisov (Nikolai and Petya Rostov), statesmen like Tsar Alexander I (the same), and Roman Gaius Mucius Scaevola (Nikolenka Bolkonsky).
33. O, rin' menia na boi, ty, opytnyi v boiakh,
Ty, golosom svoim rozhdaiushchii v polkakh
Pogibeli vragov predchuvstvennye kliki,

Vozhd' Gomericheskii, Bagration velikii!
Prostri mne dlan' svoiu, Raevskii, moi geroi!
Ermolov! ia lechu—vedi menia, ia tvoi:
O, obrechennyi byt' pobed liubimym synom,
Pokroi menia, pokroi tvoikh perunov dymom!

—Borodinskoe pole. Elegiia

34. I refer to Raevsky's legendary heroic stand with his two adolescent sons at the battle of Saltanovka, July 11, 1812, and Ermolov's charge on the Raevsky Redoubt during the battle of Borodino, during which he purportedly threw St. George crosses to his men to inspire them. Compare *War and Peace*, III.1.xii (PSS 11:55–56) and III.2.xxxii (PSS 11:236) with Davydov, "Zamechaniia na nekrologiiu N. N. Raevskogo," 1860, I:9; 1895, III:115 and his *Dnevnik partizanskikh deistvii 1812 goda*, 1860, I:9–10; 1895, II:33–34 respectively.

35. See especially Bagration's letter to A. A. Arakcheev complaining about Barclay de Tolly interpolated into the text, *War and Peace* III.2.v (PSS 11:124–126); but also the analysis by the narrator, III.2.i (PSS 11:101). For Davydov's criticism of Bagration's jealousy of Barclay de Tolly as it affected the 1812 campaign, see "Materialy dlia istorii sovremennykh voin" (Materials for the History of Contemporary Wars), 1860, II:60–62, and 1895 I: 133–135. This is part of the same extended description of Bagration from which, as we shall see, Tolstoy borrowed.

36. "Meeting with Field Marshall Count Kamensky," 1860, II:47; 1895, I:122–123.

37. Quotations from "Materials," 1860, II:57–63; 1895, I:129–135. We can be sure Tolstoy noticed the description in "Materials" because there is a long note on the battle of Schöngraben appended to it from which, as Apostolov notes (*Lev Tolstoi nad stranitsami istorii*, 93–94), he borrowed an important detail about the battle.

38. Quotations from "Materials," 1860, II:129–130; 1895, I:199–200. For another version of the same sequence of events, see "Memoir of the Battle of Preussisch-Eylau," 1860, II:204–207; 1895, I:265–267.

39. Note that Tolstoy uses a slightly different expression—*kartuz s smyshkami*—for Bagration's distinctive hat than Davydov (whose phrase is *kartuz iz seroi smushki*).

40. In another example that Tolstoy would have read, in "Lesson for a Scamp," Bagration, "whose goodness of heart did not take second place to the elevated qualities of a heroic soul," is very concerned about the fate of his foolish young adjutant; 1860, II:191; 1895, I:255.

41. "This Achilles of the Napoleonic Wars," "Materials," 1860, II:62; 1895, I:135.
42. "Meeting with Kamensky," 1860, II:39–40; 1895, I:115.
43. "Vospominaniia o pol'skoi voine 1831 goda,"1895, II:204. This memoir was only published in 1872 in *Russkaia starina* (July, 1–38, and October, 309–405) and therefore was unavailable to Tolstoy when he was writing his novel. For the history of this text and another version of the passage, see M. I. Gillel'son, *Ot arzamasskogo bratsva k Pushkinskomu krugu pisatetei* (Leningrad: Izdatel'stvo "Nauka" Leningradskoe otdelenie, 1977), 56–59. I have corrected Gillel'son's reference to the wrong volumes of *Russkaia starina* in 1972.
44. See his letter to N. M. Iazykov of November 13, 1835, 1895, III:209; quoted in 1940, 434. As with Bagration, "Napoleon's energy and his presence of mind increased as the danger became greater." See "Memoir of the Battle of Preussisch-Eylau," 1860, II:214; 1895, I:274.
45. "Byl vek burnyi, divnyi vek, / Gromkii, velichavyi; / Byl ogromnyi chelovek, / Rastochitel' slavy." See also "Vospominaniia o pol'skoi voine 1831 goda," 1895, II:278. "Generals of the stature of Frederick, Napoleon, and Suvorov stake on a single card the capital of all the immense victories achieved by them, and they win states or parts of the world, or they lose everything including their own life and their own freedom, as Napoleon and Hannibal did, having nothing left to nourish their glory except immortality."
46. At Tilsit, Davydov observed and described in detail Napoleon's abilities as an actor, but unlike Tolstoy he does not regard these as base, and he approvingly quotes another observer (Prince de Lille) that "everything is remarkable in a man who does and says nothing by chance and without a goal"; see *Til'zit v 1807 godu* (Tilsit in 1807) 1860, II:260–266, quotation 265; 1895, I:315–320, quotation 319. Tolstoy probably borrowed from this memoir to create the scenes at Tilsit. For Napoleon and his origins in the novel, see Kathryn B. Feuer, *Tolstoy and the Genesis of War and Peace*, ed. Robin Feuer Miller and Donna Tussing Orwin (Ithaca, NY: Cornell University Press, 1996), 170–172, and passim.
47. Leighton, "Denis Davydov," 34.
48. For the reactions of contemporary military readers to Tolstoy's portrayal of them, see Orwin, "*War and Peace* from the Military Point of View," in *Tolstoy on War: Narrative Art and Historical Truth in "War and Peace"*, ed. Rick McPeak and Donna Tussing Orwin (Ithaca, NY: Cornell University Press, 2012), 167–169.

49. III.3.iii; PPS 11:274–275, emphasis added. I slightly alter the translation by Richard Pevear and Larissa Volokhonsky.
50. Bogdanovich did in fact borrow from Davydov's memoirs (Apostolov, *Lev Tolstoi nad stranitsami istorii*, 140). For information about Bogdanovich, see *Voennaia entsiklopediia* (St. Petersburg: Sytin Publishing, 1911–15), vol. 4.
51. *O Bogdanoviche nel'zia govorit'—nichego samostoiatel'nogo.*
52. On Bogdanovich and *War and Peace*, see Orwin, "Military Point of View."
53. Note the reference to 1868 in the draft, for instance, and references in the draft to the theme in "A Few Words" of the genre of the novel.

Works Cited

Apostolov, N. N. *Lev Tolstoi nad stranitsami istorii*. Moscow: Komissiia po oznamenovaniiu stoletiia so dnia rozhdeniia L. N. Tolstogo, 1928.

Biblioteka L'va Nikolaevicha Tolstogo v Iasnoi Poliane. Vol. 1, *Knigi na russkom iazyke*. Part 1. Moscow: Izdatel'stvo Sovetskoi Rossii, 1958.

"Bogdanovich, Modest Ivanovich." *Voennaia entsiklopediia*. Vol. 4. St. Petersburg: Sytin Publishing, 1911–15.

Brojde, A. M. *A. V. Druzhinin. Zhizn' i tvorchestvo*. Copenhagen: Rosenkilde & Bagger, 1986.

Chukovskii, K. "Druzhinin i Lev Tolstoi." *Kornei Chukovskii. Liudi i knigi*. 2nd ed., 44–97. Moscow: Gosudarstvennoe izdatel'stvo khudozhestvennoi literatury, 1960.

Cuddon, J. A. *Dictionary of Literary Terms and Literary Theory*. Revised by C. E. Preston. 4th ed. New York: Penguin Books, 1999.

Davydov, Denis. *Sochineniia Denisa Vasil'evicha Davydova. Izdanie chetvertoe, ispravlennoe i dopolnennoe po rukopisiam avtora*. 3 vols. Moscow: V tipografii Bakhmetova, 1860.

Davydov, Denis. *Voennye zapiski*. Edited by Vl. Orlov. Moscow: Gosudarstvennoe izdatel'stvo "Khudozhestvennaia literatura," 1940.

"Davydov Denis Vasil'evich." *Russkie pisateli, 1800–1917*. Vol. 2. Moscow: Nauchnoe izdatel'stvo "Bol'shaia Rossiiskaia Entsiklopediia," 1992.

Druzhinin, A. V. "'Metel'—'Dva gusara'—povesti L'va Tolstogo." Biblioteka dlia chteniia 7, no. 9 (1856): 1–30.

Druzhinin, A. V. *Sobranie sochinenii A. V. Druzhinina*. 7 vols. St. Petersburg: Tipografiia Imperatorskoi akademii nauk, 1865–67.

Eikhenbaum, Boris. "Ot voennoi ody k 'gusarskoi pesne.'" *O poezii*. Edited by M. I. Dikman, 148–168. Leningrad: Sovetskii pisatel', 1969.

Feuer, Kathryn B. *Tolstoy and the Genesis of War and Peace*. Edited by Robin Feuer Miller and Donna Tussing Orwin. Ithaca, NY: Cornell University Press, 1996.

Gillel'son, M. I. *Ot arzamasskogo bratsva k Pushkinskomu krugu pisatetei*. Leningrad: Nauka, 1977.

Griffin, Jasper. *Homer on Life and Death*. Oxford: Oxford University Press, 1980.

Gukovskii, G. A. *Pushkin i russkie romantiki*. Moscow: Izdatel'stvo "Khudozhestvennaia literatura," 1965.

Koshelov, V. A. "Gusar—znak i simvol russkoi kul'tury." *Znak i symbol*. Edited by Olga Glówko and N. I. Ishchuk-Fadeeva, 50–60. Łódź, Tver': Uniw. Łódźki; Tver. Gos. Un-t., 2010.

Leighton, Lauren. "Denis Davydov and *War and Peace*." *Studies in Honor of Xenia Gasiorowska*. Edited by Lauren Leighton, 21–36. Columbus, OH: Slavica, 1983.

Leighton, Lauren. "Denis Davydov's Hussar Style." *Slavic and East European Journal* 7, no. 4 (1963): 349–360.

Lotman, Iu. "Dekabrist v povsednevnoi zhizni." *Besedy o russkoi kul'ture. Byt i traditsii russkogo dvorianstva (XVIII—nachalo XIX veka)*. Edited by N. G. Nikolayuk, 331–384. St. Petersburg: "Iskusstvo-SPB," 1994.

Mikhailov, M. L. "Bibliogragiia. Sochineniia Denisa Vasil'evicha Davydova, Izd. 4-oe, ispravlennoe i dopolnennoe po rukopisiam avtora. Tri chasti. Moskva. 1860 g.," *Russkoe slovo*, June, pt. 2, 1860, 72–88.

Orlov, V. L. "Denis Davydov." *Puti i sud'by*, 61–101. Moskva-Leningrad: Sovetskii pisatel', 1963.

Orwin, Donna Tussing. "Aleksandr Druzhinin v roli posrednika mezhdu L'vom Tolstym i Denisom Davydovym." *Lev Tolstoj v Ierusalime: materialy mezhdunarodnoj nauchnoj konferentsii "Lev Tolstoï: posle iubileia"*. Edited by E. D. Tolstaia, 191–201. Moscow: Novoe literaturnoe obozrenie, 2013.

Orwin, Donna Tussing. "Suvorov v 'Voine i mire'." *Tolstoi i mirovaia literatura. Papers from Conference at Iasnaia Poliana, August 2012*, 5–21. Tula: Izdatel'skii dom "Iasnaia Poliana," 2014.

Orwin, Donna Tussing. "*War and Peace* from the Military Point of View." *Tolstoy on War. Narrative Art and Historical Truth in "War and Peace"*. Edited by Rick McPeak and Donna Tussing Orwin, 98–110. Ithaca, NY: Cornell University Press, 2012.

Pokrovskii, K. "Istochniki romana *Voina i mir*." *Voina i mir. Sbornik*. Edited by V. P. Obninskii and T. I. Polner, 113–128. Moscow: Zadruga, 1912.

Radozhitskii, Il'ia. *Pokhodnye zapiski artillerista, s 1812 po 1816 god artillerii podpolkovnika I. . . R . . . .* Vol. 2. Moscow: V tipografii Lazarevykh Instituta vostochnykh iazykov, 1835.

Sovetov, N. N. "D. V. Davydov." *Sbornik biografii kavalergardov, 1801–1826*. Edited by S. A. Panchulidzev, 28–45. St. Petersburg: Ekspeditsiia zagotovleniia gosudarstvennykh bumag, 1906. Moscow: Tri veka istorii, 2001.

Tolstoy, L. N. *Polnoe sobranie sochinenii v devianosta tomakh*. 90 vols. Moscow: Gos. izd-vo khudozh. lit-ry, 1928–58.

Vatsuro, V. E. "Denis Davydov—Poet." *Stikhotvoreniia. Biblioteka poeta*. Edited by L. S. Geyro, 5–48. Leningrad: Sovetskii pisatel', 1984.

Zhiliakova, E. M. "Denis Davydov i povest L. N. Tolstogo 'Dva gusara.'" *Russkaia povest' kak forma vremeni*. Edited by A. S. Ianushkevich, 216–226. Tomsk: Izd. Tomskogo un-ta, 2002.

5
Moscow's Urban Form and Spatial Politics in *War and Peace*

Julie A. Buckler

I. Introduction

The Latin term *civitas* refers to both government and city, evoking a conceptual and physical space where civic communities can flourish and share essential values. The Greek term *polis* similarly reflects the conviction that the urban environment and its political administration are intertwined and mutually constitutive. In the nineteenth century, although cities were understood by many as representing a concentration of humankind's most significant achievements and a locus of opportunity, accelerated development and modernization greatly exacerbated the inequities of urban life. Today, the work of postmodern urban geographers such as Edward Soja and David Harvey offers a critical spatial perspective on the structural inequalities of capital-labor relations that produce what can be termed "the urbanization of injustice."[1] The city gives rise to and perpetuates the inequities suffered by its underprivileged inhabitants.

This chapter explores Tolstoy's attitudes toward the urban environment and its inhabitants, with a particular focus on Moscow. Tolstoy consistently associated cities with human failings such as vanity and ambition, and he saw the distractions of the urban environment as hindering moral self-improvement. He later came to believe that all who profited from the labor of the urban poor bore primary responsibility for their terrible condition. For Tolstoy, the city eventually became the ground from which arise the greatest ills of society.

Tolstoy especially loathed St. Petersburg, Russia's imperial capital, and in his fictional works, he never once represented this city in a positive light. However, Moscow was a different story, at least in the 1860s, as can be seen from its largely positive representation in *War and Peace*. And Tolstoy certainly spent more time in Moscow than in St. Petersburg: it is estimated that Tolstoy visited Moscow more than 150 times between the years 1837 and 1910.[2] Tolstoy's great-grandfather Andrei Ivanovich served in Moscow in the 1770s, and Tolstoy cherished these associations with his family heritage. After the young Tolstoy spent five months indulging himself in Moscow, however, he wrote to his aunt Tatiana in December 1848, "I grew debauched in giving myself over to society life. Now all of this has wearied me terribly, and I'm dreaming again about my life in the country and intend to return to it soon" (PSS 59:25–26; my translation).

Tolstoy idealized Moscow in *War and Peace* (1865–67), but then treated city life to biting sociopolitical critique in both *Anna Karenina* (1875–77) and *Resurrection* (1899). In part 1 of *Anna Karenina*, Countess Nordstrom teases Levin about returning to the "depraved Babylon" of Moscow, and in part 7, Levin finds himself spending too much money in Moscow and wasting his energies paying social calls and attending cultural events. Tolstoy's views on the pernicious influence of the urban environment receive their fullest fictional expression in his last novel, *Resurrection*, which opens with a sweeping indictment:

> Despite the best efforts of people congregating in hundreds of thousands on one small spot to disfigure the land they had squeezed on to, despite their clogging the land with stones to make sure nothing could grow, despite their elimination of every last grass shoot, despite the fumes from coal and oil, despite the

lopping of trees and the driving out of animals and birds, spring was still spring, even in the city.[3] (PSS 32:33)

Tolstoy's long nonfictional essay "What Then Shall We Do?" (1882–86) anticipates *Resurrection* in characterizing the city as a harmful and unsuitable environment for all human life. Tolstoy's understanding of the urban environment as a "poverty generator" that degrades human morals and consciousness can be regarded as part of a tradition that includes the anti-urban thought of Tacitus, St. Augustine, Francesco Petrarch, Michel de Montaigne, and Jean-Jacques Rousseau.[4]

While large portions of Tolstoy's two major novels *War and Peace* and *Anna Karenina* are set in St. Petersburg and Moscow, Tolstoy was not interested in creating fully rendered fictional urban settings; in this, he differs markedly from Dostoevsky, the bard of St. Petersburg slums. In Tolstoy's fictional works, the action that takes place in cities—as opposed to the familiar Tolstoyan topos of the country estate and its rural surroundings—is largely confined to well-defined indoor settings such as private mansions or social and cultural institutions: civil ministries, men's clubs, opera houses, churches, assembly halls, Masonic lodges, and ballrooms. (Granted, these episodes are among the best-loved parts of Tolstoy's fictional works.) For Tolstoy, the urban setting usually serves either as a conceptual frame for intimate relationships, family life, and social events, or as a negative setting in more abstract terms. Interestingly, the careful attention to sounds and smells so evident in Tolstoy's battle sequences, hunting excursions, and midnight troika rides is almost entirely absent from Tolstoy's characterizations of city settings.

Anna Karenina does include several episodes that materialize the urban environment of Moscow as a proto-modernist stream of impressions and vignettes. Levin vividly experiences the sights and sounds of the Moscow streets the morning after he proposes to Kitty Shcherbatskaia for the second time. Anna Karenina takes a dark view of the Moscow city vignettes she glimpses from her carriage window during her fateful ride to the train station. These powerful episodes in *Anna Karenina* suggest that Tolstoy could have developed a distinctive urban poetics, had he wished to do so.

War and Peace represents a departure from Tolstoy's fictional norm, with volume 3, part 3 offering the most extended description of an urban milieu in all of Tolstoy's fiction. Although Tolstoy depicts the chaotic disorder of Moscow in 1812, however, he does relatively little to render the physical city as such. Instead, Tolstoy deploys organic metaphors to characterize the city as both beehive and anthill, each signifying a natural form of human community that will fully re-establish itself after the French invasion. In this, *War and Peace* reflects Tolstoy's desire to incorporate Moscow into the triumphal Russian national mythology of 1812. At the same time, Tolstoy's narrator is intensely critical of the Moscow city administration's handling of the crisis, condemning the powers that be for concealing the imminent danger of the French occupation and leaving the lower classes to their fate. Here Tolstoy comes close to offering a broader sociopolitical critique of spatial injustice in the city.

Tolstoy's fictional treatment of Moscow as an urban environment in *War and Peace* can be productively juxtaposed with his depiction of Moscow's underclass in his later nonfictional essay "What Then Shall We Do?," in which the urban environment lacks any redeeming features, much less the potential for a mystical communion of citizens. The passages in "What Then Shall We Do?" that describe the conditions of poverty in Moscow's might be considered an extension of the 1812 Moscow sequence in *War and Peace*, demonstrating what happens when the city administration and the urban upper classes abandon their responsibilities toward the underprivileged. "What Then Shall We Do?" makes a much more sweeping critique of the urban environment than *War and Peace*, however, rejecting any possibility of solving the social problems posed by the city and dispensing urban critique within a theoretical anticapitalist and anti-modern framework. Tolstoy proposes a radical solution that has no practical application in late-imperial, post-emancipation Russia—that all residents should abandon city life and resettle in the country to live simply without oppressing others.

II. Moscow in *War and Peace*

Unlike St. Petersburg, Moscow is treated fondly in *War and Peace*, as the center of all things Russian, figured by the hospitable and emotionally responsive Rostov family. In separate scenes, Nikolai Rostov and Pierre Bezukhov each feel deeply moved by their return to Moscow after an absence—for both men, this return is a spiritual homecoming. Still, in keeping with Tolstoy's fictional practice, the city environment itself receives minimal attention. The city of Moscow receives its fullest realization as an urban setting that contains a diverse populace only in volume 3, part 3, which treats the evacuation, occupation, and burning of Moscow.

There are only a few moments in the earlier parts of *War and Peace* that prefigure Tolstoy's treatment of the Moscow's humbler inhabitants in the second half. In volume 1, part 1, the action shuttles between the festive Rostov name-day party and the gloomy mansion of the dying Count Bezukhov. Not a glance is spared for the cityscape through which Anna Mikhailovna Drubetskaya and Pierre ride, but there is a curious moment as their carriage drives up to the back entrance of the old Count's residence:

> Just as [Pierre] was stepping out, two men in tradesmen's clothes hastily ran away from the entrance into the shadow of the wall. Having stopped, Pierre made out several more men of the same sort in the shadow of the house on both sides. But neither Anna Mikhailovna, nor the footman, nor the coachman, who could not

help seeing these men, paid any attention to them. So that is how it has to be, Pierre decided to himself. (76; PSS 9:92)

The shadowy tradesmen who hope for a funeral commission avoid drawing attention to themselves before the old Count has died, but this moment is also highly characteristic of Tolstoy's usual fictional treatment of the ordinary population—the tradespeople, vendors, laborers, and servants who were so numerous in nineteenth-century Moscow. Such people generally lurk at the farthest margins of Tolstoy's narrative, glimpsed only briefly and serving as representative "types" for specific trades or social estates.

Tolstoy made written statements in connection with *War and Peace* to justify his primary focus on the aristocracy and lack of attention to the urban lower and middle classes. The lengthiest of these statements appears in an 1864 draft chapter for volume 1, part 1 of the novel. Tolstoy begins by acknowledging that he has thus far written only about "princes, counts, ministers, senators, and their children" and does not expect to give significant attention to Russians of humbler origins:

> The life of merchants, coachmen, seminarists, convicts, and peasants appears to me to be single-faceted and boring, and all the actions of these people, so it appears to me, spring for the most part from the very same sources: envy for those in more fortunate circumstances, self-interest, and the material passions.[5] (PSS 13:238–239)

Tolstoy asserts that the life of the lower classes "carries in itself less of the imprint of the times" and that these lives are simply "unattractive":

> I can in no way comprehend what a policeman, standing at his sentry-box, is thinking, what a shopkeeper, urging one to buy his suspenders or neckties, is thinking or feeling, what a seminarist is

thinking when he is led up to be flogged with birches for the hundredth time, and so forth. I am so far from understanding all this that I cannot even understand what a cow is thinking when she is being milked, or what a horse thinks when she is pulling a barrel.

Tolstoy thus groups merchants and clergy indiscriminately with the lowest classes, casts the lower classes as animals, and asserts his elitist views to almost parodic effect. Alexander Martin argues that Tolstoy's Moscow of 1812 does not provide an accurate reflection of the city's population: "In the novel, there are hardly any merchants, artisans, markets, shops, taverns, slums—indeed, little of what made Moscow one of Europe's major cities."[6] With this omission, Tolstoy ignores the numerous literary representations of the most ordinary Russian urban-dwellers so prominent in the literature of the Natural School in the 1840s–1850s.[7]

In fact, a mere 6 percent of the population in 1812 Moscow were noble, and an even smaller fraction were wealthy aristocrats. According to Martin, "The people who gave Moscow its truly urban character were the middle strata—the 30 to 40% of Muscovites who were petty nobles, civil servants, clergy, merchants, professionals, foreigners, shopkeepers, members of the artisan guilds, and the like."[8] Most aristocrats left Moscow when it was clear that Napoleon and his army would take the city, whereas many middle-class Muscovites were among the more than six thousand Russians remaining in the city.[9]

In volume 3, part 3 of *War and Peace*, Tolstoy depicts the common people left behind in Moscow—peasant laborers and servants, as well as factory workers, artisans, and petty tradespeople. Tolstoy does not treat these lower-class Muscovites as individuals, however, only as parts of a mighty Russian collective that determines the course of history. In his scenes of Moscow being evacuated, Tolstoy does refer to looting by members of the lower classes and by Russian soldiers who separate themselves from their evacuating regiments but provides only a few glimpses that suggest these acts are committed by a limited number of disorderly individuals. If Tolstoy is to cast the general population as part of a patriotic collective whole, he cannot linger over or otherwise emphasize mob violence and social disorder that would contradict this view.

In his 1868 essay "Some Words about *War and Peace*," Tolstoy responded to criticism that he presented a rosy picture of Russian behavior in 1812 Moscow and did not accurately represent the violent character of those times:

> Studying letters, diaries, legends, I did not find all the horrors of that brutality in a greater degree than I find them now or at any other time.... If in our minds we have formed an opinion of the arbitrariness and crude force characteristic of that time, it is only because the legends, memoirs, stories, and novels that have come down to us record only the most outstanding cases of violence and brutality.[10] (1217–1218; PSS 16:8)

Tolstoy consulted memoirs and eyewitness accounts by members of the aristocracy for the research that undergirded *War and Peace*, but he did not refer to those written by members of the middle strata who also experienced Moscow in 1812.[11] As a result, some veterans of 1812 criticized Tolstoy's depiction of the period.[12] *War and Peace* does include angry talk among the lower orders left behind in abandoned Moscow, expressing their resentment toward aristocrats safely ensconced at their country estates and toward Moscow governor general Rostopchin's misleadingly reassuring propaganda leaflets and decrees. But the novel underplays the looting, violence, drunkenness, and civil disorder that, according to the historical record, took place among the Russian populace. Tolstoy also neglects to mention the degradation in sanitary conditions and pervasive stench from excrement and rotting corpses that marked the breakdown in public order.[13]

The first instance of a crowded urban scene in *War and Peace* hints at the potential for violence and disorder, but ultimately comes down on the side of fervent communal feeling. When young Petya Rostov goes to Red Square on his own in hopes of pleading his case as a would-be military volunteer to the tsar, he finds himself hemmed in by the crowd, surrounded by diverse urban townsfolk: "Next to Petya stood a peasant woman, a footman, two merchants, and a retired soldier" (672–673; PSS 11:87–88). The common people of Moscow fill the square, "on the glacis, on the roofs, everywhere," and Petya hears their "joyful talk," noticing on all faces "the same general expression of tenderness and rapture." As the crowd pushes forward, Petya "rolled his eyes out wildly, and rushed forward," seeing "exactly the same wild faces" all around him and swept along with them. Petya is nearly crushed by the surging crowd, but is rescued by a clergyman, who behaves protectively toward the "young gentleman" and elicits the crowd's sympathy, perching Petya on the Tsar-Cannon, where he has an excellent view. Petya rejoins the crowd when the tsar tosses biscuits from the palace balcony: Petya "rushed and tripped up a little old woman" to seize a biscuit.[14] Tolstoy lards this episode with irony, making it clear that Petya finds himself at physical risk alone in the crowd, but that his social standing, visible to all despite his attempted disguise, works to his advantage. Petya himself lacks any self-awareness regarding his privileged status. Tolstoy does depict the crowd's wildness and disorder, but their behavior is motivated by a passionate shared desire to glimpse Alexander I and to capture a biscuit touched by his royal hand.

There are two episodes in volume 3, part 3 that depict an unruly Russian mob in Moscow after it has become clear that the city would be surrendered. Of these, the first serves as a prelude to the second, which renders the horrific scene of Vereshchagin's death. Chapter 23 opens inside a tavern where "drunken shouting and singing was heard" from nearly a dozen Russian factory workers: "Drunk, sweaty, bleary-eyed, straining and opening their mouths wide, they were all singing some song" (880; PSS 11:336–337). Tolstoy does not take the trouble to individuate these men or to give them names. After a brief bloody fight between the factory workers and a group of blacksmiths, the entire group, joined by a community of cobblers, sets off as an impromptu mob to express their anger to "the authorities." Tolstoy gives the reader a sampling of voices from the crowd: "What, the gentry and the merchants have all gone, and we're to perish for that? What, are we dogs or something?" (882–883; PSS 11:340). This single emblematic scene of disorder functions as a lead-up to the episode in which the prisoner Vereshchagin, accused of treason, is murdered by the mob.

The Vereshchagin episode is the only episode that depicts Russian urban mob violence in *War and Peace*. And yet, even here, Tolstoy casts primary blame upon Rostopchin for deliberately inciting the murder to distract the mob and deflect their anger toward him. When Rostopchin first declares it necessary to punish "the villain who has brought ruin to Moscow," the crowd is initially uncertain: "Only in the back rows . . . came grunts, groans, the sounds of shoving and the stamping of shifting feet." Rostopchin must repeatedly incite the crowd to violence, intentionally building the "wave" that rises among those gathered: "To hold on to each other, to breathe in that infected atmosphere, having no strength to stir, and to wait for something unknown, incomprehensible, and dreadful, was becoming unbearable" (888–889; PSS 11:347).

When an officer strikes Vereshchagin on the head with the flat of his broadsword, the prisoner cries out in surprise and a "groan of surprise and horror passed through the crowd." This moment of sympathy cannot prevent the unstoppable wave of violence that follows. Tolstoy clearly views the crowd as fellow victims, at the mercy of Rostopchin's machinations and helpless to resist a natural force arising from the intolerably tense circumstances:

> The barrier of human feeling, strained to the utmost in holding back the crowd, instantly broke. The crime had begun, it was necessary to go through with it. The pitiful moan of reproach was stifled by the menacing and wrathful roar of the crowd. Like the

seventh and last wave that breaks up ships, this last irrepressible wave surged from the back rows, raced towards the front ones, knocked them down, and engulfed everything. (890; PSS 11:348)

The crowd's response resembles the passion that Petya Rostov witnesses at the Kremlin—a "natural" communal reaction that does not allow for individuation.

The crowd is swept away by the wave. This phenomenon is similar to yet different from the Foucauldian "it" that Pierre later senses on the execution field at Devichye field (966–967; PSS 12:40–43). For the French soldiers at Devichye, the inhuman force that guides their cruel actions is systemic and impersonal, whereas the Russian mob in Rostopchin's courtyard, composed of confused and angry citizens, is led astray by a tyrant who uses them as an unwitting instrument of social control. When Vereshchagin is nearly dead, the crowd looks upon him with "horror, reproach, and astonishment," with "painfully pitying expressions," and they shrink from the corpse as it is dragged out.

In contrast to the two mob episodes in volume 3, part 3 of *War and Peace*, Volume IV Part 4 represent Moscow more broadly as an urban system. Tolstoy contrasts urban institutions as empty forms with the urban environment closer to the ground, where common people perform the useful functions that define them, bringing the city back to life.

Tolstoy's elaborate beehive metaphor counters Napoleon's view of Moscow from the Poklonnaya Hill, where Napoleon believes he can see "the quivering life in the city" and feel "the breathing of that big and beautiful body." For Russians, Moscow is a "mother," and every foreigner "must feel the feminine character of this city." For Napoleon, Moscow as a soon-to-be-occupied city is like "a young girl who has lost her honor," and he gazes with desire at "the Oriental beauty lying before him," in what Tolstoy frames as a grotesque and unnatural misperception suggesting the rape of a mother (871; PSS 11:326).

In a lengthy, materially manifested metaphor, Tolstoy counters Napoleon by casting Moscow as an empty queen-less hive, an abandoned urban structure without life. The deity-like "beekeeper," whose discerning eye provides the observed details, taps on the hive's wall and examines the lower chamber, the "superhive" in the upper chamber, and finally the nest within the two central frames. But some essential component of life is absent. The half-alive remaining bees are "sitting over the sacred thing they were guarding, which is no longer there," in a state of senseless unknowing, moving about pointlessly and sluggishly, "having lost the awareness of life" (875; PSS 11:331). Ensuring that the reader makes the connection, Tolstoy follows his beehive metaphor with the observation, "In various corners of Moscow only a few people still stirred meaninglessly, keeping to old habits and not understanding what they were doing" (875; PSS 11:331). The image of the beehive manifests Tolstoy's principle of "swarm life" and his bottom-up view of history as the sum of infinitesimal elements—history as produced by an unconscious swarm-like intelligence that is linked to natural law, to national destiny, and perhaps to divine will.[15]

As a counterpart to the meaningless movement of the remaining bees in the hive, Tolstoy reproduces a proclamation from Napoleon, which fails to persuade the Russian populace to restore urban order:

> Stillness is returning to the capital, and order is being restored in it.... Citizens! Return with confidence to your dwellings: you will soon find ways to satisfy your needs! Craftsmen and labor-loving artisans! Go back to your handiwork: houses, shops, and protective guards are waiting for you, and you will be duly paid for your work!... Depots are being set up in the city, where peasants can bring their surplus stocks and plants of the earth. The government has taken ... measures to provide them with a free market.... Immediately means will be employed for the restoration or normal trade. (1004–1005; PSS 12:86–87)

According to Tolstoy's narrator, these hollow phrases "did not touch the essence of the matter, however, but, like the hands of a clock with the mechanism removed, turned arbitrarily and aimlessly, without catching the gears" (1005; PSS 12:88). The clock metaphor, which recalls the earlier tower-clock metaphor for the battle of Austerlitz, reflects Tolstoy's rejection of top-down methods in urban government as well as national history. Throughout the novel, the narrator asserts that decisions taken far away in St. Petersburg have no influence on the course of the war, since they have little connection to the reality on the ground. The return to the clock metaphor in volume 4, this time cast as ineffectual rather than inexorable, will be countered by Tolstoy's characterization of Moscow in volume 4, part 4 as a self-regenerating anthill reborn after the French occupation.

When Pierre and the other Russian prisoners in the French convoy walk through the city as they begin their retreat, Tolstoy hints at the reclamation of Moscow, evoking specific places and their names: the lanes of Khamovniki, the Kaluga Road curving around the Neskuchny Garden, Kamenny Bridge, Bolshaya Ordynka, Krymsky Ford, and the square where Zamoskvoretskaya and Kaluga Streets meet. Here Tolstoy asserts the city's continued existence as a grounded place that can be mapped as objective reality despite the vast damage from the occupation.

When Pierre returns to Moscow after his convalescence in Orel, he sees that the city is indeed rising again, and understands that the ruins of the fire are the source of Moscow's renewal:

> Driving along the streets amidst the charred ruins of houses, he was astonished at the beauty of these ruins. The chimney stacks of the houses, the broken-down walls, picturesquely reminiscent of the Rhine and the Colosseum, were strung out, hiding each other, through the burnt quarters. Cabbies and their passengers, carpenters notching frames, market women and shopkeepers all glance at Pierre with merry, beaming faces. (1120; PSS 12:226)

In his reading of this scene, Andreas Schönle emphasizes "the restorative social functions of ruins," which offer hope for moral regeneration and social transformation, releasing the energy bound by the inflexible institutions about which Tolstoy was so skeptical.[16] For Schönle, "The ruin is the authentic form of the city," the common ground from which an even more authentic urban community can arise. Despite the universally merry faces that Pierre notices, however, there is little indication that reborn Moscow will have the interests of its humbler inhabitants at heart.

In setting up a sharp contrast between Russian and French approaches to establishing an urban order, Tolstoy's narrator declares that the occupying French had found Moscow empty "but with all the forms of a city leading an organically regular life, with its various functions of trade, crafts, luxury, state government, religion. These forms were lifeless, but they still existed." The longer the French stayed, however, "the more these forms of city life were obliterated, and in the end it all merged into one indistinct, lifeless field for looting" (1109; PSS 12:212). Empty urban structures without the animating content of Russian inhabitants correspond to Napoleon's hollow proclamation, the lifeless forms of urban life akin to official but empty words.

In volume 4, part 4, the people of Moscow rebuild their city spontaneously, seemingly with little help from any institutions of government, in an organic process that Tolstoy describes with recourse to his second entomological metaphor of the anthill:

> Just as it is hard to explain why and where ants hurry to from a demolished anthill . . . so it would be hard to explain the reasons that made the Russian people, after the departure of the French, crowd into the place which was formerly called Moscow. But just as, when looking at the ants scattered around the destroyed anthill, despite its complete obliteration, one can see by the tenacity, the energy, the countless numbers of swarming insects, that everything has been destroyed, except for something indestructible,

> immaterial, which made for the whole strength of the anthill—so Moscow, in the month of October, despite the fact that there were no authorities, no churches, no holy objects, no wealth, no houses, was the same Moscow it had been in August. Everything was destroyed, except for something immaterial but mighty and indestructible. (1108–1109; PSS 12:211)

Unlike the inhuman force of a European system of ideology or government imposed from above, this mighty and indestructible Russian energy arises naturally and represents a kind of common property. This energy, which also leaves no room for dissent, reflects the potent Russian mythology of 1812, casting this moment as a major unifying event in the ascendance of the Russian nation.[17]

At times, Tolstoy's determination to see all Russian actors in a positive light approaches the absurd. Tolstoy's narrator had asserted that those who abandoned the city as the French approached were performing a latent patriotism that ultimately led to Napoleon's expulsion, and here he declares that the longer Russian looting went on and the greater the number of people who participated, "the more quickly it restored the wealth of Moscow and the regular life of the city." Looting, a lawless activity, nevertheless gives rise to a restorative Russian energy that results in the common good: "Besides looters, the most varied people, some drawn by curiosity, some by official duties, some by calculation—house owners, clergy, high- and low-ranking officials, tradesmen, artisans, muzhiks—flowed into Moscow from all sides, like blood to the heart" (1109; PSS 12:212). And within a week,

> Muzhiks coming with empty carts to carry things off were stopped by the authorities and forced to cart the dead bodies out of the city. Other muzhiks . . . came to the city with wheat, oats, hay, and beat each other down to prices lower than before. Teams of carpenters, hoping for high pay, entered Moscow every day, and on all sides there were new houses under construction

and burned-down houses being repaired. Merchants opened their stalls for trade. Cookshops and inns were set up in burnt houses. The clergy resumed services in many churches that had not burned down. (1109–1110; PSS 12:212–213)

Whether characterized as a great wave, beehive, anthill, or human body brought to life by the circulation of healthy blood, the Russian people in *War and Peace* exist to serve a broader national purpose. They are not individuated or given voice—apart from random scraps "overheard" in the narrative—and exist only as members of castes who perform specific functions in the urban environment.

This moment of great hope toward the end of *War and Peace* was indeed realized by the post-1812 transformation and modernization of Moscow. The Moscow city center was rebuilt in more European style: new boulevards were laid out, and new squares, plazas, and parks appeared, including the Alexander gardens by the Kremlin's western walls. Many of these improvements suggested that Moscow was becoming a modernizing urban environment with more public spaces for all to enjoy.[18] During the final decades of the nineteenth century, after the Emancipation in 1861, however, this hopeful moment was overtaken by an uncontrolled expansion of Moscow's population that gave rise to the enormous increase in urban poverty that Tolstoy documented in "What Then Shall We Do?"

In *War and Peace*, Moscow becomes a symbol of Russian identity—determined, resilient, hopeful, generative, and communal. The Moscow sequences in volumes 3 and 4 correspond to the battlefield episodes elsewhere in the novel, requiring Tolstoy to manage a vast number of human participants within a complex panoramic setting. Tolstoy represents battles as pointless and chaotic mass events, however, whereas he casts Moscow as the locus of shared Russian national potential. This largely positive representation of an urban setting is unique in Tolstoy's oeuvre. *War and Peace* can be productively juxtaposed with the extended nonfictional essay that Tolstoy produced some twenty-five years later. With its focus on urban poverty, "What Then Shall We Do?" paints a dark view of the Russian urban population in mid-1880s Moscow, more than seventy years after its triumphant post-1812 rebuilding. In essence, "What Then Shall We Do?" repudiates the very possibility of an urban *communitas* whose spiritual core nourishes and is nourished by all urban residents in equal measure.

III. "What Then Shall We Do?"

The rapid and uncontrolled expansion of modern cities had enormous social consequences, with accelerating industrialization and mass migration from the countryside resulting in mass urban poverty. As Jan C. Behrends has argued, these changes were most severe on the periphery of the Western world, where growth was fastest and least moderated by the state, as was the case in both Russia and the United States.[19] During the final decades of the nineteenth century, Moscow numbered among the fastest-growing cities worldwide, but social welfare programs, whether funded by the state or private charities, were woefully inadequate to the problems of the urban poor—joblessness, homelessness, alcoholism, prostitution, and crime.[20]

In the fall of 1881, at his wife's urging, Tolstoy and his family moved to Moscow for their children's education and social development. He was anguished by the scale of the poverty he saw on the streets of Moscow. In October 1881, Tolstoy wrote in his diary:

> Unfortunates! And there is no life. Stench, stones, luxury, poverty. Debauchery. Villains have come together, robbing the common people; they have arranged for soldiers and law courts to protect their orgies, and they feast. As for the common people, there is nothing more they can do other than take advantage of

the passions of these others and lure back from them what has been stolen. (PSS 49:58; my translation)

In late January 1882, Tolstoy began working with a group carrying out the Moscow census. He hoped that the corps of young volunteers ready to go into Moscow's poorest quarters to interact with the needy and identify opportunities to better their lot would be more effective than merely collecting charitable donations from Moscow's wealthiest citizens.[21] After a short time, however, Tolstoy grew disillusioned with the potential for well-intended efforts to remedy the condition of the urban poor, dismissing the possibility that he could personally help even a few individuals. He came to believe that all such efforts were doomed to reproduce the very social divisions they proposed to address.

In hopes of disseminating his bold ideas, Tolstoy worked on the long nonfictional essay eventually titled "What Then Shall We Do?" ("Tak chto zhe nam delat'?"), during the period 1882–86. The essay consists of twenty-four chapters, the first twelve of which describe the condition of the urban poor in Moscow. In his conversations with Moscow's indigent, Tolstoy recorded many individual stories and circumstances, in a departure from his previous fictional practice. Later chapters present a more expansive and abstract critique of Russian society, the capitalist system of labor and production, and money itself as a primary source of unequal wealth.[22] One of Tolstoy's early working titles for this piece was "Life in a Christian City," suggesting a connection with Augustine of Hippo's fifth-century *De civitate Dei contra paganos* (*The City of God*), but also a direct link with his own seminal experience witnessing a public execution in Paris, a connection that Tolstoy makes explicit in "What Then Shall We Do?":

> Thirty years ago, in the presence of a thousand spectators, I saw a man decapitated by a guillotine in Paris. . . . By my presence and lack of interference, I approved this sin, and participated in it. Just

as now, at the sight of this starvation, cold, and humiliation of thousands of people, I understood, not with my reason, nor with my heart, but with my whole being, that the existence of tens of thousands of such people in Moscow is a crime, not committed a single time, but unceasingly committed—no matter what the wise men of the world tell me about this being unavoidable—while I, with other thousands, gorge myself on fillet and sturgeon, and cover horses and floors with cloth coverings and carpets, and that I, with my luxury, am not only present for this, but am also a direct participant in it.[23] (PSS 25:190)

"What Then Shall We Do?" represents Tolstoy's attempt to address what Inessa Medzhibovskaya calls "the daily genocide of rich against the poor."[24] In it, Tolstoy poses two central questions, the first of which is "Why should I go to see the sufferings of men whom I am unable to help?" (PSS 25:186). Tolstoy poses this first question to himself after seeing a policeman arrest a beggar and then following them to the police station to inquire fruitlessly about the situation. Tolstoy promptly answers himself in the text with "another voice," asserting that it is his responsibility as a Moscow-dweller to bear witness. Irina Paperno links his answer with "Come and see," the New Testament commandment from Revelation 6:1.[25] The second question is self-focused: "Who am I who wishes to help people?" (PSS 25:245). Paperno observes, "Rather than make efforts to improve other people's lives, Tolstoy decides to change his own."[26] Tolstoy describes the "daily genocide" as a moral eyewitness, but then chooses to withdraw into his own thinking and writing and to repudiate his aristocratic privilege by living as simply as possible.

The most vivid chapters in "What Then Shall We Do?" describe Tolstoy's visits to the Khitrov market, Liapinsky dosshouse, and Rzhanov Fortress, the last a large tenement building on Protochnyi Lane.[27] Tolstoy was appalled by the degradation and immorality that he witnessed:

> The spectacle was terrible because of the crowding ... and the intermingling of men and women. The women who were not dead drunk were sleeping with men. Many women with children were sleeping with strange men on narrow cots. Terrible was the spectacle in its poverty, filth, raggedness, and the frightened condition of these common people; and mainly terrible because of the enormous number of people who were in this condition. One apartment, then another just like it, and a third, and a tenth, and a twentieth, and there was no end to them. (PSS 25:219)

The residents of the tenement lodging-house were of diverse origins, constituting a kind of cosmos of the Moscow underclass, pushed toward this fate by a common social force:

> The residents of these houses compose the lowest urban population, of whom there are probably more than one hundred thousand in Moscow. Here, in this building, there representatives of this population of every sort: there are small proprietors and artisans, bootmakers, brush-makers, joiners, turners, shoemakers, tailors, blacksmiths; there are drivers, independent hawkers and traders, laundresses, secondhand dealers, usurers, day laborers, and people with no definite occupations; and there are beggars and prostitutes. (PSS 25:202)

For Tolstoy, all city residents who profited from the labor of the urban poor were responsible for their dire circumstances. He poses another central question: "What is urban life and urban poverty?" In a doomed quest, common people moved from the country, "that is, away from those places where there are forests and fields, and grain, and livestock, where the whole wealth of the land is located," to make a living "in that place where there are neither trees, nor grass, nor even soil, but only stone and dust" (PSS 25:227–228). Migrants from the countryside were drawn by seemingly easier earnings and better living in the city but fell into drunkenness and profligate ways. Social problems resulted directly from "the passing of the wealth of the producers into the hands of the non-producers and the accumulation of wealth in the cities." Thus, concluded Tolstoy, "We, through our luxurious life, directly spread [infection] among those people whom we wish to help" (PSS 25:232). Those familiar with Tolstoy's thought will recognize the "infection" metaphor as part of his discourse on art, but here infection represents an immoral assumption of privilege. In fact, Tolstoy returns to the anthill metaphor from *War and Peace* to characterize urban poverty as a violation of natural law:

> I see that what is taking place resembles what would happen in an anthill, if the society of the ants had lost the feeling of a common law, if individual ants from the base of the hill should start dragging the fruits of labor to the top, straitening the base and widening the apex, and in this way, also compelling the other ants to move themselves from the base to the apex. (PSS 25:244)

The rebuilding of Moscow is portrayed as a natural phenomenon, whereas the hierarchy of wealth in Russian urban society is a crime against nature.

In asserting that the economic and social structures that sustain Moscow are the primary cause of mass urban poverty, Tolstoy concluded that the rich should give up their wealth and leave the city for a simpler life that leveled economic inequities. The views at which Tolstoy arrived differed greatly from those of Henry George, whose 1879 book *Progress and Poverty* Tolstoy had admired when he read it in 1885. George supported the nationalization of land through a single land tax, an idea that Tolstoy found promising, but Tolstoy did not share George's vision of a city that could serve all residents once the unequal distribution of wealth had been thereby solved. George imagined the urban future in utopian terms:

> We could establish public baths, museums, libraries, gardens, lecture rooms, music and dancing halls, theaters, universities, technical schools, shooting galleries, playgrounds, gymnasiums, etc. Heat, light, and motive power, as well as water, might be conducted through our streets at public expense . . . and in a thousand ways the public revenues made to foster efforts for the public benefit.[28]

Tolstoy was no proponent of socialism, which he saw as a pernicious institutionalization of social order that was antithetical to moral growth in a Christian spirit. "What Then Shall We Do?" thus represents a repudiation of the nationalist myth in *War and Peace* that coalesced around the image of reborn Moscow, as well as a rejection of the ideal conception of a Christian city with which Tolstoy began his project in the 1880s.

Although Tolstoy's wholesale rejection of urban life did not prove influential in Russia, his ideas about urban spatial justice inspired others, among them Jane Addams, founder of Chicago's Hull House in 1889. Addams's 1893 book *The Subjective Necessity for Social Settlements* reflected Tolstoy's belief that traditional practices of charity were inadequate to the widespread problem of urban poverty. Addams posed a solution that emphasized American ideals of democracy and citizenship.[29]

IV. Conclusion

In *War and Peace*, Tolstoy renders the lower classes of 1812 Moscow as anonymous and largely dehumanized, members of a vast insect community who perform their biologically determined functions. It is precisely this blindly dismissive attitude toward Moscow's poorer inhabitants that Tolstoy so fiercely denounces in "What Then Shall We Do?," in transcribing the life-stories and situations of individuals during his participation in the Moscow census. This project of individuated understanding proved so disturbing to Tolstoy, however, that he withdrew both his physical presence and his reformist energies from the plight of the urban poor, completing his long essay with its increasingly abstract ideas after he had already disengaged.

After completing "What Then Shall We Do?," Tolstoy lost interest in the urban environment both as an object of written representation and as a site for real-life advocacy. In "What Then Shall We Do?" the city is irredeemable. By its very nature, the urban environment cannot serve the needs of its humbler inhabitants but can only exploit them and ignore their suffering. *War and Peace* contains the seeds of this critique in its quasi-sympathetic account of the Russian lower classes who remained in occupied Moscow, but the novel in no way suggests that Tolstoy would arrive at a thorough condemnation of the modernizing late-imperial city. Tolstoy, for whom social justice and social ills were such pressing concerns, was unable to accept the urban environment as an inevitable fact of modern human life, the product of technological advancement regarded by so many as progress; much less could he imagine how the city could be improved in meaningful ways for all urban dwellers. The hopeful and "natural" rebuilding of Moscow in *War and Peace* is thus a Tolstoyan aberration, fueled by wishful nationalist mythology. In this sense, the angrily bewildered humble inhabitants of abandoned Moscow prefigure the fate of the urban poor under late-imperial Russian rule.

Notes

1. See, for example, Edward W. Soja, *Seeking Spatial Justice* (Minneapolis: University of Minnesota Press, 2010), 49.
2. N. S. Rodionov, *L. N. Tolstoi v Moskve* (Moscow: Moskovskii rabochii, 1958), 3.
3. The English version is from Anthony Briggs's translation of *Resurrection* (New York: Penguin Books, 2009), 5.

4. Andrzej Dudek, "Leo Tolstoy's Urban Anthropology," *Rusycystyczne Studia Literaturoznawcze* 26, no. 3 (2016): 86.
5. The translation is from Kathryn B. Feuer, *Tolstoy and the Genesis of War and Peace*, ed. Robin Feuer Miller and Donna Tussing Orwin (Ithaca, NY: Cornell University Press, 1996), 146–147.
6. Alexander M. Martin, "Moscow in 1812: Myths and Realities," in *Tolstoy on War: Narrative Art and Historical Truth in "War and Peace,"* ed. Rick McPeak and Donna Tussing Orwin (Ithaca, NY: Cornell University Press, 2012), 43.
7. For very different literary representations of the Moscow population, see such works as I. T. Kokorev, *Ocherki Moskvy sorokovykh godov*, ed. N. S. Ashukin (Moscow, 1932); A. Levitov, *Moskovskie nory i trushchoby*, 2nd ed. (St. Petersburg, 1869); M. N. Poliakov, *Moskvichi doma, v gostiakh i na ulitse: Razskazy iz narodnago byta* (Moscow, 1858); and P. Vistengof, *Ocherki Moskovskoi zhizni* (Moscow, 1842).
8. Martin, "Moscow in 1812," 47–48. See also L. V. Koshman, "The Meshchanstvo in Nineteenth Century Russia," *Russian Social Science Review* 57, no. 5 (September–October 2016): 320–349.
9. Martin, "Moscow in 1812," 48. See also Andrei G. Tartakovskii, "Naselenie Moskvy v period frantsuzskoi okkupatsii," *Istoricheskie Zapiski* 93 (1973): 356–379.
10. For a nuanced consideration, see Dan Ungurianu, "The Use of Historical Sources in *War and Peace*," in *Tolstoy on War: Narrative Art and Historical Truth in "War and Peace"*, ed. Rick McPeak and Donna Tussing Orwin (Ithaca, NY: Cornell University Press, 2012), 26–41. On pages 37–38 of his article, Ungurianu assesses Viktor Shklovsky's wholesale dismissal of Tolstoy's historical method in Shklovsky's *Material i stil' v romane Tolstogo "Voina i mir"* (Moscow, 1928; reprint, The Hague, 1970), ultimately concluding that despite mistakes and idiosyncrasies, *War and Peace* does rest on a solid factual foundation.
11. For a list of works that Tolstoy did consult, see "Spisok knig, kotorymi polzovalsia L. N. Tolstoi vo vremia pisaniia 'Voiny i mira'" (PSS 16:141–145). *Rasskazy ochevidtsev o dvenadtsatom gode*, ed. T. Tolycheva [E. V. Novosiltsova], 2nd ed. (Moscow, 1912), first published in 1865, is one example of an alternative source of views that Tolstoy could have chosen to consult.
12. For details, see Dan Ungurianu, "Visions and Versions of History: Veterans of 1812 on Tolstoy's *War and Peace*," *Slavic and East European Journal* 44,

no. 1 (2000): 48–63. See also A. V. Gulin, *Lev Tolstoi i puti russkoi istorii* (Moscow: IMLI RAN, 2004), 213–230.
13. Martin, "Moscow in 1812," 53–54.
14. For a discussion of this episode in relation to documented history, see Ungurianu, "Use of Historical Sources," 34.
15. For discussion of the beehive metaphor and its significance in *War and Peace*, see Andreas Schönle, "Modernity as a 'Destroyed Anthill': Tolstoy on History and the Aesthetics of Ruins," in *Ruins of Modernity*, ed. Julia Hell and Andreas Schönle (Durham, NC: Duke University Press, 2010), 89–102. See also Thomas Newlin, "Swarm Life and the Biology of *War and Peace*," *Slavic Review* 71, no. 2 (Summer 2012): 359–384.
16. Schönle, "Modernity as a 'Destroyed Anthill,'" 96–97.
17. For a broader discussion of the anthill and its significance in Russian intellectual history, see Vladimir Wozniuk, "In the Shadow of the Anthill: Religious Faith, Individual Freedom, and the Common Good in the Thought of V. S. Solov'ev," *Russian Review* 67 (October 2008): 623–637.
18. For a description of Moscow before and after 1812, see Albert J. Schmidt, *The Architecture and Planning of Classical Moscow: A Cultural History* (Philadelphia, PA: American Philosophical Society, 1989).
19. Jan C. Behrends, "Visions of Civility: Lev Tolstoy and Jane Addams on the Urban Condition in Fin de Siècle Moscow and Chicago," *European Review of History—Revue européenne d'histoire* 18, no. 3 (2011): 337.
20. For information about the urban condition in late-imperial Moscow, see Joseph Bradley, *Muzhik and Muscovite: Urbanization in Late Imperial Russia* (Berkeley: University of California Press, 1985); Robert Johnson, *Peasant and Proletarian: The Working Class of Moscow in the Late Nineteenth Century* (Leicester: Leicester University Press, 1979); and Adele Lindenmeyr, *Poverty Is Not a Vice: Charity, Society and the State in Imperial Russia* (Princeton, NJ: Princeton University Press, 1996).
21. Tolstoy lays out the problem in his January 1882 article "O perepisi v Moskve," which was published in *Contemporary News*. The text can be found in PSS 25:173–181.
22. Individual chapters and fragments appeared in the journal *Russian Wealth* and in Tolstoy's collected works from 1886, but the essay was not published in full in Russia until the Posrednik publishing house put it out in 1906. A partial version was published in Geneva in 1886 and a full version in 1889. An English translation can be found in *The Complete Works of Count Tolstoy*, vol. 17, trans. Leo Wiener (Boston: Dana Estes, 1904).

23. All English translations of passages from "What Then Shall We Do?" are my own.
24. Inessa Medzhibovskaya. *Tolstoy and the Religious Culture of His Time: A Biography of a Long Conversion, 1845–1887* (Lanham, MD: Lexington Books, 2008), 266.
25. Irina Paperno, *"Who, What Am I?": Tolstoy Struggles to Narrate the Self* (Ithaca, NY: Cornell University Press, 2014), 103. Chapter 5 is devoted to a reading of "What Then Shall We Do?"
26. Paperno, *Who, What Am I?*, 106.
27. For a remarkable description of the situation at Khitrov Market, see the chapter "Khitrovka" in V. A. Giliarovskii, *Moskva i moskvichi: Vospominaniia* (Moscow: Vserossiiskii soiuz poetov, 1926).
28. Henry George, *Progress and Poverty: An Inquiry into the Cause of Industrial Depressions and of Increase of Want with Increase of Wealth: The Remedy* (New York: National Single Tax League Publishers, 1905), 454. See also Jesse Stavis, "Double Thoughts on the Single Tax: Tolstoy, Henry George, and the Meaning(s) of Progress," *Tolstoy Studies Journal* 28 (2016): 75–93.
29. Cf. Behrends, "Visions of Civility," 346.

Works Cited

Behrends, Jan C. "Visions of Civility: Lev Tolstoy and Jane Addams on the Urban Condition in Fin de Siècle Moscow and Chicago." *European Review of History / Revue européenne d'histoire* 18, no. 3 (2011): 335–357.

Bradley, Joseph. *Muzhik and Muscovite: Urbanization in Late Imperial Russia*. Berkeley: University of California Press, 1985.

Dudek, Andrzej. "Leo Tolstoy's Urban Anthropology." *Rusycystyczne Studia Literaturoznawcze*, no. 26 (2016): 75–86.

Feuer, Kathryn B. *Tolstoy and the Genesis of War and Peace*. Edited by Robin Feuer Miller and Donna Tussing Orwin. Ithaca, NY: Cornell University Press, 1996.

George, Henry. *Progress and Poverty: An Inquiry into the Cause of Industrial Depressions and of Increase of Want with Increase of Wealth: The Remedy*. New York: National Single Tax League Publishers, 1905.

Giliarovskii, V. A. *Moskva i moskvichi: Vospominaniia*. Moscow: Vserossiiskii soiuz poetov, 1926.

Gulin, A. V. *Lev Tolstoi i puti russkoi istorii*. Moscow: IMLI RAN, 2004.

Johnson, Robert. *Peasant and Proletarian: The Working Class of Moscow in the Late Nineteenth Century*. Leicester: Leicester University Press, 1979.

Kokorev, I. T. *Ocherki Moskvy sorokovykh godov*. Edited by N. S. Ashukin. Moscow, 1932.

Koshman, L. V. "The Meshchanstvo in Nineteenth Century Russia." *Russian Social Science Review* 57, no. 5 (September–October 2016): 320–349.

Levitov, A. *Moskovskie nory i trushchoby*. 2nd ed. St. Petersburg, 1869.

Lindenmeyr, Adele. *Poverty Is Not a Vice: Charity, Society and the State in Imperial Russia*. Princeton, NJ: Princeton University Press, 1996.

Martin, Alexander M. "Moscow in 1812: Myths and Realities." *Tolstoy on War: Narrative Art and Historical Truth in "War and Peace."* Edited by Rick McPeak and Donna Tussing Orwin, 42–58. Ithaca, NY: Cornell University Press, 2012.

Medzhibovskaya, Inessa. *Tolstoy and the Religious Culture of His Time: A Biography of a Long Conversion, 1845–1887*. Lanham, MD: Lexington Books, 2008.

Newlin, Thomas. "Swarm Life and the Biology of *War and Peace*." *Slavic Review* 71, no. 2 (Summer 2012): 359–384.

Paperno, Irina. *"Who, What Am I?": Tolstoy Struggles to Narrate the Self*. Ithaca, NY: Cornell University Press, 2014.

Poliakov, M. N. *Moskvichi doma, v gostiakh i na ulitse: Razskazy iz narodnago byta*. Moscow, 1858.

Rodionov, N. S. *L. N. Tolstoi v Moskve*. Moscow: Moskovskii rabochii, 1958.

Schmidt, Albert J. *The Architecture and Planning of Classical Moscow: A Cultural History*. Philadelphia, PA: American Philosophical Society, 1989.

Schönle, Andreas. "Modernity as a 'Destroyed Anthill': Tolstoy on History and the Aesthetics of Ruins." *Ruins of Modernity*. Edited by Julia Hell and Andreas Schönle, 89–102. Durham, NC: Duke University Press, 2010.

Shklovskii, Viktor. *Material i stil' v romane Tolstogo "Voina i mir"*. Moscow, 1928; reprinted The Hague, 1970.

Soja, Edward W. *Seeking Spatial Justice*. Minneapolis: University of Minnesota Press, 2010.

Stavis, Jesse. "Double Thoughts on the Single Tax: Tolstoy, Henry George, and the Meaning(s) of Progress." *Tolstoy Studies Journal* 28 (2016): 75–93.

Tartakovskii, Andrei G. "Naselenie Moskvy v period frantsuzskoi okkupatsii." *Istoricheskie Zapiski* 93 (1973): 356–379.

Tolstoy, Lev. *The Complete Works of Count Tolstoy*. Vol. 17. Translated by Leo Wiener. Boston: Dana Estes, 1904.

Tolstoy, Lev. *Polnoe sobranie sochinenii*. Edited by V. G. Chertkov. 90 vols. Moscow: Khodozhestvennaia literatura, 1928–58.

Tolycheva, T. *Rasskazy ochevidtsev o dvenadtsatom gode*. 2nd ed. Moscow, 1912.

Ungurianu, Dan. "The Use of Historical Sources in *War and Peace*." *Tolstoy on War: Narrative Art and Historical Truth in "War and Peace"*. Edited by Rick McPeak and Donna Tussing Orwin, 26–41. Ithaca, NY: Cornell University Press, 2012.

Ungurianu, Dan. "Visions and Versions of History: Veterans of 1812 on Tolstoy's *War and Peace*." *Slavic and East European Journal* 44, no. 1 (Spring 2000): 48–63.

Vistengof, P. *Ocherki Moskovskoi zhizni*. Moscow, 1842.

Wozniuk, Vladimir. "In the Shadow of the Anthill: Religious Faith, Individual Freedom, and the Common Good in the Thought of V. S. Solov'ev." *Russian Review* 67 (October 2008): 623–637.

6
Life Immersed in Love
Natasha, Andrei, and Pierre

Predrag Cicovacki

I. Love as the Essence of Life?

Tolstoy is not known as a "poet of love." *Anna Karenina* may lead some to reconsider this view, but we do not readily suspect that *War and Peace* may do so as well. Yet buried deep in the last part of *War and Peace*, Tolstoy makes a surprising statement: "Suddenly [Natasha's] love for her mother showed her that the essence of life—love—was still alive in her." Then, after proclaiming so decisively that love is the essence of life, Tolstoy concludes the paragraph with yet another intriguing claim: "Love awoke, and life awoke" (1080; PSS 12:177).

Perhaps under the influence of his later works of nonfiction, we should expect that Tolstoy would relate any claim about the essence of life to morality or religion, not love. Yet Tolstoy's claim, worthy of Plato, is one of the most philosophically interesting claims made in *War and Peace*. Maybe his claim has received minimal interest from philosophers because love has not been a primary topic of philosophical discussions. Let us then give Tolstoy's claim more attention by first examining his declaration that the awakening of love leads to the awakening of life.

We ordinarily think of the relationship of love and life in the opposite order: love happens—or comes, or enters into our lives—when the time or situation in life is ripe for it. In the spring, for example, after a long slumber during the winter season, life awakens, and it usually leads to a revitalization of all of our capacities, including that for love. In a person's youth, which corresponds to the spring season and is accompanied by a great impetus for love, a similar thing happens. In the novel, Tolstoy depicts a period in the life of the Rostov family, when "Vera was a beautiful twenty-year-old girl; Sonya a sixteen-year-old, with all the loveliness of a just-opened flower; [and] Natasha, half young lady, half child, now childishly funny, now girlishly bewitching" (330; PSS 10:43). As Tolstoy describes it metaphorically,

> Never had the amorous air in the Rostovs' house, the atmosphere of being in love, manifested itself so strongly as during these festive days. "Seize the moments of happiness, make them love you, fall in love yourself! That is the only real thing in this world—the rest is all nonsense. And that is the one thing we're taken up with here," said the atmosphere. (331; PSS 10:45)

Whether or not love is the essence of life, and what exactly Tolstoy had in mind when making this claim, cannot be established without further inquiry. In a novel as complex as *War and Peace*, it is to be expected that Tolstoy would deal with a whole spectrum of manifestations of love: from the love of one's lover, friends, parents, or children to that of one's nation, as well as the love of life or God. It is difficult to believe that all such forms of love could justify the claim that love is the essence of life. To further probe Tolstoy's claim, I will focus my considerations on the experience of love of his three central characters: Natasha Rostova, Andrei Bolkonsky, and Pierre Bezukhov. I will further narrow my inquiry to three forms of love, which I will call ecstatic, devotional, and sublimated.

The initial love of Prince Andrei and Natasha provides a good illustration of ecstatic love: it leads first to their engagement and, later, due to Natasha's infidelity, to their breakup. Pierre's realization that he loves Natasha, despite his being married to Hélène

Kuragina and Natasha's being engaged to his best friend, represents devotional love: out of his loving devotion for Natasha, Pierre decides to hide his feelings from her and removes himself from her life. Sublimated love is the relationship that Tolstoy describes as occurring after the experience of great suffering or some personal tragedy. Tolstoy believes not only that such experiences can lead to important insights about life as a whole but also that they prepare one to recognize the most elevated form of love described in this novel. Such love occurs between the dying Prince Andrei and Natasha, several years after their experience of ecstatic love. Even more clearly, sublimated love develops between Pierre and Natasha after their recovery from the traumas of the last months of the war. Since this form of love is likely of the greatest philosophical relevance, in trying to understand how this form of love may support Tolstoy's claim that love is the essence of life, I will rely on some of the views of Iris Murdoch. A novelist and a philosopher as well as a great admirer of Tolstoy, Murdoch has some profound insights about the relevance of love and the nature of the sublime. They will assist us in properly appreciating Tolstoy's understanding of the relevance of love in human life.

II. Ecstatic Love

The passages in which Tolstoy describes how Prince Andrei and Natasha fell in love are some of the most romantic in the novel. Their first encounter occurs at the Rostov estate, when one night, through an open window, Prince Andrei accidentally overhears Natasha's excited singing and talking coming from the floor above. Natasha could not understand how her best friend Sonya, or anyone else, could sleep on such a beautiful spring night, when the moon is shining so radiantly and everyone should be thinking about flying into the sky! Prince Andrei is then thirty-one, Natasha about sixteen. Prince Andrei had been married previously, but his wife died during childbirth; after her death, he sealed his already cold heart in order to dedicate himself to "more important things in life." Even before that, in one of the first pages of the novel, Prince Andrei displays his pessimistic attitude about marriage and love by advising Pierre:

> Never, never marry, my friend. Here's my advice to you: don't marry until you can tell yourself that you've done all you could, and until you've stopped loving the woman you've chosen, until you see her clearly, otherwise you'll be cruelly and irremediably mistaken. Marry when you're old and good for nothing.... Otherwise all that's good and lofty in you will be lost. (28; PSS 9:34)

Prince Andrei is a man of strong will and sharp intellect. He advises Pierre not only against marriage but also against ecstatic love. Such love is too irrational: it takes control of our lives. Despite Prince Andrei's firm conviction and iron will, which he shares with his father, Natasha's charming singing and innocent chatter that starry night evoke in his soul "a tangle of youthful thoughts and hopes, contradictory to his whole life" (422; PSS 10:157). His love for Natasha does not develop right away, but already on the way home from the Rostov estate, "a causeless spring-time feeling of joy and renewal came over him" (423; PSS 10:158).

The ecstatic love between Prince Andrei and Natasha develops during and immediately after Natasha's first ball. Pierre, a clumsy youth and terrible dancer himself, understands what this ball means to Natasha and is pained as much as she is about her not being approached by a single dance partner. Pierre nudges Prince Andrei to dance with his overexcited friend, and the emotions of Prince Andrei and Natasha heat up with every rhythmic movement on the dance floor, leading to their passionate love and engagement. "I wouldn't have believed it," Prince Andrei confesses to Pierre a few days later, "if someone had told me I could love so much" (475; PSS 10:222).

In his description of ecstatic love, Tolstoy does not mention the word "beauty." Neither Prince Andrei nor Natasha is characterized as beautiful. We can imagine Prince Andrei as impeccably dressed and behaved, but not necessarily good-looking or attractive. When Tolstoy first introduces Natasha, as a thirteen-year-old girl, he presents her to us as "the dark-eyed, big-mouthed, not beautiful, but lively girl" (39; PSS 9:47). Everything is funny to her as she runs wild through the house, even in the presence of guests, instead of behaving like a young lady with well-groomed and graceful manners. Her love of life seems endless and contagious. She attracts everyone's attention, even admiration, but not because of her beauty. Her sister Vera, who evokes hardly any of our curiosity or sympathy, is described as beautiful, but not Natasha.

In *War and Peace*, as in Homer's *Iliad*, the prototype of the exemplary human beauty is named Helen. But in Tolstoy's work, despite the admiring attention she receives from every male—and the envy she evokes in every female—we do not see Hélène fall in love. She does not even seem capable of love, unless it is love of herself. Unlike his Greek predecessors, Tolstoy seems to have believed that beauty—especially extraordinary physical beauty—is an obstacle to love. But if not beauty, what leads to ecstatic love?

The word "ecstasy" comes from the Greek *ekstasis*, which literally means "standing outside oneself." We can understand it as rapturous delight that makes us feel like we have lost control of ourselves and are heading toward an adventure with an unknown destination. Ecstasy, I should add, characterizes a marginal state: between pleasure and pain, love and war, sanity and madness, sanctity and pollution, cosmos and chaos, being and nonbeing.

In *War and Peace*, the naturally passionate Natasha is more prone to ecstasy than the strong-willed Prince Andrei. Tolstoy uses Natasha to show how ecstatic love can also have a negative side. When Prince Andrei's father opposes his son's marriage to Natasha because she is so young and demands that they wait for a year, in the absence of Prince Andrei Natasha develops a sudden irresistible passion for Anatole Kuragin. This irresponsible and idle man, who is already secretly married and is as frivolous as his sister Hélène, seduces Natasha and asks her to elope with him. The impressionable Natasha is enchanted by Anatole to the extent that she is willing not only to break her marriage engagement but also to run away from home with a man she barely knows. One could hardly describe better the hazards of ecstatic love than Tolstoy does in Natasha's response to Sonya's shock that Natasha could be so madly in love with someone she has only known for three days:

> "Three days," said Natasha. "It seems to me I've loved him for a hundred years. It seems to me I've never loved anyone before him. And never loved anyone the way I love him. You can't understand it, Sonya. Wait, sit here." Natasha embraced and kissed her. "I've been told it happens, and you've probably heard it, but only now have I experienced this love. This isn't like before. As soon as I saw him, I felt that he was my master and I was his slave, and that I couldn't help loving him. Yes, slave! What he tells me to do, I'll do. You don't understand it. What am I to do? What am I do to, Sonya?" Natasha said with a happy and frightened face. (577; PSS 10:347)

Tolstoy does not tell us that ecstatic love must lead to such adversity. But he suspects that this form of love is unstable and that the price we have to pay for it is too high, with its consequences being more negative than positive. Despite our romantic inclinations, such ecstatic madness cannot have led Tolstoy to declare that love is the essence of life.

III. Devotional Love

Tolstoy much admired Plato's *Symposium*, and in *War and Peace* there is a scene that Tolstoy may have written with this dialogue in mind. In occupied Moscow, Pierre and the French officer Ramballe drink heavily and talk about love.[1] Plato believes that, when drunk, we cannot but speak the truth. Tolstoy follows suit. Ramballe describes some of his many love affairs, which can roughly be considered ecstatic love. When it is his turn to speak, Pierre tells the story of his life. He confesses that he has loved only one woman—Natasha—although she could never belong to him. He has loved her, he professes, from an early age, but "had not dared to think of her because she was so young and he was an illegitimate son without a name." Later, when his status improved, he again "had not dared to think of her because he loved her too much, placed her too high above the whole world, and the more so, therefore, above himself" (912; PSS 11:376). The drunk French officer may have compared Pierre's love to that of Dante toward Beatrice, but instead, he only murmurs: "Platonic love, clouds" (913; PSS 11:377). Ramballe could not approve of such helpless devotion to one unreachable woman when there are so many who are attractive and willing. He is struck far more by the revelation that Pierre is fabulously rich than by the unhappiness of his love life.

Tolstoy certainly thinks more highly of devotional than of ecstatic love. Devotional love demands knowledge, loyalty, and sacrifice. Pierre knows well who Natasha is, and his love for her does not make him blind to her shortcomings. It is Pierre who has to reveal to the spellbound Natasha that Anatole is already married, and he also frightens Anatole so that he stays away from her.

Devotional love involves making a conscious decision to dedicate ourselves to the well-being of another person—even if that means removing ourselves from that person's life. Tolstoy probably understood that sacrifice represents the basis of all religious life. To sacrifice is to make sacred, as Pierre does by putting Natasha on that high, and for him unreachable, pedestal. If, symbolically speaking, we can say that Ramballe treats every woman like the fallen Mary Magdalene, Pierre treats Natasha like the Madonna.

Pierre is not the only character in *War and Peace* who is capable of devotional love. We also find it in Sonya's love for Natasha's brother Nikolai and in Princess Marya's devotion to her father, brother, nephew (Prince Andrei's son), and, ultimately, God. Tolstoy never openly mocks Princess Marya, even though we feel his disapproval—perhaps because it is directed not so much toward her devotion itself but toward its extent. In its extreme cases, this form of love again reminds us of slavery, of which Natasha spoke with regard to her ecstatic devotion to Anatole. The slavery of devotional love is not mad and spontaneous, but desperate and calculated. It is an act of self-coercion, disguised through the transformation of a living object into something sacred. Despite its seemingly positive connotation, it may not be a coincidence that one of the meanings of the verb "devote" is "to doom" or "to consign to destruction"—whether it is the destruction of the object of devotion, or, even more likely, of the one who is so "selflessly" devoted.

Tolstoy does not take his story in the direction of such murky waters. Sonya does not become destructive, and Nikolai is most grateful to Sonya, not just for her steady feelings and devotion, but for all that she has done to help the struggling Rostov family. Sonya is beyond reproach, approaching perfection. And yet perfection can be admired but not loved. After years of adolescent affection for her, Nikolai could not love Sonya any more, nor could he perceive their relationship as that of love: "In her there was everything for which people are appreciated; but there was little what would make him love her. And he felt that, the more he appreciated her, the less he loved her" (1140; PSS 12:249).

Natasha, who is the most intuitive and perceptive character in the novel, senses the negative side of devotional love even more strongly than her brother. We first see it in her intense initial dislike of Princess Marya, but also later in her attitude toward Sonya.

In a remarkable passage in the epilogue, when Nikolai is already married to Princess Marya, Natasha calls her sister-in-law's attention to that always thought-provoking declaration in the Gospel of Matthew (25:29): "To him who has will be given, from him who has not will be taken." Speaking in her spontaneous, yet sometimes crude manner, Natasha proclaims:

> [Sonya's] the one who has not—why, I don't know, but from her will be taken, and everything has been taken. I feel terribly sorry for her sometimes; I used to want terribly for Nicolas to marry her; but I always had a sort of presentiment that it would never be. She's a sterile blossom, you know, like on strawberries? Sometimes I feel sorry for her, but sometimes I think she doesn't feel it the way we would. (1148–1149; PSS 12:259–260)

The astonished Princess Marya tries to explain to Natasha that this biblical passage should be understood differently, but in her heart, she also knows that "Sonya . . . was completely reconciled with her destiny as a *sterile blossom*" (1149; PSS 12:260).

There is something opposed to vitality in the very nature of devotional love, something akin to the process of sterilization, of turning what is vibrantly alive into a static symbol or a dead abstraction. If love is to be the essence of life, it has to be a very different kind of love.

IV. Sublimated Love

The long years of wars, the years of destruction and deprivation, take their toll on the protagonists of *War and Peace* and change them. They devastate the world with which they are familiar and, even more importantly, transform their perspectives on life as a whole. Toward its end, Tolstoy's novel acquires the flavor of a Greek tragedy, in which human limitations become all too obvious and unsurpassable, yet the main protagonists are not broken by these limitations, at least not in the spiritual sense. Quite the contrary, some of these individuals seem to find a new source of belief, a new source of inspiration—some of them, but by no means all.

At the battle of Borodino, Prince Andrei is mortally wounded. By a miracle of fate, the escort of the wounded soldiers, among which is Prince Andrei, retreats along the same path as those who are escaping from the soon-to-be-occupied Moscow, including the Rostovs. Prince Andrei and Natasha meet again, several years after their breakup. Without a second thought, Natasha dedicates her attention to the injured man, and the sparks of mutual attraction soon fly again. Both of them are more mature now, especially Natasha, and the situation in which they find themselves is far more solemn. Not wine but the tragic destiny of their country and its people, together with the shadow of Prince Andrei's looming death, lead them to be thoughtful and truthful to the highest degree.

While Prince Andrei is lying severely injured, his thoughts turn toward understanding the role love plays in that hardly comprehensible and tragicomic interplay of living and dying:

> In those hours of suffering solitude and half-delirium that he spent after being wounded, the more he pondered the new principle of eternal love revealed to him, the more, though without feeling it himself, he renounced earthly life. To love everything, everybody, always to sacrifice oneself for love, meant to love no one, meant not to live this earthly life. And the more imbued he was with this principle of love, the more he renounced life and the more completely he destroyed that dreadful barrier which, without love, stands between life and death. When, in that first time, he remembered that he had to die, he said to himself, "Well, so much the better." (982; PSS 12:61)

Prince Andrei is far from always being so sure that dying is preferrable to living. As he is seriously wounded at Borodino, so is

Anatole Kuragin. Seeing his severely wounded rival, whose leg has just been amputated, Prince Andrei swallows his pride and forgives him for destroying his relationship with Natasha. When a few days later his secret wishes are answered and Natasha begins to care for him, Prince Andrei's convictions shift once more: "When in his half delirium she whom he wished for appeared before him, and when, pressing her hand to his lips, he wept quiet, joyful tears, love for one woman crept imperceptibly into his heart and again bound him to life" (982; PSS 12:61). Yet Prince Andrei feels that his life is being taken away from him, against his powerful will: "Can it be that fate brought us together so strangely only so that I should die? . . . Can it be that the truth of life was revealed to me only so that I should live in a lie? I love her more than anything in the world. But what am I to do if I love her?" (983; PSS 12:61).

There is not much Prince Andrei can do, but the awareness of his tragic life leads him to even deeper insights that bring us closer to understanding why Tolstoy would claim that love is the essence of life:

> "Love? What is love?" he thought. "Love hinders death. Love is life. Everything, everything I understand, I understand only because I love. Everything is, everything exists, only because I love. Everything is connected only by that. Love is God, and to die—means that I, a part of love, return to the common and eternal source." (984; PSS 12:63)

Prince Andrei has come a long way from being the prudent and self-sufficient man we meet at the beginning of the novel. That man believed not only in the power of the will but also in the historic role of someone like Napoleon. In the course of the novel, Prince Andrei learns to admire General Kutuzov much more, despite knowing his limitations. In addition to preferring Kutuzov to Napoleon, Prince Andrei accepts the limitations of the human ability to direct the course of history. He recognizes the existence of the cosmic dimension of love and the supremacy of that love over the will. At the end of his life, he surrenders to this force that he now believes holds the world together. To love is to accept both life and death, for death is nothing but the return to the common and eternal source, which we may call the world soul. It is as if Prince Andrei comes to realize that life has to enter into the realm of love within the world soul, rather than the other way around. This could be how it is that, when love awakens, life awakes as well.

Profound as Prince Andrei's thoughts are, the narrator makes it clear that they need not be last thoughts, ultimate insights: "These thoughts seemed comforting to him. But they were only thoughts. Something was lacking in them, there was something one-sidedly personal, cerebral—there was no evidence. And there was the same uneasiness and vagueness. He fell asleep" (984; PSS 12:63). And not long after, he died.

Prince Andrei died, and it was left to the living to further ponder his thoughts on the significance of love for life. They—Natasha and Pierre in particular—had to test the realizations of Prince Andrei: not at the cerebral level, but in the way they lived and related to each other.

After Prince Andrei's death, the emotionally drained Natasha spends the next several months consoling her mother. The Rostovs lived beyond their means, and Natasha's mother worried for years that her elder son, Nikolai, might marry Sonya, the girl without a dowry. The father of the family, Count Ilya Rostov, was not capable of providing more for the family, while the older son Nikolai was going from one military campaign to another. As if these problems were not enough, the younger son Petya, who was still a child, also enlisted and was killed during the final battles of the war.

Pierre also undergoes much in the months after the battle of Borodino. His wife dies. While Moscow is burning, Pierre is arrested and held in custody. There he meets Platon Karataev, who has a profound impact on how Pierre looks at life. After their mock execution, the murder of Platon by the retreating French soldiers, the death of Petya, and the end of the military hostilities, Pierre becomes seriously ill. The three months of recovery bring him a different perspective on life:

> All his life he had looked off somewhere, over the heads of the people around him, yet there was no need to strain his eyes, but only to look right in front of him.... Now he had learned to see the great, the eternal, and the infinite in everything, and therefore, in order to see it, to enjoy contemplating it, he had naturally abandoned the spyglasses he had been looking through until then over people's heads, and joyfully contemplated the ever-changing, ever-great, unfathomable, and infinite life around him. And the closer he looked, the calmer and happier he became. The terrible "Why?" which formerly had destroyed all his mental constructions, did not exist for him now. Now, to this question "Why?" a simple answer was always ready in his soul: because there is God, that God without whose will not a single hair falls from a man's head. (1104; PSS 12:205)

If ecstasy is a "marginal stage," in the sense of touching multiple planes of existence, and if devotion means a separation of these planes, here we have a phenomenon of intertwining: of the ordinary and the extraordinary, of freedom and destiny, of the human and the divine.

Pierre experiences this change in perspective as liberating and life-enhancing. Tolstoy describes it as manifest in Pierre's inner peace, a powerful surge of vitality, and a smile that does not depart from his face. Even someone far less perceptive than Natasha would have noticed the change, but she had her own peculiar way of describing it to Princess Marya, with "a mischievous smile" on her face: "He's become somehow clean, smooth, fresh—as if from the bathhouse, you understand?—morally from the bathhouse."

Prince Andrei lost his life but found his soul. Pierre found his soul and a new life as well. As with Natasha, love awoke, and life awoke as well.

Plato would have said that Pierre climbed up the ladder of Beauty, from the initial attraction to the "marble beauty" of Hélène," to something that he called Beauty in Itself. Dante could have said that the pilgrim Pierre Bezukhov went through Inferno and Purgatory and was now ready to follow his Beatrice through Paradise. Tolstoy puts those silly words in Natasha's mouth, and they lead Princess Marya to grasp the possibility of deep and lasting love between Natasha and Pierre. They have both arrived "as if from the bathhouse."

But Pierre's transformation went deeper than Natasha understood, and the narrator describes it more precisely: "Love overflowed [Pierre's] heart, and, loving people without reason, he discovered the unquestionable reasons for which it was worth loving them" (1124; PSS 12:230). This is the best characterization of sublime love we find in *War and Peace*: love comes before life and infuses it with its own qualities. Like Empedocles, Tolstoy elevates love to a metaphysical principle. But then, must he not also elevate Empedocles's *polemos*—whether translated as strife or war—to a cosmic principle?[2] And if so, would not an appropriate title for Tolstoy's novel be "War and Love"?

V. The Sublime

Sublimated love is based on something quite different from ecstatic and devotional love. We are not simply drawn to the object of our desire, nor do we detach from it by an act of will, because there are obstacles to our open and direct loving of it. Rather, based on some profound and often tragic experiences, we are drawn into a different dimension of love. Tolstoy thinks that it is not accidental that we need to be "prepared" for such experiences of love through suffering. The root meaning of the verb "to suffer" is "to feel keenly." What we end up feeling so keenly—far more so than how we do in ordinary situations—is something that indicates to us the presence of a force, or a dimension of reality that is substantially different from what is familiar to us in our everyday life. In feeling so keenly, yet without having a good grasp of the nature of what we are feeling, we are overcome and surrender. We then take something else, and not just human beings and human life, to be of central importance in the grand scheme of things. Instead of love being "added" to our lives, it is as if our lives are immersed in a dimension of reality that is somehow infused with love.

Tolstoy's message seems to be that human lives do not have intrinsic value on their own. Only when our lives are immersed in the realm of love can we claim that love is the essence of life. The poetic expression of this state of affairs is Pierre's inner peace and the smile that never departs from his face. If this is what Tolstoy had in mind, we can understand why, while reading *War and Peace*, we are left with the impression that Tolstoy is highly critical of both anthropocentrism and humanism.[3]

Sublime love is both rare and replete with an otherworldly dimension. This is why our ordinary language fails when we try to capture that larger picture with our limited concepts. There are good reasons to rely on Iris Murdoch in this context, for, somewhat surprisingly, her views roughly correspond to the central orientations of Prince Andrei, Pierre, and Natasha and help us articulate them both individually and all together.

Although the sublime is normally understood as an aesthetic category—as the highest degree of the beautiful—that is not how Murdoch sees it.[4] She relates the sublime far more to good than to beauty. Understood in this sense, the sublime relates to the matters of highest concern: to the art of living and dying, and to the presence of an order of things that we sense to be superior to anything we could design or implement. The sublime may reveal to us the highest and noblest, but also the darkest aspects of reality, while at the same time not forcing us to label or classify them by means of categories suitable for social morality and the ordinary ways of life.

Among Tolstoy's characters in *War and Peace*, Prince Andrei is the one that assumes a similar attitude toward life. Unlike his sister, who is a devout Christian, Prince Andrei comprehends the world in less-defined categories, while also recognizing the presence of a strongly felt yet unspecified transcendence.[5]

Murdoch describes our experience of the sublime in terms of both the upsetting glimpse of the boundlessness of nature and the revival of our spiritual power arising from the vast formless strength of the natural world. During the battle of Borodino, Prince Andrei could also fully subscribe to such views, but with one addition: faced with an enormous mass of armed humanity, divided into two camps with the two sides hurling themselves at each other with a rage that defies reason, he extended that boundlessness of nature to include humanity as well. His experience of that battle sharpened his spiritual power and attuned him not to judgment of humanity and its actions, but more to what Murdoch calls "un-self-centered agnosticism."[6] That agnosticism now leads him toward a tacit acceptance of all of the manifestations of life, including death, instead of toward a sense of righteousness, which we would expect from Prince Andrei in the first three-quarters of the novel.

Murdoch puts an emphasis on moral vision, instead of choice, as most contemporary moral philosophers do. In the spirit of Plato, she interprets the central point of our moral vision as the "Good." That Good is the magnetic center toward which we gravitate.[7]

Prince Andrei is so deeply entrenched in the struggle between life and death that the nature of this transcendent center seems to escape him. While he is naturally skeptical about any possible innate goodness in human nature, Pierre is not. Pierre drifts through most of his life seeking that goodness and suspects that it may hide in various aspects and manifestations of life. Although he is often disappointed, he never seems to lose faith in at least the potential goodness of humanity—even in the midst of the most brutal destructions of the war. In the last months of the war, and during his convalescence, Pierre finally stops straying from one idea to another and begins to feel this center both within and around himself.

George Steiner offers an illuminating clarification of this point by comparing Tolstoy with Homer:

> War and mortality cry havoc in the Homeric and Tolstoyan worlds, but *the centre holds*: it is the affirmation that life is, of itself, a thing of beauty, that the works and days of men are worth recording, and that no catastrophe—not even the burning of Troy or of Moscow—is ultimate.[8]

If the center still holds, we can sense it and affirm life through love. This is yet another, and perhaps the most important, insight that we can learn from Murdoch and apply to Tolstoy. Murdoch connects love with a heightened attentiveness to the reality of individuals and things. Tolstoy is a superbly perceptive artist, who seems to see every detail and every nuance of things: nothing escapes him, and his scenes and characters vibrate with life. Fully in the spirit of Tolstoy, although following Simone Weil's guidance, Murdoch's "categorical imperative" is that we ought to be lovingly attentive to reality. She argues that love plays a crucial role in seeing things how they are. Love prevents the self from getting in the way of our perception of things: love is not about us, about what we want, or about the objects of our devotion. Removal of the self from the central position opens the way for love and the experience of the sublime. Approaching the world with loving attentiveness removes the "in-between," the separateness of beings. Love makes us realize that the alleged disconnectedness of things and individuals is a consequence, rather than the source, of our problematic attitude toward life.[9]

Among Tolstoy's characters in *War and Peace*, Natasha is the most attentive. She is also the most erotic—which can hardly be said of Prince Andrei or Pierre. Natasha does not think about any transcendent order, nor whether the center may or may not hold. She is simply grounded in reality by being so perceptive and lovingly attentive toward everything that comes her way.

For Natasha, as for Murdoch, the contingency of the world does not imply its meaninglessness. Natasha would not understand the modern view about the discontinuity of moral agents and their world (which Murdoch ascribes to existentialism), because with her entire being, with all her penetrating intuition and loving attentiveness, Natasha experiences the world and human beings as inseparably interconnected.

Murdoch believes that love consists in the tension between the imperfect soul and the magnetic perfection that she calls the Good and that we experience as the sublime. Such experience "is the unmistakable sign that we are spiritual creatures, attracted by excellence and made for the Good."[10]

None of Tolstoy's characters in *War and Peace* would arrive at this view individually. By weaving together the views of Prince Andrei, Pierre, and Natasha, however, we come close to it.

This does not mean that the positions of Murdoch and Tolstoy do not differ. Murdoch believes that the Good is sovereign to love. For Tolstoy, they are intertwined: love is infused with and inseparable from the Good. Through such an integration, in *War and Peace*, Tolstoy elevates love even higher than Murdoch.

VI. Life Infused with Love

In the epilogue of *War and Peace*, Tolstoy describes the later life of Natasha and Pierre. They are married and have four children. Natasha's life is fully dominated by her roles as a wife and mother:

> She felt that the charms which her instinct had taught her to make use of before would not only be ridiculous in the eyes of her husband, to whom, from the first moment, she had given herself

entirely—that is, with her whole soul, not leaving one little corner that was not open to him. She felt that her bond with her husband held, not by those poetic feelings that had attracted him to her, but by something else, indefinite but firm, like the bond between her own soul and body. (1155; PSS 12:267)

A comparable transformation happens to Pierre. Although from an outside point of view he dedicates himself to political and intellectual pursuits, he is completely under "his wife's heel," and happy with that state of affairs.

After seven years of married life, Pierre felt a joyful, firm consciousness that he was not a bad man, and he felt it because he saw himself reflected in his wife. In himself he felt all the good and the bad mixed together and obscuring each other. But only what was truly good was reflected in his wife; all that was not entirely good was rejected. And this reflection came not by way of logical thinking, but otherwise—as a mysterious, unmediated reflection. (1157; PSS 12:270)

Does the marriage of Natasha and Pierre, as described in the epilogue, provide a blueprint for the realization of Tolstoy's vision that love is the essence of life? Tolstoy likely believed that at the time of writing it, but it need not be so.

Recall that at the beginning of the novel, the older and already married Prince Andrei advises Pierre never to marry. Prince Andrei seems to separate marriage, love, and the pursuit of "all that's good and lofty in [us]" (28; PSS 9:34), the latter corresponding roughly to the sublime. Contrary to Prince Andrei's warning, in the epilogue, Tolstoy brings all three together. In reconstructing a vision of life based on love, with the marriage of Natasha and Pierre, Tolstoy joins love and the pursuit of "all that's good and lofty." These two intertwined, with or without the presence of marriage, are the key to love being the essence of life. Marriage in general, and the marriage of Pierre and Natasha in particular, does not seem to be a prerequisite for love being the essence of life.[11]

Given our previous considerations, we can now reconstruct Tolstoy's view on love in *War and Peace*. He does not accidentally talk about love as the essence of life. Among his tacit assumptions is the view that at least some things have what used to be called an essence—or "true nature." And everything that has a true nature must have a "false nature" as well, in the sense that it may appear in a way that covers up or misrepresents what it is meant to be. Tolstoy believes that neither military valor nor the fashionable life of high society reveals the true nature of humanity. Quite the contrary, they delude us into living in an unnatural way, to be untrue to ourselves. Socially accepted values and morals—military or civilian—often make it more difficult for us to realize who we are and how we are supposed to love and live.

An indispensable element in our attempt to discover our true nature and live in accordance with it is love. By love, Tolstoy does not mean the erotic passion that is so celebrated in society, nor does he mean devotion to an abstraction—whether of our own making or our collective imagining. Tolstoy's central characters find their true nature only through one kind of love—sublime love. Such love presupposes a capacity to feel keenly and see clearly, and thus to know what people and reality are genuinely like.

Tolstoy's views of sublime love and of love as the essence of life put him in the company of Plato and Meister Eckhart, of Dante and Goethe. Unlike most of those who defend similar views, Tolstoy does not think of sublime love as requiring any ascent or descent. Metaphorically speaking, we can stay where we are, but we need to learn to look at the world with lovingly attentive eyes. When we do so, love becomes the capacity to connect with other people and reality as a whole. It builds bridges, but it also transforms—those who love, as well as those who are loved. Tolstoy believes that this kind of transformation happens by love directing us toward the world's cosmic dimension and its invisible order. Although love can be ignited by what is beautiful, it is more naturally directed toward what is good—or the Good, as Murdoch insists.

Tolstoy rightly believes that we sense most keenly what Good is when we are confronted with its opposite. Our experience of suffering and of tragic events need not destroy us, physically or spiritually. Rather, it can purify us and present us with a vision of who and what truly matter. Tolstoy does not understand the world as homocentric, but nor does he believe that humanity can be reduced to the temporal dimension of reality. Through sublime love, our lives are infused with the dimension of eternity.[12]

Sublime love is less directly related to the choices we make than to our overall vision of life. There are many contingent and loose parts in the world, just as there are many experiences that are far from what we hope for or desire. Yet if love can reveal the presence of Good in this complex and never fully understandable whirlwind of events, we can feel keenly that the center holds and that, despite its numerous obstacles and disappointments, life enhances us and is worth living. When love awakens, life awakens as well.

Temporarily or permanently, life can exist without love, and too many lives are neither guided by love nor filled with it. Many such lives are shattered physically on the battlefields or wasted spiritually in the gossip clubs of high society. By claiming that love is the essence of life Tolstoy is not making a descriptive statement. The kind of love that he envisions as the essence of life is not common, nor is it easy to obtain. A life guided by and filled with love is an ideal and a task.

Many would be critical of the vision of life immersed in love that Tolstoy outlines in *War and Peace*. They may find it naive, or too idealistic. Despite such criticisms, we should realize that this vision is not arbitrary insofar as it addresses some of our deepest longings. And those are longings that we recognize in virtually every epoch and every culture, even if not always in every individual. It is possible, as ever more vocal critics of the vision of life immersed in love assert, that despite such longings being so deeply rooted, we may be better off if we outgrow them. Nevertheless, the intricacies of sublime love, as presented in *War and Peace*, may make us wonder whether this rich conception of love does not deserve more of our attention and appreciation than it has been given, even by Tolstoy himself.

As is well documented, Tolstoy was critical of this vision in his later life. His criticism did not lead him to abandon the vision entirely, but rather to replace it with one based on his reading of the New Testament. The cosmic dimension of love and the element of eternity are preserved in his later vision, but faith is claimed to be the essence of life. Tolstoy proposes that love, interpreted as agape, is grounded on less indeterminate and better-known footing and that the role of love can be defined as the law of love. As he articulates in his late book *The Law of Love and the Law of Violence*,

> It is this recognition of the law of love as the highest law of human life, and the clearly expressed guidance for conduct that follows from the Christian teaching on love, applied equally to enemies and those who hate, offend and curse us, that constitutes the peculiarity of Christ's teaching. The precise and definite meaning given to the doctrine of love and the guidance resulting from it inevitably involves a complete transformation of the established structure of life, not only among Christian nations, but among all the nations of the world.[13]

The role of love in human life is now definitely redefined. Even the title, *The Law of Love and the Law of Violence*, sounds like a reversal of the title *War and Peace*. Yet it is questionable both whether Tolstoy's earlier conception of sublime love is but his immature substitute for religion, and whether our understanding of love is enhanced when it is hiding behind the alleged authority of the divine law. As Tolstoy makes a case for it in *War and Peace*, love may be at its best when it combines the spontaneity and vitality of the young Natasha, the earnestness and thoughtfulness of Prince Andrei, and the sincerity and goodness of Pierre.

Notes

1. There is a similar "banquet" in *Anna Karenina* (part 1, chap. 11; PSS 18:46), in which Stiva and Levin discuss love, and Stiva refers explicitly to Plato's *Symposium*. For a valuable discussion of this episode, and of Plato's influence on Tolstoy in general, see Donna Orwin, "Taming the Author: The Platonic and the Turgenevian Moments in Tolstoy's Fiction," in Orwin, *Consequences of Consciousness: Turgenev, Dostoevsky, and Tolstoy* (Stanford, CA: Stanford University Press, 2007), 57–75. For an illuminating discussion of love in Tolstoy's opus, see Richard F. Gustafson, *Leo Tolstoy: Resident and Stranger* (Princeton, NJ: Princeton University Press, 1986), 3–213.
2. For two original renderings of this important topic, see Dudley Young, *Origins of the Sacred: The Ecstasies of Love and War* (New York: St. Martin's Press, 1991); and James Hillman, *A Terrible Love of War* (New York: Penguin Books, 2004).
3. For further discussion, see Nikolai Berdyaev, *The Russian Idea*, trans. R. M. French (Hudson, NY: Lindsifarne Press, 1992), chap. 4, "The Problem of Humanism," especially page 110.
4. For a discussion of the sublime as the highest degree of beautiful, see Nicolai Hartmann, *Aesthetics*, trans. E. Kelly (Boston: de Gruyter, 2014), chaps. 30–32, pp. 392–421. Let us also notice that, unlike Tolstoy, Murdoch does not have a negative attitude toward beauty; cf. Murdoch, "On 'God' and 'Good,'" and "The Sovereignty of Good Over Other Concepts," both in *Existentialists and Mystics: Writings on Philosophy and Literature*, ed. Peter Conradi (London: Penguin Books, 1999), 337–385.
5. This point may also underscore how little Christian doctrine and terminology there is in *War and Peace*. In *Anna Karenina*, by contrast, we are prepared for it right away: the epigraph for the novel is a quotation from the Bible.
6. Murdoch, "The Sublime and the Beautiful Revisited," in *Existentialists and Mystics*, 283.
7. As Murdoch puts it succinctly, "Good, not will, is transcendent"; "On 'God' and 'Good,'" 356.

8. George Steiner, *Tolstoy or Dostoevsky: An Essay in the Old Criticism*, 2nd ed. (New Haven, CT: Yale University Press, 1996), 78.
9. Murdoch believes that we thereby address the greatest problem of modernity, which she also describes as the separation of being and morality, by addressing the growing mistrust of the world. Hannah Arendt offers an illuminating discussion of this point in *The Human Condition*, 2nd ed. (Chicago: University of Chicago Press, 1998), 242ff.
10. Murdoch, "Sovereignty of Good," 384.
11. Tolstoy's view of marriage, as described in the epilogue, has been criticized as "parochial" and even "suffocating"; a thoroughly domesticated Natasha, with all her vitality tamed, has been compared to "a breeding fish." Cf. Ruth Crego Benson, *Women in Tolstoy: The Ideal and the Erotic* (Urbana: University of Illinois Press, 1973), 65–68. Tolstoy himself offered a powerful criticism of marriage as in institution later in *The Kreutzer Sonata* and the epilogue that he wrote to that novella.
12. My understanding of the relationship of the temporal and eternal dimensions of reality relies on Erazim Kohák, *The Embers and the Stars: A Philosophical Inquiry into the Moral Sense of Nature* (Chicago: University of Chicago Press, 1984); and Henry Bugbee, *The Inward Morning: A Philosophical Exploration in Journal Form* (Athens: University of Georgia Press, 1999).
13. Tolstoy, *The Law of Love and the Law of Violence*, in Tolstoy, *A Confession and Other Religious Writings*, trans. Jane Kentish (New York: Penguin Classics, 1987), 174 (PSS 37:169).

Works Cited

Arendt, Hannah. *The Human Condition*. 2nd ed. Chicago: University of Chicago Press, 1998.

Benson, Ruth Crego. *Women in Tolstoy: The Ideal and the Erotic*. Urbana: University of Illinois Press, 1973.

Berdyaev, Nikolai. *The Russian Idea*. Translated by R. M. French. Hudson, NY: Lindisfarne Press, 1992.

Bugbee, Henry. *The Inward Morning: A Philosophical Exploration in Journal Form*. Athens: University of Georgia Press, 1999.

Gustafson, Richard. *Leo Tolstoy: Resident and Stranger*. Princeton, NJ: Princeton University Press, 1986.

Hartmann, Nicolai. *Aesthetics*. Translated by Eugene Kelly. Boston: de Gruyter, 2014.

Hillman, James. *A Terrible Love of War*. New York: Penguin Books, 2004.
Kohák, Erazim. *The Embers and the Stars: A Philosophical Inquiry into the Moral Sense of Nature*. Chicago: University of Chicago Press, 1984.
Murdoch, Iris. *Existentialists and Mystics: Writings on Philosophy and Literature*. Edited by Peter Conradi. London: Penguin Books, 1999.
Orwin, Donna. "Taming the Author: The Platonic and the Turgenevian Moments in Tolstoy's Fiction." Orwin, *Consequences of Consciousness: Turgenev, Dostoevsky, and Tolstoy*, 57–75. Stanford, CA: Stanford University Press, 2007.
Steiner, George. *Tolstoy or Dostoevsky: An Essay in the Old Criticism*. 2nd ed. New Haven, CT: Yale University Press, 1996.
Tolstoy, Leo. *The Law of Love and the Law of Violence. A Confession and Other Religious Writings*. Translated by Jane Kentish, 151–229. New York: Penguin Classics, 1987.
Young, Dudley. *Origins of the Sacred: The Ecstasies of Love and War*. New York: St. Martin's Press, 1991.

7
War and Peace and the Origins of Tolstoy's Religion

Lina Steiner

I. Tolstoy's Youth: Between Enthusiasm and Unbelief

Tolstoy grew up in an age when faith and the authority of the church were no longer taken for granted by the Russian elite. Although respect for the Orthodox faith had been part of the official national ideology since the beginning of Nicholas I's reign, even conservative Slavophiles were deeply steeped in post-Kantian German philosophy, which reconciled Christian faith and science. Libertinism still flourished in aristocratic circles, whereas Ludwig Feuerbach and August Comte became spiritual fathers of the emergent radical intelligentsia. Describing the upbringing of a typical son of the century in *Childhood*, *Boyhood*, and *Youth*, Tolstoy showed that Nikolai Irten'ev's loss of religious faith was a byproduct of his education and acculturation. Thus in *Boyhood* Nikolenka makes his first forays into philosophy, which makes him abandon his old beliefs. His philosophizing brings him to the point of complete skepticism, so that "besides myself I imagined no one and nothing existed in the whole world" (PSS 2:57). In one of the drafts of chapter 19 of *Boyhood* Nikolenka confessed:

> I was also an atheist. With the arrogance strikingly characteristic of that age, which, once allowing religious doubt, [made me]

ask myself why God would not prove it to me that all what I have been taught is true. And I prayed to Him sincerely, so that He would prove to me His existence either in myself by some miracle or somehow else. Brushing aside all beliefs inculcated in me since childhood I was drawing up my own, new beliefs. It was hard for me to part with a comforting idea about the future immortal life; while considering that nothing vanishes but only changes shape in reality, I have arrived at the pantheist idea, the one about an infinite and forever changing ladder of beings, I was so gripped by this idea that I became seriously preoccupied by the question what I had been before I became a man—a horse, a dog, or a cow. This thought in its turn, was replaced by another idea, Pascal's idea that even if all that religion teaches us were untrue, we would lose nothing by following it, by not following it, on the other hand, we risk receiving eternal damnation instead of eternal bliss.[1] (PSS 2:287)

Irten'ev's struggles with doubt do not receive much attention in the published text. Furthermore, chapter 12 of *Youth* describes him as an enthusiastic believer obsessed with self-perfection. Thus in chapter 6, "The Confession," failing to confess some of his peccadillos, he feels repentant and decides to make another confession. The next chapter describes Irten'ev's trip to the monastery, where he finds his confessor, a monk, and disburdens his conscience. However, as soon as Irten'ev enters Moscow University, he abandons his self-absorbed quest for moral purity and embarks on the path of socialization. His encounters with students from middle-rank families raise his awareness about social differences and inequality. The final, fourth, part of Tolstoy's educational narrative, which transformed into *The Cossacks*, suggests that the hero's attempt at socialization ended in a profound inner discord and disillusionment. Hence his Rousseau-inspired escape from society in search of natural morality, friendship, and love. Rousseau's Savoyard Vicar is the philosophical mentor of the protagonist,

Olenin, whose belief in the intrinsic order and purposefulness of nature leads him to loathe himself, a "problematic individual" unable to win the love of the Cossack maiden and find a niche in the organic world of the Cossacks community.[2]

The end of the Crimean War and the beginning of the Great Reforms deepened Tolstoy's interest in sociopolitical issues. He conceived another novel about a young Russian landowner of his generation.[3] The surviving sketches suggest that in this Bildungsroman Tolstoy wanted to link the hero's quest for personal authenticity to those for social responsibility and justice. In 1856 Tolstoy also started drafting a historical novel about Russia's first revolutionaries, the Decembrists. Tolstoy was undoubtedly interested in the liberal ideas of the gentry revolutionaries. At the same time, he was intrigued by the piety of the surviving Decembrists and wanted to uncover the roots of their religiosity.[4] *The Decembrists* eventually metamorphosed into *War and Peace*, Tolstoy's first epic-scale project, which absorbed and transformed the key motifs from his early fiction. The central plot lines, focused on Pierre Bezukhov, Andrei and Marya Bolkonsky, Natasha and Nikolai Rostov, are all shaped as novels of education that reflect Tolstoy's keen interest in Plato and Rousseau, whom Tolstoy read assiduously in the 1840s, and in other philosophers he discovered in the 1850s–1860s.

The deeper Tolstoy probed the history of the early nineteenth-century Russia, the stronger was his wish to define his own religious convictions. Tolstoy's earliest essay on religion, which remained unfinished, dates back to 1865 (PSS 7:125–127). Inspired by Montaigne, this essay discusses the insufficiency of our religious knowledge and the shortcomings of various arguments for the existence of God, including those of the eighteenth-century deists whose ideas he finds most convincing. However, he stops short of recommending a leap of faith or a transformative religious experience of the kind he described in part 8 of *Anna Karenina* and in his *Confession*. As my essay will argue, it was in *War and Peace* that Tolstoy first attempted to narrate religious experience. Thus several crucial scenes in the novel are centered on the epiphanic and mystical experiences, which transform the characters' worldviews and lives. And yet Tolstoy's fascination with religious experiences did not undermine his Enlightenment-based view of religion as a means of human betterment. In fact, the tension between the rationalistic "natural religion" and skeptical fideism that harked back to Montaigne and Pascal remained unresolved in Tolstoy's oeuvre even after his so-called religious turn in the late 1870s.

II. Traditional Belief and Its Enlightened Despisers

While researching and writing *War and Peace* Tolstoy began to develop his unique vision of Russia's path toward Enlightenment, which led him to question both Orthodoxy and the existing approaches to modernization. The future Decembrist Pierre Bezukhov, his friend Andrei Bolkonsky, and the woman they both love, Natasha Rostova, represent the "young Russia" awakened by the Napoleonic Wars, whose historical fate the author tries to divine. It is this group of characters that bear the bulk of Tolstoy's historiosophical vision. The uniqueness of their trajectories can be fully appreciated against the background of the world from which they come. The old Count Bezukhov and the Rostov family represent the patriarchal Moscow gentry, where gentry customs and Orthodox traditions are thoroughly intertwined. We catch only a few glimpses of the Bezukhov household before the old Count, a grandee of Catherine II's age, dies, whereas the Rostovs occupy a central place in the narrative. Count Rostov and his wife live unselfconsciously, guided by their feelings and established opinions. The Countess is a kindly and outwardly pious woman who does not realize that the way she treats her ward Sonya smacks of hypocrisy. A product of this milieu, Sonya accepts her inferiority and never questions her benefactress's attitude to her. The Count is more honest with himself. He regrets his profligacy, but the force of habit is stronger than his scruples.

Much more enlightened than the Rostovs, the Bolkonskys offers rich material for discussing Russia's secularization. This family includes both skeptics like Prince Andrei and his father, and the pious and sentimental Marya. Modeled on Tolstoy's maternal grandfather, Prince Nikolai Volkonsky, the old Prince is a remnant of the epoch when the French *philosophes* were the masters of the progressive part of society. Thought enlightened, the Prince is a household tyrant. Prince Andrei spends three-fourths of the novel away from his father's estate, leaving his sister to bear the full weight of parental despotism, which she endures with a saintly patience. Marya resembles the autobiographical hero of *Boyhood* insofar as she, too, longs to be a good Christian. But while Nikolenka's passionate pursuit of self-perfection stems from overabundant self-love, Marya, whose individuality is stifled, clings to religion as the only sphere where she can express herself. By nature, Marya is as proud and dignified as her brother, but having been brought up in the country, she is humble and unambitious. She does, however, have a rebellious side: by receiving the holy fools in the manor house at Lysye Gory she violates her father's orders. We are also told that Marya dreams of escaping from home and becoming a vagrant herself (486; PSS 10:236).

"God's people" are not merely a charity object for Marya. Like Pierre, she is genuinely curious about the common people whose language and beliefs appear to be full of mysterious depth. The tales of the vagrants are no less interesting to her than the sufferings of Rousseau's heroes from *Julie, or the new Héloïse*, the novel that provides a model for Marya's correspondence with her only society friend, Julie Karagina. This is not to say that Rousseau does not play a big role in Marya's life. Unlike the phony Julie, for whom Rousseau is just a fashionable novelist du jour, Marya becomes influenced by Rousseau's ideas. The depth of this influence becomes clear at the end of the novel, when during Prince Andrei's illness

Marya develops a passionate friendship with Natasha.[5] Their relationship reminds us of Julie's friendship with Claire, her cousin and confidante who shares her sentimental "religion of the heart." Finally, in the first epilogue to *War and Peace*, Rousseau's Julie becomes a model for Marya as a wife and mother. A thoughtful reader of Rousseau, Marya has a humanizing influence on her husband Nikolai Rostov, checking and moderating his violent outbursts against the serfs. She also teaches her children to strive toward goodness and be their own moral judges.

The fact that Nikolai Rostov recognizes his wife's moral superiority suggests that Tolstoy was not as misogynist as many critics have claimed. However, to understand Marya's role in the moral universe of *War and Peace*, one should closely examine her relationship with her intellectual brother. Prince Andrei loves his sister but finds her religiosity naive. Of course, we should bear in mind that Prince Andrei follows Marya's development into an adult from a distance. Sometimes instead of really listening to Marya he mimics his father's condescending attitude to her. Thus before going to war in 1805 he almost mocks her when she begs him to accept an amulet, which their grandfather had worn in the battles. However, seeing genuine emotion in Marya's beautiful eyes, he lets her hang the icon over his neck. Several months later, when Prince Andrei regains consciousness in the French bivouac hospital after the battle of Austerlitz, he notices the little icon on his chest and thinks:

> "It would be good, if everything was as clear and simple, as it seems to Princess Marya. How good it would be to know where to look for help in this life and what to expect after it, there, beyond the grave! How happy and calm I'd be, if I could say now: Lord, have mercy on me! . . . But to whom shall I say it? Either it is an indefinable, unfathomable power, which I not only cannot address, which I cannot express in words—the great all or nothing," he said to himself, "or it is that God whom Princess Marya has

sewn in here, in this amulet? Nothing, nothing is certain, except the insignificance of everything I can comprehend and the grandeur of something incomprehensible and most important." (239; PSS 9:359)

Fixated on the meaninglessness of all human striving in the face of eternal nature—an insight that occurred to him when he lay wounded on the battlefield—Prince Andrei resembles Pascal's thinking reed. He has nearly lost his life, and yet he is still trying to embrace the whole world in his mind. The narrator neither agrees nor disagrees with Prince Andrei, who dismisses Marya's naive faith without allowing the thought that her prayers may have been heard, because he is still alive, to cross his mind. It is not Prince Andrei, but the author who seems to be playing with the idea of Pascal's wager in this episode, pitting Prince Andrei's doubt against Marya's faith. A reader who knows that at the end of the novel Prince Andrei too will find God cannot but see in this scene a foreshadowing of Andrei's conversion.

Tolstoy returns to the problem of icon worship several times throughout the novel, every time drawing a line between mere superstition and genuine religious feeling. The scene that drives home this difference most powerfully occurs in chapter 21 of part 2, volume 3, which describes a religious procession and prayer to the Smolenskaya Mother of God icon before the battle of Borodino. The whole army, from the commander in chief Kutuzov to simple soldiers, lines up to kiss the icon. In this episode the narrator's irony is directed not at the praying Russians, but at the German generals who understand that this ceremony is important for raising the soldiers' morale, but cannot share the feelings of those who are getting ready to die for their land (763; PSS 11:196). In this scene Pierre, too, acts as an observer. Although he admires the soldiers' resolute calm on the eve of the battle, he cannot yet comprehend their naive faith. Only after many trials and tribulations will Pierre come to realize that faith does not require reasonable justification, anticipating the insight articulated by Tolstoy's *Confession* that faith is the very force that impels one to live and to act (PSS 23:131).

Among the characters of *War and Peace* are also a number of morally indifferent and spiritually inert people. Some of them are portrayed as banal (Boris Drubetskoy, Anna Scherer, Berg), whereas others as downright vicious (the Kuragins, Napoleon). None of them, however, is Satanic. Even Tolstoy's Napoleon is a pompous narcissist rather than a Promethean God-wrestler of the Romantic tradition. I will not devote any special attention to these characters, but only discuss them insofar as their actions affect the destinies of the major characters.

III. Pierre's Path toward Freedom

In the earliest drafts of the opening scene of *War and Peace*, which takes place in the St. Petersburg salon of Anna Scherer, there appears a young man named Léon who is said to be an illegitimate son of the immensely rich Count Bezukhov. "Léon" is the Gallicized version of Tolstoy's first name, by which his family often referred to him in childhood and youth. It is also the name of the protagonist from Nikolai Karamzin's unfinished Bildungsroman *The Knight of Our Time*, with whom Pierre shares some character traits.[6] Karamzin was a major influence on Tolstoy throughout the 1840s and 1850s.[7] While researching the history of the Napoleonic Wars, the writer broadened his horizon, acquiring firsthand knowledge of the European thinkers Karamzin popularized in Russia. Thus in his portrayal of Pierre's spiritual wanderings Tolstoy draws on Christoph Martin Wieland and Johann Gottfried Herder, both of whom Karamzin admired and visited during his European tour.[8]

Pierre's story calls to mind Wieland's novel *The History of Agathon*, often regarded as the first Bildungsroman. It presents a fictional biography of the tragedian who appears in Plato's *Symposium*. An illegitimate son of a wealthy Athenian, Agathon is raised in the Temple of Apollo at Delphi, where he studies Platonic philosophy, which makes him a mystic and a dreamer. Kidnapped by pirates and sold as a slave to the Sophist Hippias, who tries to turn him into an Epicurean, Agathon relinquishes his naive belief in the inherent beauty and goodness of mankind and develops a new understanding of *kalokagathia* as a virtuous character shaped by experience. Most critics agree that the point of Wieland's novel is to critique *Schwärmerei*, or excessive enthusiasm. The term "enthusiasm" gained currency in the seventeenth-century Protestant theology, where it was used as a synonym for divine inspiration. In his *Letter Concerning Enthusiasm* Shaftesbury associates enthusiasm with Platonic mysticism. The distinction between enthusiasm and *Schwärmerei* emerged in the German Enlightenment circles critical of Pietism.[9] The *Aufklärer* like Wieland dismissed the Pietists as fanatical and countered their mysticism with their "reasonable" natural religion.

In a letter to Alexander Herzen dated March 14, 1861, Tolstoy described the Decembrist hero of his new novel as "an enthusiast, a mystic, and a Christian" (PSS 60:374). Having studied Joseph de Maistre's *Conversations in St. Petersburg* and some other works of conservative Catholic thinkers that were in vogue in Russia in the 1800s, Tolstoy ultimately drew the line between the Christian mysticism that held sway in Petersburg salons and the Decembrist ideology.[10] Maistre appears in the novel under the name of Abbé Morio, a distinguished guest in Anna Scherer's salon with whom Pierre clashes over the question of eternal peace.[11] Enthusiasm, on the other hand, remained a crucial element of Pierre's character. By drawing on Wieland's nearly forgotten novel, Tolstoy was able to create the image of the "beautiful soul" in the original eighteenth-century sense of the term, that is to say, a pure-hearted, magnanimous idealist. But even though Tolstoy does not make a sharp distinction between enthusiasm and *Schwärmerei*, his hero also undergoes a self-formation through experience, which anchors his passion for truth and justice in historical reality.

Whereas Agathon is raised in Delphi, Pierre is raised in Switzerland, the center of modern enlightened pedagogy. With his head full of progressive ideas, he is completely unprepared for life in Russian society. Unprepared to handle the vast fortune his father leaves him, Pierre surrounds himself with fortune seekers and sycophants. He lets Prince Vasilii Kuragin manipulate him into marrying his beautiful but depraved daughter Hélène, whose affair with Dolokhov prompts Pierre's first spiritual crisis. After challenging Dolokhov to a duel and injuring him, Pierre feels horrified. Leaving Hélène in Moscow, he goes to St. Petersburg, but at a coach station between the two capitals he encounters the leader of the Moscow Masons, Osip Bazdeev. The old man notices Pierre's despair and tries to convert him, an unbeliever, to the Masonic belief. The narrator makes it clear, however, that it is not the mystical metaphysics of the Masons, inherited from Gnosticism, but their ethics focused on moral self-purification and brotherly love that inspires Pierre to become a Mason.

At the height of his Masonic career Pierre meets with his old friend Prince Andrei, who by this point in the story has already experienced the bitter disillusionment of Austerlitz and the death of his wife. Having withdrawn from society, Prince Andrei looks for consolation in Stoic ideas. But Pierre, armed with the arguments derived from Herder's *Naturphilosophie*, tries to convince his friend that the universe is teleological, that God exists, and therefore that life has a meaning.[12] Although Pierre's argument does not convince his skeptical friend, his infectious enthusiasm cheers him up. In the wake of Pierre's visit, Prince Andrei makes a business trip, during which he spends a night at Count Rostov's estate. There he encounters Natasha, who awakens him to a new life.

Meanwhile, Pierre seeks ways to implement his idealistic dreams by reforming the Masonry and expanding its activities beyond philanthropy. Unsurprisingly, his attempts to politicize Masonry meet with the resistance of most Brothers, who are wary of political activism. When the French invade Russia, Pierre's eagerness to become a conscious historical agent and a benefactor of humanity leads him to conceive a plan to assassinate Napoleon, but Pierre's plan backfires and instead of killing Napoleon he gets arrested along with other suspected arsonists and barely escapes execution. Pierre is spared only because Marshal Davout, who happens to interrogate him, realizes that he is a man of quality who could be of some use. Pierre survives, but his optimistic worldview crumbles.

Just as Pierre begins to succumb to nihilism, his soul is revived and transformed through an encounter with an old soldier, Platon Karataev. This encounter is couched in mythological symbolism and resembles a theophany. After his interview with Davout Pierre finds himself in a dark shed, where he at first cannot see anything. The smell of sweat makes him recognize a little round man next to him. Always cheerful and busy, Karataev has no regrets or fears. Over time, Pierre comes to see Karataev, with his round gestures, round face, and illogical but persuasive speech, as "the unfathomable, round, and eternal embodiment of the spirit of simplicity and truth" (974; PSS 12:50).[13] The night following Platon's execution, Pierre has a dream that critics have long seen as the culmination of Pierre's metaphysical quest:[14]

> Again the events of reality combined with dreams, and again someone, he himself or some other person, spoke thoughts to him, and even the same thoughts that had been spoken to him in Mozhaisk.
>
> "Life is everything. Life is God. Everything shifts and moves, and this movement is God. And while there is life, there is delight in the self-awareness of the divinity. To love life is to love God. The hardest and the most blessed thing is to love this life in one's suffering, in the guiltlessness of suffering."
>
> "Karataev!" Pierre recalled. And suddenly a long-forgotten, meek old teacher, who had taught him geography in Switzerland, emerged in Pierre's mind as if alive. "Wait!" said the old man. And he showed Pierre a globe. This globe was a living, wavering ball of

no dimensions. The entire surface of the ball consisted of drops tightly packed together. And these drops all moved and shifted, and now merged from several into one, now divided from one into many. Each drop strove to spread and take up the most space, but the others, striving to do the same, pressed it, sometimes destroying, sometimes merging with it.

"This is life," said the old teacher.

"How simple and clear it is," thought Pierre. "How could I not have known before?"

"In the center is God, and each drop tries to expand in order to reflect Him to the greatest measure. And it grows, merges, and shrinks, and is obliterated on the surface, goes into depths, and again floats up. Here he is, Karataev, see, he spread and vanished." (1064–1065; PSS 12:158–159)

The mention of a "Swiss" teacher led some scholars to conclude that this dream alludes to Rousseau's Savoyard Vicar, whose deism informs Tolstoy's early works. But while the Vicar believes in the transcendent Architect of the world, the dream's imagery illustrates a monistic metaphysics. Similar imagery is found in *God, Some Conversations*, one of Herder's most important works that Karamzin discussed in his *Letters of the Russian Traveler*.[15] Tolstoy probably knew that *God, Some Conversations* played a key role in the famous Pantheism Controversy, and that it was Herder's interpretation of Spinoza that German Romantics adopted in their efforts to reconcile Fichte's principle of absolute subjectivity with Spinoza's metaphysics. The passage that resembles Pierre's dream is found in the Fifth Conversation, where Theophron discusses the laws of physics governing the universe, comparing planets and the solar system to drops of liquid.[16] Given Pierre's familiarity with Herder, one could expect him to remember this text.

Assuming that Pierre's dream alludes to Herder's treatise, we can look at Karataev not only as the embodiment of organic Russianness, but as an exemplary wise man in Spinoza's sense of the term, that is, someone who does not worry too much about death because he feels at one with the world. Karataev embodies Spinoza's understanding of freedom as life in agreement with one's nature. He illustrates a compatibilist solution to the problem of freedom versus necessity that Tolstoy addresses directly in the second epilogue, but implicitly throughout the novel. The encounter with Karataev resolves Pierre's metaphysical doubts:

> This seeking for a purpose had only been a seeking for God; and suddenly he had learned in his captivity, not through words, not through arguments, but through immediate sensation, what his nanny had told him long ago: that God is here, right here, everywhere. In captivity he learned that God in Karataev was much greater, more infinite and unfathomable, than in the Arkhitechton of the universe recognized by the Masons. (1103–1104; PSS 12:205)

After his liberation from captivity, Pierre loses a sense of time and tarries in the joyful sensation of the fullness of life. However, it is not in Pierre's nature to spend the rest of his life in blissful indolence. His turn to radical politics, described in the first epilogue, fits well with his Spinozism, the religion of the democratic Enlightenment.[17] But unlike Wieland's Agathon, who at the end of the story finds himself in the utopian republic of Tarent, Tolstoy's hero only glimpses but never reaches the coast of utopia. Tolstoy's story ends five years before the Decembrist Uprising, the event whose significance the writer pondered for decades after finishing *War and Peace*.

IV. Andrei's Quest for Immortality

While Pierre was originally conceived as a philosophical seeker, Andrei Bolkonsky first appeared in the drafts of *1805* as a brilliant officer who died heroically on the battlefield of Austerlitz. His death was supposed to put into question the chivalric or romantic conception of heroism. But eventually the author decided to restore the mortally wounded hero to life and made him one of the vehicles of his critique of modernity. A son of a typical Enlightenment rationalist, Prince Andrei must have received a formal philosophical education that strengthened his skeptical propensity. His skepticism comes across most clearly in his dialogues with Pierre in volumes 1 and 2, where it serves as a perfect foil for Pierre's enthusiasm.

Prince Andrei's disappointment with Napoleon and the romantic ideal of heroism, combined with the collective humiliation of the Russian army at Austerlitz and his wife's death in childbirth, lead to a melancholia that forces him to resign and retreat from society. He settles down on his estate, Bogucharovo, and tries to find fulfillment in the role of a good landowner, but his attempts to engage with the dysfunctional serf economy only deepen his misanthropy. Pierre's visit to Prince Andrei in Bogucharovo sheds a ray of light into Prince Andrei's soul—not because Andrei agrees with Herder's optimistic philosophy, but because Pierre's enthusiasm is infectious. Yielding to the impulse to break out of the shell he built to protect himself from the world, Prince Andrei makes a business trip to the estate of Count Rostov, where he encounters Natasha for the first time. As we will see, this chance meeting changes Andrei's trajectory, but does not completely transform his character.

One of the most famous scenes in the novel describes Prince Andrei eavesdropping on Natasha, who chatters with Sonya, sings, and dreams perched on the window sill in Otradnoe. All energy and life, Natasha wants to fly to the sky. She is vexed at Sonya, who is not stirred by the beauty of the night and wants to sleep. "'She doesn't care at all about my existence!' Prince Andrei thought all the while he was listening to her talk," says the narrator without explaining whether Andrei's desire to be included in this girl's thoughts comes from loneliness or from injured amour propre (422; PSS 10:157). In any case, after this meeting he decides to end his self-imposed isolation and goes to Petersburg where he gets involved with Speransky's committee that was developing a liberal reforms project. However, after a single visit to the war minister, Arakcheev, Prince Andrei loses his optimism about any future reforms. What keeps him in Petersburg throughout the season is not his work with Speransky, but his love for Natasha, whom he meets again at a brilliant ball where she stands out against the background of fashionable ladies like Hélène Bezukhova.

In contrast to the statuesque Hélène, Natasha looks thin and angular. Nevertheless, she is irresistibly charming, especially when she sings. The erotic potential of singing was a popular aesthetic topos in eighteenth- and early nineteenth-century literature. Thus in Wieland's Bildungsroman, Danae seduces the idealistic Agathon through a singspiel that appeals to his soul as well as his senses.[18] Natasha's singing, however, produces an even more powerful impact on Prince Andrei's soul, one that can be compared to a religious experience.

> After dinner Natasha, at Prince Andrei's request, went to the clavichord and began to sing. Prince Andrei stood by the window, talking with the ladies, and listened to her. In the middle of a phrase, Prince Andrei fell silent and suddenly felt choked with tears, which he did not know was possible for him. He looked at the singing Natasha and something new and happy occurred in his soul. He was happy, but at the same time he felt sad. He had decidedly nothing to weep about, but he was ready to weep. About what? His former love? The little princess? His disappointments? . . . His hopes for the future? . . . Yes and no. The main thing he wanted to weep about was a sudden, vivid awareness of the terrible opposition between something infinitely great and indefinable that was in him, and something narrow and fleshly that he himself, and even she, was. This opposition tormented him and gladdened him while she sang. (467; PSS 10:212)

Back in Otradnoe, Natasha's singing stirred in Prince Andrei's soul long-forgotten youthful desires. But now the emotional maelstrom produced in his soul by her voice results in deeper insights. He becomes aware, as we have seen, of the "terrible opposition between something infinitely great and indefinable that was in him, and something narrow and fleshly that he himself, and even she, was." Moved by Natasha's song, Prince Andrei recognizes both in Natasha's soul and in his own a yearning for the infinite. Given Andrei's skepticism and mature age (he is about five years older than Pierre and sixteen years older than Natasha), the scenes describing his Romantic longing are particularly poignant.[19] Observing his friend, Pierre comes to the realization that Andrei has been transformed: "Prince Andrei seemed and was quite a different, new man. Where was his anguish, his contempt for life, his disillusionment?" (475; PSS 10:222). Andrei himself compares what has happened to him to an enlightenment: "The whole world is divided for me into two parts: one is she, and there is all happiness, hope, light; the other is where she is not, and there everything is dejection and darkness" (475; PSS 10:222).

Prince Andrei's spiritual awakening is akin to a religious experience as discussed in Schleiermacher's *On Religion: Speeches to Its Cultures Despisers*. Tolstoy owned the collected works of Schleiermacher, and although references to Schleiermacher's works began to appear in Tolstoy's works only in the 1880s, he might have been familiar with *On Religion* already in the 1860s.[20] At any rate, the parallels between Schleiermacher's groundbreaking work and the religious sensibility that Prince Andrei begins to develop in volume 2 are noteworthy. Thus in the second speech Schleiermacher famously claims that the essence of religion "is neither thinking nor acting, but an intuition and feeling."[21] Schleiermacher goes on to define religion as "intuition of the universe." A neo-Spinozist, by "intuition of the universe" he means the experience of becoming aware of one's participation in the "One-and-All."[22] In the fourth speech Schleiermacher points out that music is especially conducive to developing this intuition. Similarly, in *War and Peace* music not only charms but elevates and frees the soul of the listener.[23] There are other parallels between Schleiermacher's and Tolstoy's texts. I would also argue that Tolstoy's definition of the essence of religion as the individual's relationship to the world as a whole in *What Is Religion and of What Does Its Essence Consist?* is also indebted to Schleiermacher.[24]

Despite his feelings for Natasha, Prince Andrei yields to the demand of his arrogant father, who does not regard a Rostova as a proper match for his son, to postpone the wedding for a year. Andrei goes abroad without announcing their engagement, which creates an emotionally challenging situation for his bride-to-be. Filled with desire but forced to spend a year in a limbo—neither a fiancée nor a free woman—Natasha pines away for months until she falls into a trap laid out by the skilled seducer Anatole Kuragin and his sister Hélène. Although Natasha's elopement with Anatole is averted by Sonya's quick and decisive actions, her letter, in which she breaks her engagement to Bolkonsky, does reach its addressee. Deeply insulted, Prince Andrei tells Pierre that forgiving her and renewing their engagement is unthinkable for him.

Prince Andrei's failure to understand and forgive Natasha surprises Pierre. He reminds his friend about their old argument, where Prince Andrei had suggested that "a fallen woman should be forgiven" (597; PSS 10:371). Their discussion seems to have been theoretical. Although the New Testament is the obvious reference, their debate may have been inspired by a fashionable literary work. The motif of the "fallen woman" deserving forgiveness is central to many eighteenth-century novels, including *The History of Agathon*. Thus at the end of the story, Agathon cannot decide whether he should marry a reformed courtesan and his former mistress Danae or have a chaste friendship with her instead. As Pierre points out, Natasha can hardly be called a "fallen woman." But the point of the discussion is not the degree of the woman's "fall," but rather her beloved's attitude. Agathon loves Danae but hesitates to marry her, because he fears that carnal love would always remind him about her past and undermine his respect for her. In Andrei's case, sympathy is completely blocked by pride. Although their engagement was unofficial, Natasha's inconstancy humiliated him in the eyes of the few people who knew about it, including his father, and in his own eyes.

A careful reader would discern that the love between Prince Andrei and Natasha is not ruined overnight. It is stifled over the entire period of Bolkonsky's absence from Russia, during which genuine communication between the lovers gets interrupted. Although Natasha regularly receives detailed letters from Prince Andrei, she does not enjoy them, but feels offended by the fact that he lived a real life seeing new places and people while she was pining away in the countryside.

> Her own letters to him not only did not furnish her with any comfort, but were a boring and false duty.... She was unable to write, because she could not conceive the possibility of truthfully expressing in a letter even a thousandth part of what she was used to expressing with her voice, smile, and gaze. (534; PSS 10:294)

We do not know how much Prince Andrei himself missed Natasha. His readiness to take offense and break off all communication with his fiancée suggests that during his absence he has lost touch with her soul. The moments of shared longing for the infinite did not produce the kind of spiritual bond that would neutralize the egoistic drives of two individuals. After their breakup Prince Andrei succumbs to misanthropy, which only a stronger passion—the hatred of the French invaders—could supplant. Re-entering military service, he turns down the opportunity to join the staff and becomes a regimental commander.

During the battle of Borodino Prince Andrei's regiment is stationed in the reserves, under constant bombardment. Pacing across the meadow, and watching the cannonballs fall at some distance, Prince Andrei suddenly sees a spinning cannonball next to him. Remembering that he is being watched, he remains standing and gets severely wounded in the stomach. It is not Romantic love, but death that finally frees Prince Andrei from his amour propre. His conversion occurs in a makeshift hospital, where among the wounded and dying he sees Anatole Kuragin. The sight of the sobbing Anatole, whose leg has just been amputated, evokes a memory of Natasha as he first saw her at the ball three years ago. Love and tenderness awaken in his soul, giving rise to an even more powerful feeling of rapturous pity and love for his suffering enemy:

> Prince Andrei could no longer restrain himself, and he wept tender, loving tears over people, over himself, and over their and his own errors.
> "Compassion, love for our brothers, for those who love us, love for those who hate us, love for our enemies—yes, that love which God preached on earth, which Princess Marya taught me, and which I didn't understand; that's why I was sorry about life, that's what was still left for me, if I was to live, but now it's too late. I know it!" (814; PSS 11:257–258)

Before Prince Andrei dies, he gets a chance to see Natasha and communicate with her soul again. When she suddenly appears before him in Mytischi and asks his forgiveness, Prince Andrei no longer remembers his grudge. As long as his body fights the gangrene, their souls dwell in a blissful harmony. But as his vital force dwindles, his consciousness also begins to transform. Prince Andrei finds himself straddling two worlds: the realm of creaturely life and the realm of spirit. Andrei's train of consciousness echoes the image of the liquid globe from Pierre's dream. He, too, seems to be in dialogue with the teacher whose message implied that happiness is to be found in the intellectual love of God:

> "Love? What is love?" he thought. "Love hinders death. Love is life. Everything, everything I understand, I understand only because I love. Everything is, everything exists, only because I love. Everything is connected only by that. Love is God, and to die—means that I, a part of love, return to the common eternal source." These thoughts seemed comforting to him. But they were only thoughts, something was lacking in them, there was something one-sidedly personal, cerebral—there was no evidence. (984; PSS 12:63)

As long as he feels attached to a particular being, the love of God remains a cold, cerebral idea. Conscious of his earthly identity, he cannot join the eternal source of life. But one night he falls asleep and dreams that he has already died and that death is an awakening from life. From this point on, everything that he held dear in this life begins to lose its importance for Prince Andrei.

While Prince Andrei experiences his detachment from life as a liberation, those around him are frightened by his transformation. The fact that he is half-dead is brought home to Princess Marya, when she arrives at her brother's deathbed, bringing his son along.

> "André, would you li . . ." Princess Marya suddenly said in a shuddering voice, "would you like to see Nikolushka? He talks about you all the time."
>
> Prince Andrei smiled barely perceptibly for the first time, but Princess Marya, who knew his face so well, understood with horror that this was a smile not of joy, not of tenderness for his son, but of quiet, mild mockery of Princess Marya, who, in his opinion, was using her last means of bringing him to his senses. (980; PSS 12:58–59)

When Prince Andrei's spirit finally departs, Natasha closes his eyes and presses her lips to "what was her nearest reminder of him," asking: "Where has he gone? Where is he now?" (986; PSS 12:65).

Unlike Marya, a pious Christian who firmly believes in the dogma of resurrection, Natasha is unsure about the shape of the afterlife. Her question harks back to a philosophical dialogue about memory and immortality in chapter 10, part 4 of volume 2. It is Natasha who begins this dialogue, inviting Nikolai and Sonya to share their earliest memories. It may appear strange that Natasha, whom even Pierre who adores her sees as enchanting, but hardly intelligent, is the one to introduce such a hefty philosophical topic. This is, however, no accident. The heroine who inspires the love of the two co-protagonists is not only the symbol of the Eternal Feminine, but also a vehicle of Tolstoy's budding philosophy of life.

V. Natasha, or Life

The dialogue about immortality in Otradnoe recalls the above-cited episode from the drafts to *Boyhood*, which describes Nikolenka's fascination with pantheism. In *War and Peace* it is Sonya who mentions the Egyptians' belief in metempsychosis, to which Natasha replies that their souls could not have been in animals, but were probably in angels. When Nikolai asks ironically why their souls end up in a lower realm, she objects with conviction: "Not lower, who told you it's lower? . . . How do I know what I used to be? . . . The soul is immortal . . . which means, if I will live forever, then I also lived before, lived for the whole eternity" (522; PSS 10:578). Dimmler remarks that it is hard for humans to imagine eternity, but Natasha retorts: "Why is it hard to imagine eternity? . . . There will be today, there will be tomorrow, there will be always, and there was yesterday, and there was the day before" (522; PSS 10:578). Unable to think abstractly, Natasha imagines eternity not the way the Judeo-Christian tradition conceives of it, namely as timelessness, but as perpetuity.

Suddenly, the old Countess interrupts her daughter's naive philosophizing and asks her to sing. Reluctant at first, Natasha gives one of her best performances ever. Throughout the novel the musical Rostov family, with their charm and hedonistic proclivity, are represented as "the locus for the irresponsible fullness of the present."[25] But the Rostovs' musicality is also the key to their emotional receptivity. Natasha in particular is gifted with the emotional sensitivity that compensates for her impulsiveness, allowing her to evolve from a charming girl into a wise woman. Unlike Goethe's Ottilie from *Elective Affinities* or Makarie from *Wilhelm Meister's Journeyman Years*, who also divine nature's secret wisdom, Natasha never records her thoughts or pontificates. Her grasp of the laws of the universe is expressed through her actions that cerebral individuals like Prince Andrei find bewildering. But on closer inspection, Natasha's spontaneous outbursts turn out to conform to the hidden logic of life. The novel's central dramatic event, Natasha's betrayal of Prince Andrei's faith, provides an illustration to Tolstoy's understanding of determinism versus freedom that became the backbone for his mature religious philosophy. I will now briefly analyze this drama and its philosophical ramifications.

From the very beginning of Prince Andrei's courtship, Countess Rostova feels uneasy about her vivacious Natasha marrying Bolkonsky. Known for their intellectual snobbism, Prince Andrei and his father are the opposites of Natasha's prodigal father and her loving, but limited, mother. The conflict between these different worlds seems written in the stars. Natasha's visit to the opera where she meets Anatole occurs immediately after her humiliating visit to the old Prince's house. Thus her attraction to Anatole, whose attention boosts her self-confidence, is natural. It compensates her for the months of isolation and the humiliation she has endured at the Bolkonskys. Only Pierre, who understands the volatility of emotions and secretly loves Natasha, can understand Natasha's feelings. The rest of the world condemns her impulsive behavior that could dishonor herself and her family—hence her profound sense of guilt, which causes deep suffering and illness. This crisis awakens Natasha's moral conscience, transforming her from an impetuous girl into a mature woman who would one day become the Decembrist's wife, a figure who in the Russian cultural imagination has always had the aura of martyrdom.

Watching Natasha pine away, her parents surround her with doctors, but medications have no effect on Natasha, whose illness has spiritual causes. When a neighbor from the country comes to Moscow to venerate holy relics, Natasha welcomes this opportunity to atone for her sins and receive Holy Communion. For days she gets up at dawn to attend the matins. This is the first time we see Natasha opening her soul before God. In chapter 18 of part 1, volume 3, the author "goes behind" Natasha as she takes part in a Sunday liturgy. Conducted at Count Razumovsky's house chapel, this service offers the first sketch of Tolstoy's destructive critique of the institutionalized Christianity in *The Resurrection* and other late works. At first distracted by society gossipers and fashionable ladies, Natasha is eventually able to get absorbed in her prayers. She follows the words of the deacon, substituting the ones she does not understand with her own. However, in the middle of the mass the priest starts reciting a new prayer he has just received from the synod, which curses Russia's enemies. Natasha is bewildered:

> With her whole soul she participated in the petition about a right spirit, about the strengthening of hearts with faith, hope, and inspiring them with love. But she could not pray about trampling her enemies under her feet, when a few moments before she had wished to have more of them, so as to love and pray for them. (663; PSS 11:77)

Natasha does not dare question the rightness of this prayer. However, after this church visit she seems to lose an interest in official religion.

That Natasha matures into a naturally pious person whose impulses seem to coincide with the moral law becomes clear in subsequent chapters that describe the advent of war in Russia. In one of the novel's most memorable scenes Natasha defies her mother by ordering the servants to unload thirty carts containing her parents' possessions and give them to the wounded officers, so that they can flee Moscow. When in the epilogue Natasha is transformed into a mother of a large family, she resembles her mother, and yet we cannot doubt that this penny-pinching matron would sacrifice her family's comfort to save other people. Natasha's helping save the wounded foreshadows the woman who would give up the life of luxury to share her husband's exile not only out of love for him, but also out of intuitive respect for his genuinely Christian cause: the abolition of serfdom. In the epilogue Natasha emerges as a woman who not only gives and sustains life, but also grasps its hidden teleology, which Tolstoy links to the emergence of Humanity, the Brotherhood of the Spirit. Unlike Karataev, who would not have understood Pierre, she realizes that his restlessness in the midst of family happiness has to do with his need for a higher form of perfection: he cannot be at peace in a country of slaves.

VI. Conclusion: Tolstoy's Religion

In the 1870s and 1880s Tolstoy became immersed in the study of ethics, theology, the Bible, and biblical criticism. His quest for a new religious philosophy was motivated by two overwhelming desires: to conquer death, or the fear of death, and to eradicate slavery. In his treatises, beginning with *On Life*, Tolstoy offered his new vision of human formation that culminated with the liberation from the fear of death and transition to a wholly spiritual life.[26] In *On Life* moral perfection is virtually synonymous with immortality. Revisiting Herder's idea that a "human being is formed to expect immortality," he calls this state of rational perfection "reasonable consciousness" and suggests that one should strive to achieve it before confronting death.[27] "Reasonable consciousness" also harks back to Spinoza's concept of the mind's eternity. By ascending to the perspective of the One-and-All, one escapes anxiety and reaches ultimate freedom. This vision of self-transcendence is not to be confused with the ecstasies of agape. As evidenced by Tolstoy's analysis of Prince Andrei's consciousness in chapter 16, part 1, volume 4, the intellectual love of God that overcomes his consciousness at the brink of death is very different from the rapturous love he felt for Anatole Kuragin. It is hardly a feeling, but a chilling thought that turns one into a living dead. Striving toward this kind of immortality while still alive seems cruel to those around one.

In *War and Peace* Tolstoy had found a way around this problem by shifting his attention to another kind of immortality: the survival of one's image in the memory of those who knew and loved one. Thus Prince Andrei's spiritual image lives on in the hearts and thoughts of those who loved him. The novelistic epilogue concludes with Nikolushka Bolkonsky's dream, which comes across as a prophecy of the Decembrist Uprising. In this dream, the images of Prince Andrei and Pierre merge with the images of the defenders of the Roman republic immortalized by Plutarch. Waking up, Nikolushka calls out "Father! Father!" and vows to do something that would make his father, whose memory he worships, proud of him.

This novelistic ending anticipates the story of the child Christ in Tolstoy's *Gospel in Brief*. Nikolushka's prayer-like apostrophe to his father foreshadows Tolstoy's description of Jesus Christ as an orphan yearning for an absent father.[28] A lonely child projects a divine Father and imagines himself to be a spiritual hero, a messiah. When approached as a piece of biblical criticism, Tolstoy's retelling of the Gospel comes across as a Feuerbachian critique of Christ's divinity. However, when approached as a literary work, it reveals the same yearning for God one finds at the heart of all of Tolstoy's auto-psychological narratives.

Despite late Tolstoy's insistence on stripping Christianity of the belief in the supernatural and centering religion on the moral reform of individuals and nations, his later fiction and diaries suggest that he never stopped hoping for a religious experience akin to

Pascal's. It is telling that *Pensées* was one of the books Tolstoy left on his desk when he fled his home on October 28, 1910. His death at a railway station became a fitting conclusion to a life of a God-seeker who for over half a century shared his illuminations with the world while keeping diaries where he recorded his continual struggle with doubt.

Notes

1. The English translation is quoted from Inessa Medzhibovskaya, *Tolstoy and the Religious Culture of His Time: A Biography of a Long Conversion, 1845–1887* (Lanham, MD: Lexington Books, 2008), 37.
2. Donna Tussing Orwin analyses Rousseau's influence on the young Tolstoy in *Tolstoy's Art and Thought, 1847–1880* (Princeton, NJ: Princeton University Press, 1993), 85–98.
3. This project was titled "Roman russkogo pomeshchika."
4. In 1860 Tolstoy met the famous Decembrist and his relative Sergei Volkonsky. He also read various historical materials on the Decembrists published by Alexander Herzen and Nikolai Ogarev. I discuss this issue in Lina Steiner, "A Revolutionary as a Beautiful Soul: Lev Tolstoy's Path to Ethical Anarchism," *Studies in East European Thought* 71, no. 1 (2019): 43–62.
5. For a discussion of this relationship see Anne Eakin Moss, *Only among Women: Philosophies of Community in the Russian and Soviet Imagination, 1860–1940* (Evanston, IL: Northwestern University Press, 2019), chap. 2.
6. N. M. Karamzin, *Rytsar'nashego vremeni*, in *Sochineniia v 2-kh tomakh*, vol. 1 (Leningrad: Khudozhestvennaia literatura, 1984), 64–92.
7. For a detailed discussion of Karamzin's influence on Tolstoy see Boris Eikhenbaum, *Molodoi Tolstoi* (Munich: Fink, 1968), 14–20.
8. N. M. Karamzin, *Letters of a Russian Traveler*, trans. Andrew Kahn (Oxford: Voltaire Foundation, 2003), 99–106.
9. Joe Lee Davis, "Mystical versus Enthusiastic Sensibility," *Journal of the History of Ideas* 4, no. 3 (1943): 301–319.
10. Isaiah Berlin argued that Maistre's ideas had a big influence on Tolstoy's historiosophy. See Berlin, "The Hedgehog and the Fox," in *Russian Thinkers*, ed. Henry Hardy and Aileen Kelly (London: Penguin, 1978), 22–81. This opinion can be contested. Tolstoy always rejected such pivotal

Maistrian ideas as the creation of the universal church and the attainment of perpetual peace through the balance of powers.
11. Tolstoy's portrayal of Maistre is discussed in Vera Miltchyna, "Joseph de Maistre in Russia: A Look at the Reception of His Work," in *Joseph de Maistre's Life, Thought, and Influence*, ed. Richard A. Lebrun (Montreal: McGill-Queens University Press, 2011), 241–270; cf. especially page 243.
12. *War and Peace*, volume 2, part 2, chapter 12. I discuss this scene in Steiner, *For Humanity's Sake: The Bildungsroman in Russian Culture* (Toronto: University of Toronto Press, 2011), 106–108.
13. Jonathan I. Israel, *Radical Enlightenment: Philosophy and the Making of Modernity, 1650–1750* (New York: Oxford University Press, 2001).
14. See, for example, Richard Gustafson, *Leo Tolstoy: Resident and Stranger* (Princeton, NJ: Princeton University Press, 1986), 81.
15. Karamzin, *Letters of a Russian Traveler*, 100.
16. Johann Gottfried Herder, *God, Some Conversations*, trans. Frederick H. Burkhardt (Indianapolis, IN: Library of Liberal Arts, 1940), 178–179.
17. Israel, *Radical Enlightenment*, 159–174.
18. Christoph Martin Wieland, *Geschichte des Agathon*, in *Sämtliche Werke*, vol. 1 (Hamburg: Stieftung zur Förderung von Wissenschaft und Kultur, 1984), 687.
19. Friedrich Schleiermacher, *On Religion: Speeches to Its Cultured Despisers*, trans. and ed. Richard Crouter (New York: Cambridge University Press, 1996), 75.
20. See *Biblioteka L'va Nikolaevicha Tolstogo v Iasnoi Poliane. Bibliograficheskoe opsanie*, 3 vols. (Tula: Iasnaia Poliana, 1999), 1:312.
21. Schleiermacher, *On Religion*, 22.
22. For a detailed analysis of Schleiermacher's neo-Spinozism see Julia A. Lamm, *The Living God: Schleiermacher's Theological Appropriation of Spinoza* (University Park: Pennsylvania State University Press, 1996).
23. Schleiermacher, *On Religion*, 75.
24. Cf. PSS 35: 161–162.
25. Caryl Emerson, "Tolstoy and Music," in *Anniversary Essays on Tolstoy*, ed. Donna Tussing Orwin (New York: Cambridge University Press, 2010), 8–32, 15.
26. Tolstoy, "*O zhizni*" is published in PSS 26:313–442.
27. Chapter 7, book 4 of Johann Gottfried Herder's *Ideen zur Philosophie der Geschichte der Menschheit* (Berlin: Holzinger, 2017), 433–436.
28. Cf. PSS 24:69.

Works Cited

Berlin, Isaiah. "The Hedgehog and the Fox." *Russian Thinkers*. Edited by Henry Hardy and Aileen Kelly, 22–81. London: Penguin, 1978.

Biblioteka L'va Nikolaevicha Tolstogo v Iasnoi Poliane. Bibliograficheskoe opsanie. 3 vols. Tula: Iasnaia Poliana, 1999.

Davis, Lee. "Mystical versus Enthusiastic Sensibility." *Journal of the History of Ideas* 4, no. 3 (June 1943): 301–319.

Eakin Moss, Anne. *Only among Women: Philosophies of Community in the Russian and Soviet Imagination, 1860–1940*. Evanston, IL: Northwestern University Press, 2019.

Eikhenbaum, Boris. *Molodoi Tolstoi*. Munich: Fink, 1968.

Emerson, Caryl. "Tolstoy and Music." *Anniversary Essays on Tolstoy*. Edited by Donna Tussing Orwin, 8–32. New York: Cambridge University Press, 2010.

Gustafson, Richard. *Leo Tolstoy: Resident and Stranger*. Princeton, NJ: Princeton University Press, 1986.

Herder, Johann Gottfried. *God, Some Conversations*. Translated by Frederick H. Burkhardt. Indianapolis, IN: Library of Liberal Arts, 1940.

Herder, Johann Gottfried. *Ideen zur Philosophie der Geschichte der Menschheit*. Berlin: Holzinger, 2017.

Israel, Jonathan I. *Radical Enlightenment: Philosophy and the Making of Modernity, 1650–1750*. New York: Oxford University Press, 2001.

Karamzin, N. M. *Letters of a Russian Traveler*. Translated by Andrew Kahn. Oxford: Voltaire Foundation, 2003.

Karamzin, N. M. *Rytsar'nashego vremeni. Sochineniia v 2-kh tomakh*. Vol. 1, 64–92. Leningrad: Khudozhestvennaia literatura, 1984.

Lamm, Julia A. *The Living God: Schleiermacher's Theological Appropriation of Spinoza*. University Park: Pennsylvania State University Press, 1996.

Medzhibovskaya, Inessa. *Tolstoy and the Religious Culture of His Time: A Biography of a Long Conversion, 1845–1887*. Lanham, MD: Lexington Books, 2008.

Miltchyna, Vera. "Joseph de Maistre in Russia: A Look at the Reception of His Work." *Joseph de Maistre's Life, Thought, and Influence*. Edited by Richard A. Lebrun, 241–270. Montreal: McGill-Queens University Press, 2011.

Orwin, Donna Tussing. *Tolstoy's Art and Thought, 1847–1880*. Princeton, NJ: Princeton University Press, 1993.

Schleiermacher, Friedrich Daniel Ernst. *On Religion: Speeches to Its Cultured Despisers*. Translated and edited by Richard Crouter. New York: Cambridge University Press, 1996.

Steiner, Lina. *For Humanity's Sake: The Bildungsroman in Russian Culture*. Toronto: University of Toronto Press, 2011.

Steiner, Lina. "A Revolutionary as a Beautiful Soul: Lev Tolstoy's Path to Ethical Anarchism." *Studies in East European Thought* 71, no. 1 (Spring 2019): 43–62.

Tolstoy, L. N. *Polnoe sobranie sochininenii v 90 tomakh*. Edited by V. G. Chertkov. 90 vols. Moscow: Khudozhestvennaia literatura, 1928–58.

Wieland, Christoph Martin. *Geschichte des Agathon. Sämtliche Werke.* Vol. 1. Hamburg: Stieftung zur Förderung von Wissenschaft und Kultur, 1984.

8
Death and Infinity

Jeff Love

Everyone who has read *War and Peace* remembers Prince Andrei seriously wounded and supine on the Pratzen heights after the battle of Austerlitz:

> "*Voilà une belle mort*," said Napoleon, looking at Bolkonsky.
> Prince Andrei understood that it had been said about him, and that it was Napoleon speaking. He heard the man who had said these words being addressed as *sire*. But he heard these words as if he was hearing the buzzing of a fly. He not only was not interested, he did not even notice, and at once forgot them. He had a burning in his head; he felt that he was losing blood, and he saw above him that distant, lofty, and eternal sky. He knew that it was Napoleon—his hero—but at that moment, Napoleon seemed to him such a small, insignificant man compared with what was now happening between his soul and this lofty, infinite sky with clouds racing across it. (291; PSS 9:356–357)

Apocalyptic, existential (*Grenzsituation*), epiphanic, transcendent, sublime: this scene invites interpretations that have in common the identification of the eruption of the infinite, the indeterminate—death itself—into the carefully modulated structure of the Tolstoyan text. What had hitherto been so important for Prince Andrei, Napoleon and the mastery of warfare exhibited by Napoleon's impressive string of victories, dissipates almost instantly into the "buzzing of a fly." Such an extraordinary transformation in Prince

Andrei's attitude to Napoleon confers a significance on this scene disproportionate to its length; and, indeed, Prince Andrei remains haunted by the image of the "lofty, infinite" sky throughout the remainder of his narrative. In the words of Jorge Luis Borges, "There is a concept which corrupts and upsets all others. I refer not to Evil, whose limited realm is that of ethics; I refer to the infinite."[1]

What haunts Prince Andrei haunts or "upsets" the novel more generally. Accordingly, I investigate in this chapter several ways in which the infinite appears in the novel and, in particular, the peculiar association of the infinite with determinism and death. First, I look at the infinite as it appears abstractly in the critique of historians and the narratives that they create. Second, I take two "cases" that show the impact of the infinite on the concrete form of characters' lives, specifically, those of Prince Andrei and his friend Pierre Bezukhov. To conclude, I consider the persona of the narrator as also reflecting the impact of the infinite on the novel's narrative structure itself. This approach to the narrative frame of the novel allows me to bring together important strands of the preceding presentations to indicate to what extent the infinite corrupts the narrative of *War and Peace*, thereby raising questions about the novel's capacity to right the wrongs of historians critiqued within it.

I. Of Infinite Causes and Motion

The critique of historians that becomes increasingly explicit in *War and Peace* has had a polarizing effect on both readers and critics.[2] While often dismissed in the nineteenth century, this critique received a good deal of attention in the twentieth century largely thanks to Sir Isaiah Berlin's pioneering essay, "The Hedgehog and the Fox."[3] This is a somewhat ironic result. Though Berlin takes Tolstoy's critique of historians seriously in terms of the fictional text, he assumes a rather dismissive attitude to Tolstoy's "theorizing."[4] Nonetheless, Tolstoy's theorizing should not be so lightly dismissed, nor should the deeper thrust of his critique of historians. Both rely on arguments drawing on the infinite, in the case of the calculus proposal, on infinite or continuous motion, and, in the case of the critique of historians, on infinite causation.[5] I shall take up the critique of historians first and then Tolstoy's calculus proposal.

The first chapter of the third book of *War and Peace* contains one of the most direct statements of the argument about causation relative to historical narratives. The narrator raises the question of causation in connection with the various reasons given for Napoleon's choice to invade Russia. The narrator asks, "What produced this extraordinary event? What were its causes?":

> For us descendants—who are not historians, who are not carried away by the process of research and therefore can contemplate events with unobscured common sense—a countless (*neischislimoe kolichestvo*) number of causes present themselves. The deeper we go in search of causes, the more of them we find, and each cause taken singly or whole series of causes present themselves to us as equally correct in themselves, and equally false in their insignificance in comparison with the enormity of the event, and equally false in their incapacity (without the participation of all other coinciding causes) to produce the event that took place. (604; PSS 11:4–5)

Tolstoy's argument against historical narratives holds that they are *reductive* and cannot be anything but reductive because the causes that come together to produce them are "countless"—that is, they are infinite in number. No matter what explanation a historian gives for an event, it must mislead to the extent it claims authority to explain the event completely because it is a specific narrative selecting aspects of an event as determinative of the event as a whole. The dominant criterion for selection that Tolstoy interrogates is famously the notion that one person can direct a historical event. In other words, Tolstoy's critique of historians is also a critique of human agency and the notion that one human being can have an adequate appreciation of an event so as to be able to direct it. Put more bluntly, Tolstoy's insistence on infinite causation demands that anyone claiming to direct historical events have an infinite or "Laplacean" mind capable of seeing the whole as it is "in advance" or as if sub specie aeternitatis. Yet the problem of the infinite cannot be resolved since the infinite cannot constitute a whole or, at least, only in a very problematic sense.[6]

Hence, the skeptical views about historical narratives that both Berlin and others attribute to Tolstoy arise from an argument, of ancient provenance, for infinite causation.[7] This argument results in a pervasive nominalism whereby any construction of events cannot avoid accusations of reductiveness or partiality based on an arbitrarily chosen criterion of selection. No historical narrative can be true, then, if truth requires something like absolute, unlimited, or infinite knowledge,[8] itself a notion, attributed to God, that suffers when applied to human beings: the divine mind, unlike the human mind, intuits all without regard to time. The best a historical narrative can do is to provide an account that cannot claim superiority to other accounts as an *absolutely complete* account of an event. And if Hegel is right when he says that the "truth is the whole," all narratives fall short of the truth. They are stories that one may choose to believe or reject, and Tolstoy's narrator suggests that we may have to reject them all if what we seek is a final and indubitably true account.

But is that in fact the position the narrator takes? Another chapter in the third book suggests otherwise:

> For human reason, absolute continuity of movement is incomprehensible.
> Man begins to understand the laws of any kind of movement only when he examines the arbitrarily chosen units of that

movement. But at the same time it is from this arbitrary division of continuous movement into discrete units that the greater part of human errors proceeds.

The passage continues:

> By taking smaller and smaller units of movement, we only approach the solution of the problem, but never reach it. Only by allowing for an infinitesimal quantity and the ascending progression from that up to one tenth, and by taking the sum of that geometrical progression, do we arrive at the solution of the problem. A new branch of mathematics, having attained to the art of dealing with infinitesimal quantities in other, more complex problems of movement as well, now gives answers to questions that used to seem insoluble.
>
> This new branch of mathematics, unknown to the ancients, in examining questions of movement, allows for infinitesimal quantities, that is, such as restore the main condition of movement (absolute continuity), and thereby corrects the inevitable error that human reason cannot help committing when it examines discrete units of movement instead of continuous movement.
>
> The same thing happens in the search for the laws of historical movement.
>
> The movement of mankind, proceeding from a countless number of human wills, occurs continuously.
>
> To comprehend the laws of this movement is the goal of history. (821; PSS 11:266–267)

Tolstoy takes a different course in this chapter. The argument against causation holds that no causal account of an event can claim to be final. Indeed, if all causal accounts are equally plausible and implausible or equally correct and incorrect, there is no possibility of establishing any persuasive normative criterion for determining the truth of a given historical account. To emphasize the point again, in the infinite there can be no correct perspective on anything at all—the infinite cannot allow any decisive or final perspective—all perspectives are *necessarily* equal.

Yet, as the preceding passage indicates, Tolstoy does not leave it at that. To the contrary, he seeks to create a new kind of history analogous to calculus. To put this more directly, he seeks to apply to human behavior a method of analysis that applies to all physical processes as processes involving continuous motion. He thus puts in question the significance of human freedom as the freedom to act in a manner not subject to law. The modern notion that a human being may initiate a causal series is put doubly in question. Not only does Tolstoy's account of causation eliminate from consideration the possibility that any historical actor can claim to initiate, and thereby control, a causal series, but he also affirms this claim by advocating an approach to history based on a method that likens human behavior to that of any physical object in motion.

In both cases, the infinite is fundamental, and fundamentally estranging, because the infinite shows no concern for human beings in the simple sense that human beings can claim neither that they direct events nor that their perspective is in fact a correct or true one. The infinite, as Borges notes, corrupts all concepts as constructions of a finite creature, limited and determined by factors of which it is frequently scarcely conscious.

We may then ask: How can calculus offer a "better" picture of history? How is the calculus analogy helpful in overcoming the problem of infinite causation? In the second part of the epilogue the narrator claims that the end of history should be to proclaim the laws of history; that is, the laws governing human movement in history (1212–1215; PSS 12:338–341). Such laws, like calculus, would be more accurate and final because they could take into account the movement of an infinite set of persons. All persons would in fact be treated as equally relevant and irrelevant or equally important or unimportant in the production of movement—no one selection of persons or "causes" would have agency or influence on the event superior to any others. By taking into account all these movements as essentially equal, the historian may come to determine a law governing all persons that allows for some understanding of history, though the narrator, for other reasons, sheds doubt on the possibility of establishing a complete self-perpetuating model of historical motion (1200–1203; PSS 12:322–327).[9]

It is not my task to evaluate the merits of this proposal (Berlin, for one, does not take it seriously). Important for my purposes is this: the proposal offers additional evidence of the centrality of the infinite to the narrative of *War and Peace* as *the* primary problem, not only for historians, but for any narrative that makes claims for its own authority by affirming that it is true or complete. If the critique of historians raises the problem of the infinite as unsettling narratives, it also puts in question assumptions about human freedom. Despite the fact that causation is infinite, Tolstoy still advocates that there is causation. Indeed, by claiming that causation is infinite, Tolstoy affirms a determinist model allowing no space for human freedom conceived primarily in the Kantian spirit as the capacity to initiate and control a causal sequence. The calculus proposal does nothing to controvert this determinist notion of causation; it may even presuppose the latter because, if there is to be a calculus of history, human agency, or the capacity to initiate causal sequences, has to be reduced to nil.[10]

The calculus proposal is itself ambiguous. If calculus is supposed to provide us with knowledge of historical movement, it must provide us with complete knowledge, for partial knowledge always allows the possibility of a substantial change or innovation that renders truths provisional. The infinite cannot be understood completely because it is the nature of the infinite never to be fully present to the finite mind. One can argue that this is not so, for knowing a finite set of patterns which repeat themselves infinitely is like infinite or complete knowledge understood precisely as the infinite repetition of a finite set of patterns. Georg Cantor, the inventor of set theory, distinguished between the countable or denumerable infinite and non-countable or non-denumerable infinite.[11] The former could be understood as infinite because of the possibility of marking out sets, say the natural numbers, and comparing them clearly on a one-to-one basis to other sets. Hence, one could compare and order the natural numbers and the set of even numbers, both of which could be comparable and ordered because they can be successfully counted against each other. A non-denumerable infinite set would not allow for this one-to-one counting.[12] More radically, the absolute infinite would allow for no counting of any kind. It would put in question the notion of discrete number itself. For Cantor, in other words, there are infinite sets that are clearly intelligible because they are based on the infinite repeatability of a finite set of counting rules. But there is also another infinite that cannot be made intelligible in this way. Tolstoy's notion of laws depends on the former understanding and has to exclude the latter.

Cantor's notion that one could have infinite but clearly coherent sets is still controversial.[13] I might assume for the sake of simplicity that Tolstoy's notion of calculus operates, if it is to provide laws of history, within a largely finitist perspective, that is, of the infinite as infinite repeatability of a finite rule or set of rules. A calculus of history could thus identify all the primary forms of movement in history such that history could be converted into a science. Otherwise, the calculus of history would not achieve at any given time anything else than a provisional and highly questionable picture of the laws of motion in history. These laws, as such, would be open to revision, as I have already remarked. They would give us only a rather unreliable science of history or a science that is essentially skeptical because forced to admit that it cannot come to any endpoint in invariable repeatability. There is nothing to argue that an infinite number of laws is not possible, but, for our purposes, to admit an infinite number of laws is to return to the problem of causation that Tolstoy brings out initially: everything has a cause, but if the number of those causes is not limited by any finite principle or pattern, then our understanding of history can never be complete and is thus ineluctably provisional.

The calculus analogy may bring us no closer to a model for understanding history than the causal account. Tolstoy affirms this by indicating that for a complete picture of history to appear, human freedom must be reduced to nil.[14] Yet he notes too that there is no possibility of reducing human freedom to nil because the human mind, or reason, cannot have access to the kind of immediate understanding, such as it is, that would be required to eliminate the problem of freedom. Here Tolstoy considers another basic aspect of the infinite. While he speaks for the most part of the infinite in quantitative terms, by referring to the understanding of history provided by causes and movement, both mediated through time, space, and number, he also recognizes the infinite in qualitative terms. That is, he recognizes the infinite as a completely indivisible whole present to the mind at one moment (that is not really a moment because it is and must be outside time or temporal sequence). This kind of unmediated knowledge is intuition, the *scientia* or *visio Dei* that is freed from time and space.[15] Such immediate, and thus absolute, knowledge is simply not possible within a quantitative model of physical processes, such as movement, and thus in the ultimate instance, the quantitative infinite cannot give us the infinite as it is in itself—it is still a construction, no matter whether it end up with the repeatable or the unrepeatable infinite.

The quantitative infinite, as such, does not affirm freedom or the illusion of freedom provided by immediacy (itself inexplicable). To the contrary, if there is causal infinity or uniform laws of motion, any notion of freedom we may have must be false. Even so, the belief in freedom remains stubborn and unshakable. As Tolstoy notes in the second part of the epilogue:

> However many times experience and argument have shown a man that in the same conditions, with the same character, he would do the same thing he did before, he, when he sets out for

the thousandth time, in the same conditions, with the same character, on an action that has always ended the same way, undoubtedly feels no less certain that he can act as he pleases than he did before the experience. Every man, savage or sage, however irrefutably argument and experience prove to him that it is impossible to imagine two acts in the same conditions, feels that without this senseless notion (which constitutes the essence of freedom), he cannot imagine life. He feels that, impossible as it may be, it is so; for without the notion of freedom, he not only would not understand life, but would not live for a single moment. (1201–1202; PSS 12:324–325)

This discussion leads to the lapidary statement: "It is impossible to imagine to oneself a man who has no freedom otherwise than as deprived of life" (1202; PSS 12:325).

Despite what reason or science may tell us, we refuse to accept that we are unfree. If one may have objections to specific aspects of Tolstoy's arguments, the equation of freedom with life is trenchant because it brings up the greater problem of determinism: that determinism leads to the reification or objectification of the human being, reminding us indelicately of the dominating and inevitable determining factor in our lives—death. Far from being connected to a notion of complete freedom, the infinite is connected with determinism and death because it ensures us both that we have no agency other than what appears to us because of our cognitive limitations and that, no matter what we do, we are fated to die. Now it is time to return to Prince Andrei at Austerlitz.

II. Hauntings

We might ask: Why is freedom so important to us that we refuse to recognize the many obvious determining elements in our lives? The notion that we are free to do what we wish seems blithely to ignore the many natural limitations on our freedom and also, perhaps more significant, that our desires themselves are more often than not shaped by one overweening desire: the so-called will to live. How can there be any freedom if we are dominated by the will to live? Indeed, the only freedom that would be available to us would be to resist the will to live, a freedom more oriented to resignation and inaction, if not suicide as an action that is the fullest rebellion against the will to live.

Prince Andrei

Prince Andrei beneath the "lofty, infinite sky" is utterly overwhelmed by immensity and what seems, as such, to resist the will to conquest that marks Napoleon and Prince Andrei as well, if to a lesser degree. For in Prince Andrei's eyes, it is Napoleon who knows how to assert himself, defeating his enemies, because of his superior grasp of military strategy. Napoleon's military "genius" is what permits him to turn battles to his own ends, to direct conflict toward a successful conclusion in accordance with his own will. The battle of Austerlitz crystallizes doubts about this picture of Napoleon, who appears to Prince Andrei as nothing more than a fly, simply another animal, and not a very noble one. His stature is drastically reduced when contrasted with the infinite sky and Prince Andrei's state at the edge of death. Prince Andrei experiences an epiphanic moment in which the immensity of nature and natural process becomes decisively clear, as does the inevitability of death.

> To him at that moment all the interests that occupied Napoleon seemed so insignificant, his hero himself seemed so petty to him, with his petty vanity and joy in victory, compared with that lofty, just, and kindly sky, which he had seen and understood, that he was unable to answer him. . . . Prince Andrei thought about the

insignificance of grandeur, about the insignificance of life, the meaning of which no one could understand, and about the still greater insignificance of death, the meaning of which no one among the living could understand or explain. (292–293; PSS 9:358–359)

This moment, mocking the pretensions of human agency as it does, comes to haunt Prince Andrei once he recovers from his wound. Why? If we recall the narrator's words from the second part of the epilogue, a man who has no freedom is "deprived of life." The assumption is that freedom, no matter how illusory in the face of death and natural determination, is absolutely necessary for the living human being.

Prince Andrei has only the unsettling realization that "nothing is certain, except the insignificance of everything" he can understand and the "grandeur of something incomprehensible but most important" (293; PSS 9:359). After Austerlitz Prince Andrei retreats to his estate, Bogucharovo. With his young wife having died giving birth to his son, he appears to be a broken man unable to take up new projects under the crushing weight of his vision of the lofty, infinite sky. Of course, this is hardly the end of Prince Andrei's narrative in the novel. He is famously "renewed" by his love for the young Natasha, and he once again enters the world of action and politics, this time with a peculiar epigone of the Napoleonic spirit, Mikhail Speransky. Still, the sense of the infinite does not leave him even when he is most beguiled by the young Natasha. At one point, after hearing her sing—and not yet aware, we are told, of his love for her—Prince Andrei feels compelled to weep because of a "sudden, vivid awareness of the terrible opposition between something infinitely great and indefinable that was in him, and something narrow and fleshly" (467; PSS 10:212).

Prince Andrei remains quite incapable of reconciling the "infinitely great" with his finite existence and, finally, on the eve of the battle of Borodino, he has another remarkable epiphanic moment:

The possibility of death presented itself to him, for the first time in his life, with no relation to the everyday, with no considerations of how it would affect others, but only in relation to himself, to his soul, vividly, almost with certainty, simply, and terribly. And from the height or that picture, all that used to torment and preoccupy him was suddenly lit up by a cold, white light, without shadows, without perspective, without clear-cut outlines. The whole of life presented itself to him as a magic lantern, into which he had long been looking through a glass and in artificial light. (769; PSS 11:203)

Aside from the Platonic echoes in this passage—the allusions to the cave allegory in Book VII of *Republic*—the noteworthy absence of perspective, of shadow, points to something akin to the absolute intuition to which I have already referred above as the *scientia* or *visio Dei*, a knowledge free of any mediation, knowledge that is in this specific sense absolute or infinite. That this knowledge as infinite is also the very highest form of knowledge is for Martin Heidegger characteristic of the Western metaphysical tradition:

> For Scholasticism it is the absolute intellect of God which serves as the *veritas prima*, the first truth, and as the source of all truth (cf. Aquinas's *Quaestiones disputatae de veritate*, q. I). The original truth, the totality of all true knowledge, is absolute, and is found in the *scientia Dei*.... The basic problems of modern philosophy remain completely closed to one who has no acquaintance with and understanding of these connections. The Scholastic doctrine of God is not only the key to Leibniz's logic; Kant's *Critique of Pure Reason* as well as Hegel's *Logic* become intelligible in their authentic thrusts from the viewpoint of the Scholastic doctrine of God. This is not to say that modern philosophy modeled itself on and borrowed propositions from theology. The philosophical meaning of the orientation on the "*scientia Dei*" is that God's

knowledge functions as the construct of an absolute cognition, on the basis of which finite, human cognition should be measured.[16]

Finite human cognition does not attain to the "position without a position" that is absolute knowledge, and one wonders what such pure intuition as infinite knowledge could possibly be other than portrayed as the perspectiveless and wholly present "view" so evident in Prince Andrei's epiphanic moment where the "crudely daubed figures" obscure what becomes clearest to Prince Andrei: death. Here there is a clear connection between Prince Andrei's epiphanic or immediate vision in "cold, white daylight" and the other ultimate vision he experienced while wounded on the battlefield at Austerlitz. In both cases the sense of the infinite and immediate turns away from life toward death, and Prince Andrei seems almost to offer himself up for death at Borodino when he hesitates in front of the shell about to explode. How could he continue to live in face of this vision that reduces human experience to a series of crudely daubed figures—we may say, illusions—that conceal the infinite and death as well? Moreover, those illusions draw on the basic illusion of freedom that, like a phoenix, arises ever afresh from the ashes of refutation. The final phase of Prince Andrei's narrative is ushered in by this remarkable vision of the ultimate futility of human striving as a striving to be free and freed from the chains of necessity, of an infinite immensity that is too overwhelming and too vast for the human mind to traverse, much less "tame" in action.[17]

At the very end of his life, Prince Andrei finally comes to accept the infinite in the "formless form" of divine love that has no object and, as such, is the apparently paradoxical objectless love for all things regardless of their particularity. Yet he embraces divine love rather ironically when he is no longer capable of maintaining any human contact and, to use the primary metaphor in Prince Andrei's final scene, his room has been burst open by that inscrutable *it* that is the term used both by Prince Andrei and by Pierre for the overwhelming, the infinite, and death.[18]

Pierre Bezukhov

It is no small irony that Prince Andrei's death is intertwined with Pierre Bezukhov's apparent rebirth. Pierre's own trajectory in the novel offers a continuous counterpoint to that of Prince Andrei even after the death of the latter. Prince Andrei finally throws his life away, but Pierre cannot go that far and proves to be resilient. Some identify Pierre as an almost comic character exemplifying a fascination with life rather than death. Here I wish to focus on the somewhat less explored connection between Prince Andrei and Pierre in terms of the presence of the infinite and the restless in Pierre, a sort of esoteric despair that flickers within his apparent resilience.

This sense of despair in Pierre is captured by a striking simile:

> Whatever he started thinking about, he came back to the same questions, which he could not resolve and could not stop asking himself. It was as if the main screw in his head, which held his whole life together, had become stripped. The screw would not go in, would not come out, but turned in the same groove without catching hold, and it was impossible to stop turning it. (347; PSS 10:65)

Pierre's thoughts are a "frictionless spinning in a void," in John McDowell's words, and they give him no comfort.[19] What kinds of questions lead to this spinning, an endless turning that never clicks? Pierre confronts the infinite as failure, as the absence of a ground to stand on that does not always give way to another. The allusion to the problem of infinite causation is not accidental because with Pierre the same underlying problem prevails that cannot be avoided other than through an illusion or arbitrary construction. The one certainty that Pierre mentions is death, for no one evades death. Hence, if one cannot find a way to live (or die), one is left in a purgatorial impasse in which one casts about for shelter or stability; and yet that stability relates only to one aspect of human life—its end. And what can we possibly know about this end? As Heidegger remarks with disarming irony: "Death is the most *distinctive* possibility of human being (Dasein)" ("Der Tod ist *eigenste* Möglichkeit des Daseins").[20] What is most distinctive about us, most "ours," as a possibility is death, surely an ironic response to the famous Greek γνῶθι σεαυτόν (Know thyself).

This irony accompanies Pierre's narrative. And if Prince Andrei rejects this irony as cruel and inhuman, Pierre tries to disarm it by finding a way of living that is stable, that no longer spins in the void but finds a firm footing in everyday life. While Pierre passes through several attempts to find this firm footing, surely the most famous and important of them is his meeting with Platon Karataev. This meeting occurs at a particularly low point for Pierre, who finds himself in French captivity after having witnessed an execution by firing squad:

> From the moment when Pierre saw this horrible murder performed by people who did not want to do it, it was as if the spring that upheld everything and made it seem alive had been pulled from his soul, and it had all collapsed into a heap of meaningless trash. Though he did not account for it to himself, his faith in the world's good order, in humanity's and his own soul, and in God, was destroyed. Pierre had experienced this state before, but never with such force as now. (969; PSS 12:44)

In contrast to Pierre's state, Karataev is the embodiment of lightness, speed, and roundness (an adjective applied to Karataev repeatedly). He is like a sphere whose center is everywhere, the "unfathomable, round, and eternal embodiment of the spirit of simplicity and truth" (974; PSS 12:50). He fits fluidly into whatever context he finds himself in and uses language in a peculiarly gnomic way with sayings that contradict each other but fit the contexts in which they are uttered. He shows the same affection for all around him—he fits everywhere and nowhere. In these respects, Karataev is a representation of the infinite, obviously a rather ironic one since the infinite cannot be represented.[21] Karataev is necessarily an elusive character and it is telling that Pierre turns him into an ideal thus betraying precisely what Karataev is as a being whose being is elusive, fluid, self-concealing—like nature, Karataev loves to hide.

While Karataev dies, Pierre does his best to adopt Karataev as a model for his own life. But by the first part of the epilogue, we see how far Pierre has diverged from his erstwhile ideal. Not only is Pierre absorbed in his family life with Natasha, he also becomes involved in politics: the temptations of action overcome the indifference to politics or worldly affairs that he associated with Karataev. By the end of the first part of the epilogue Pierre has returned to his previous patterns of action, looking to make a difference in the world and resembling in this respect both Napoleon and Prince Andrei. Hence, despite his much greater openness to a life that shuns the lures of finite existence, the calls to action, to exercise one's "will," Pierre cannot in the end hold to Karataev's model of life. Pierre needs grand narratives that flatter illusions of freedom; the broader suggestion is that the life of reclusion, to the extent it shatters those illusions, is one that is very hard to live. The supposed freedom of action pulls too strongly upon us, as Joseph Conrad wrote: "Action is consolatory. It is the enemy of thought and the friend of flattering illusions."[22]

That these illusions are crucial to life is something the narrator tells us, as we have seen, in the long essay contained in the second part of the epilogue. They prove pervasive in two of the primary narrative streams in the novel. Prince Andrei seems crushed by the weight of the infinite and comes out of his reclusive—and quite bitter—life at Bogucharovo on account of his burgeoning love for a particular woman, Natasha, that in turns impels him to take on a more significant role in the political world. Pierre also shows despondency when faced with the groundlessness of his own life—the simile I have mentioned—and casts about for a purpose, and almost any purpose will do. If Prince Andrei is oppressed by the poverty of human resources in the face of the infinite, so is Pierre. Neither is capable of creating a life that is worthy of death, the *it* that they both fear.

This *it* is an extraordinary aspect of *War and Peace*. Both Prince Andrei and Pierre use the term in the form of the nominative neuter pronoun, *ono*, to designate that "distinctive" (or more awkwardly "ownmost") possibility which defines human lives and does so define them much in the same way as the infinite defines Prince Andrei's life, and that of Pierre as well—that is, as uncannily undefined or estranged from definition. The most "authentic" inner self for both is not accessible to discourse at all; but it is not accessible to intuition either, for how is one to intuit death when one cannot even experience one's own death? Prince Andrei's death scene is surely compelling because of the way the narrator penetrates into the consciousness of Prince Andrei (we are reading a fiction after all) but the narrator cannot know any more than Prince Andrei or those who read the chapter what it is that bursts through the door into what is left of Prince Andrei's life so as to dissolve it. This is the *it* that no one can succeed in defining because its nature is to be elusive, to render nugatory the notion of nature as applicable to the beings we encounter. If anything, death is the *Unnatur*, or the other to nature, that cannot be understood in terms of nature or any other phenomenon that we can understand within those terms. Death remains the irreducible, enigmatic *it* that may be the most important and most resistant feature of our lives.

Prince Andrei and Pierre recoil before this manner of estrangement. They are exceptional in the novel because they are aware of the estrangement that arises from an experience like that of Prince Andrei at Austerlitz or Pierre prior to meeting Karataev. The experience can be described variably as the experience of the unlimited, sublime, and negative—the experience of "nothingness"—and it shatters the lives of both characters. The most terrible and wondrous being is the human being because the human being is the being for whom the uncanny experience of complete self-alienation is also one of returning home. To leave home is to return home; the greatest distance from home allows the utmost propinquity to it.

III. Hiddenness in Abundance

Aside from Prince Andrei (and, more comically, Pierre), the most unusually Napoleonic character in the novel is the one most hidden: the narrator. One may align the narrator with Tolstoy, but Tolstoy as a human being cannot possibly have claimed the kind of knowledge the narrator possesses in abundance. Indeed, the narrator seems to be in a position of some irony, claiming to know in a way that the narrator denies his creations. This irony is an important facet of the novel because the narrator appears to know what he claims neither Napoleon nor historians can know—indeed, the narrator creates an entire world through narrative and so successfully that it has become a placid commonplace of the novel's critical reception to praise Tolstoy's vivid, "real" characters as well as the greater social and natural reality they inhabit (1219; PSS 16:9–10).[23]

Yet, if the narrator is a Napoleonic character in this sense, the narrator also maintains a focus on the ever-evanescent present throughout the novel, even while compelling one to construct greater patterns that require time to unfold. This tension between forces of the immediate, infinite or open, present and the precariously defined or closed past, "lived" experience and reflection, immediacy and mediacy, expresses a particular experience of narrative time, of our being both "in" and "out" of it. Any given moment in the novel is thus both open and closed, a movement of both expansion and contraction. In other words, the novel defines no static structure, but one that contravenes the so-called law of contradiction by displaying at the same time and in the same respect divergent qualities, the "infinitely great" and finite exiguity. Indeed, if one accepts that the essence of narrative is to address the most devastating problem of change, that we are at any given moment living in a moment *and* dying in time, then the narrative's contradictory dynamism must be considered its most penetrating and enduring mimetic gesture.

This structural characteristic is analogous to the opposition between novelistic and epic forms of representation that Mikhail Bakhtin describes. Fundamentally at stake in this opposition is the philosophical investment of thought in the notion of genre that identifies different genres as temporal embodiments of consciousness, of an inherently reflexive attitude to the world—in this sense, epic and novel are the generic representations or crystallizations of specific forms of consciousness. By canvassing briefly the views of Bakhtin and Georg Lukács about the novel and its relation to epic, the broader implications of the peculiar narrative ambivalence of *War and Peace* may become clearer. Moreover, the fact that *War and Peace* ends with a lengthy discussion of the relation between reason and consciousness, namely, with an examination of consciousness itself as ostensibly infinite immediacy, opposed to finite reason rooted in time and space, serves as an ironic capstone to the novel's treatment of infinity. The latter appears here not as deadening but as the primary source of vitality, of the open present.

Bakhtin's conception of the novel is a peculiar formalism. Indeed, according to this conception, one might easily turn Tolstoy's concern to distance his work from specific generic categorization around to say the opposite of what it apparently wants to say (cf. 1217; PSS 16:7). For Tolstoy only confirms the essential identity of *War and Peace* as a novel by claiming that it departs from generic considerations, this being an essential trait of the novel, that it has no essential traits or, at least, that it subverts all essential traits. The novel is thus the infinite genre, the genre whose identity is infinitely elastic, like the wax Descartes famously describes in the second *Meditation*.[24] And here is the peculiarity of Bakhtin's approach: the novel is the continuously self-overcoming form, the expression of a negativity that does not annihilate itself in a final synthetic transparency, but one intrinsically open and undisciplined that takes on form only temporarily. To repeat, its essence is to have no essence. This inescapable contradiction is tremendously *productive* and serves as the lifeblood of the genre, the source of its protean flexibility. Bakhtin is surely justified in claiming that the novel is unique among literary genres because, unlike the preponderance of inherited genres, the novel tends most powerfully toward radical openness, toward the continuous transformation of form, a sort of permanent revolutionary negativity (and certainly not an easily "tamed" Aristotelian one since there is no defined telos or justifying *causa finalis*).

While the novel tends toward this inherently fluid openness, Bakhtin argues that the epic tends in the opposite direction, toward closure. For Bakhtin, the epic is primarily distinguished from the novel by the distance it creates between the present and the events it narrates. The latter are "walled off" from the present and thus constitute a discrete finite whole whose integrity is protected by virtue of distance. Epic is a genre of denial that tries to form one final hierarchical order not capable of subsequent modification. Epic reality projects a monumental, finished structure that can only be felled by violent revolution.

This revolution comes about by way of a fundamental change in the temporal limits and assumptions of narrative. Bakhtin's analysis of the difference between epic and novel is decisively shaped by an underlying distinction between the differing temporalities that govern the two genres. While epic time is a completed, Aristotelian whole, a distinct creation of closed temporal form that seeks to avoid the *distentio animi* Ricoeur discusses in *Time and Narrative*, the novel welcomes this distension, being at its most radical nothing more than a celebration of the aporias of the present, its resistance to definition, the immediacy or freedom of the free flowing "now" (*nunc fluens/stans*), of actually experienced time.[25] The epic strives toward defining the nature of time and the course of becoming and, in doing so, it turns time and becoming into a finished narrative "object" and not that immediate "in which" everything appears as such. Bakhtin maintains that "to portray an event on the same time-and-value plane as oneself and one's contemporaries (and an event that is therefore based on personal experience and thought) is to undertake a radical revolution, and to step out of the world of epic into the world of the novel." The present becomes the basic temporal quality that distinguishes the novel:

> The present, in its so-called "wholeness" (although it is, of course, never whole) is in essence and in principle inconclusive; by its very nature it demands continuation, it moves into the future, and the more actively and consciously it moves into the future the more tangible and indispensable its inconclusiveness becomes. Therefore, when the present becomes the center of human orientation in time and in the world, time and world lose their completedness as a whole as well as in each of their parts.[26]

The temporality of the novel, as Bakhtin understands it, represents a radical and permanent departure from the kind of temporal manipulation that has been the durable justification and refuge of epic narrative (a point applicable to the historians Tolstoy critiques). It is thus no surprise that Bakhtin emphasizes the uniqueness of the novel because the radical novel dispenses with the attempt to disguise the aporias of temporality through narrative structure, the attempt to tame the infinite openness of the present by denying it. The upshot is that the novel becomes the genre of immediate *freedom*, of inevitable inconclusiveness as opposed to the ostensibly closed epic.

Bakhtin's view of the novel is quite radical, and surprisingly Tolstoyan, but he characterizes the epic in ways that follow the tradition stemming from Hegel's discussions of epic poetry in his *Lectures on Aesthetics* with the one key difference: for Bakhtin, epic is not a *stage* in an inexorable progression toward a specific goal, but rather a permanent possibility of world interpretation. For Hegel, epic is the unifying narrative that establishes a basis for culture, an original whole that is the inexhaustible source from which a given people draw to define their form of life, including its temporality.[27] While Hegel goes further, claiming that the novel is one of the genres that has invaded the original domain of the epic in the modern period, he says little else about the exact significance of the novel.[28] Lukács extends and clarifies the Hegelian line of thought in *Theory of the Novel*.

For Lukács the novel is "the epic of an age in which the extensive totality of life is no longer directly given, in which the immanence of meaning in life has become a problem, yet which still thinks in terms of totality."[29] What is this totality? Lukács claims that totality in the context of the novel is inextricably tied to an essentially romantic notion of the absolute, of lost immediacy and wholeness, an all-embracing "oceanic feeling," that emerges as shattered and irretrievable in the wake of the development of self-consciousness. The novel is the genre that gives artistic expression to this modern self-consciousness, its agonizing sense of alienation from a more originary experience of life. Thus the novel as a genre both identifies this sharp awareness of alienation and attempts to redress its effects to regain in some fashion an originary or primordial unity.

Bakhtin and Lukács express opposed views of the philosophical significance of the novel. Their concern with generic categories is admittedly merely a pretext for addressing one of the great predicaments of modern thought: how to deal with the loss of faith in authority, of a firm ground for living. If Bakhtin welcomes this loss of authority, the liberation from conclusive—monologistic—narrative toward the infinite or ineffable freedom of the present, Lukács brings out a despairing view, one that reveals a longing for an essentially harmonic whole, an authoritative closure, the very closure both Prince Andrei and Pierre seem to covet in the face of the infinite.

The fundamental problematic with which Bakhtin and Lukács deal in terms of the relation of epic and novel has a central role within *War and Peace*; it provides an appropriate means of beginning to grasp the significance of the deeply ambivalent tension of infinite and finite, openness and closure. For the movement between generic categories that both apply and fail to isolate the essence of the novel is just as readily evident in the narrator's privileging of a calculus of conceptual relations over basically Aristotelian ways of characterizing the world. The view of temporality that lies under this distinction is equally indicative, since causal thinking is a major component of the creation of a linear temporality, whereas calculus creates a timeless temporality in the sense that the most powerful relations reject the purely temporal; they move the narrative out of the flow of time understood as a succession into a simultaneity that is nothing more than a continuous presentness.

But this simultaneity has two diametrically opposed consequences. On the one hand, the concealment of simple linear causality in *War and Peace* creates the same sort of open, novelistic temporality that Bakhtin describes so well. On the other hand, the ultimate fruit of that concealment, the creation of a new form of governing metanarrative, a continuous presence, is not that of the evanescent moment, but of godlike intuition in the persona (mask) of the narrator, where all objects are present at once to the divine mind—in a word, deadening epic closedness, a formidable expression of the desire to impose being on becoming, to resolve the constantly shifting present of finite consciousness into the immutable presence of an infinite one. The narrator seems to express contradiction, the same fundamental contradiction between infinite expansion and finite contraction that appears to be the inexhaustible fount of the novel's vitality and elusiveness, in its critique of historians, in its leading characters, and in its narrative structure itself.

Notes

1. Jorge Luis Borges, "Avatars of the Tortoise," in *Labyrinths*, ed. Donald A. Yates and James E. Irby (New York: New Directions, 1962), 193–198. Infinity is of course a most plastic and elusive concept. It can be expressed both qualitatively, as the absence of any determinations, or quantitatively, as an infinite series, the former being the infinite as indivisible, the latter as infinitely divisible. The infinite as indivisible is heterogeneous to finite reality; as indivisible, it tends to "dissipate" that reality in infinities of infinities. In this chapter I use the term in both senses and I mention Cantor in particular to include the most revolutionary modern approach to the infinite as infinitely divisible, the mathematical infinite. There are many histories of the concept, but I think that the best contemporary philosophical accounts of the infinite stem from Alain Badiou and those influenced by his thought. Badiou's major work, *Being and Event* (1988), takes mathematics as ontology and Cantor's theory of the infinite as determinative. See Alain Badiou, *Being and Event*, trans. Oliver Feltham (London: Continuum, 2006). See also Badiou's more recent *Immanence of Truth*, trans. Susan Spitzer and Kenneth Reinhard (London: Bloomsbury Academic, 2022). Badiou's seminars are excellent, though unfortunately many are not available in English. I have profited in particular from his seminar on the infinite from 1984 to 1985: Alain Badiou, *L'Infini: Aristote, Spinoza, Hegel* (Paris: Fayard, 2016).
2. For a useful summary of the main issues involved in regard to the generic classification of *War and Peace*, see Gary Saul Morson, *Hidden in Plain View: Narrative and Creative Potentials in "War and Peace"* (Stanford, CA: Stanford University Press, 1988), 37–65; and R. Silbajoris, *War and Peace: Tolstoy's Mirror of the World* (Woodbridge, CT: Twayne, 1995), 108–123.
3. Isaiah Berlin, "The Hedgehog and the Fox," in *Russian Thinkers*, ed. Henry Hardy and Aileen Kelly (New York: Penguin, 1978), 22–81.
4. Berlin, "The Hedgehog and the Fox," 68.
5. Employing my previous terminology, I identify the first argument with the qualitative infinite and the second with the quantitative infinite. Tolstoy in effect combines the two by defining continuous motion in mathematical terms and opening up the infinite to intelligibility as a mathematical concept.
6. The problem is the apparent contradiction expressed by "infinite whole." One could argue that an infinite set can be an actually infinite whole to the

extent it expresses only the infinite repetition of a finite set of rules. Tolstoy seems to advocate something like this in the second part of the epilogue with his notion of laws of history, though he nonetheless denies knowledge of an infinite whole in terms of a causal chain in the main body of the novel.

7. Aristotle, *Posterior Analytics*, trans. Jonathan Barnes (Oxford: Oxford University Press, 1993), 5 (72b7–16).
8. Each of these terms, though different, is brought together by a common and crucial factor: the absence of limits.
9. The primary reason is freedom understood as our cognitive incapacity to know all.
10. Cf. 1212; PSS 12:338: "Only by limiting this freedom infinitely, that is, by looking upon it as an infinitely small quantity, will we be convinced of the total inaccessibility of causes, and then, instead of searching for causes, history will set itself the task of searching for laws."
11. See Joseph Warren Dauben, *Georg Cantor: His Mathematics and Philosophy of the Infinite* (Princeton, NJ: Princeton University Press, 1990), 47–76.
12. Dauben, *Georg Cantor*, 165–168. The real numbers are an example of a non-denumerable set.
13. See Michael Hallett, *Cantorian Set Theory and the Problem of Size* (Oxford: Oxford University Press, 1984), 1–48.
14. Tolstoy equates human freedom with what cannot be made intelligible. He employs the Russian *volya* to describe will, affirming this equation. Tolstoy is also clear that the notion of will as free is nourished by ignorance and even the rejection of determinism. Tolstoy does not claim that there is an infinite that in principle is unintelligible (what Badiou would refer to as the pure multiple) but only that human beings are either unwilling or unable to accept complete intelligibility because for Tolstoy determinism and complete intelligibility are synonymous.
15. See Martin Heidegger, *The Metaphysical Foundations of Logic*, trans. Michael Heim (Bloomington: Indiana University Press, 1984), 43.
16. Heidegger, *Metaphysical Foundations of Logic*, 43.
17. Prince Andrei reflects a modern trope, that of the "Faustian" or Napoleonic man who strives restlessly for complete self-determination. Both Oswald Spengler and Heidegger discuss this notion in their differing conceptions of history, Spengler explicitly as Faustian and Heidegger more generally in his history of Being as nihilism. While Heidegger is quite critical of Spengler, several scholars have seen more continuity than distance in their assessments of Western history. See, for example, Oswald Spengler, *The Decline of the West*, 2 vols. (New York: Knopf,

1926), 1:81–84; and Martin Heidegger, *Nietzsche*, ed. David Farrell Krell, 4 vols. (New York: HarperCollins, 1991), 4:52–57, and Heidegger, *The Fundamental Concepts of Metaphysics*, trans. William McNeill and Nicholas Walker (Bloomington: Indiana University Press, 1995), 69–70. Heidegger notes the pervasive influence of Nietzsche on Spengler, an influence Heidegger engages with extensively in the over one thousand pages of his Nietzsche lectures.
18. I am indebted to Kathleen Parthé's important article on death in Tolstoy. See Kathleen Parthé, "Death Masks in Tolstoi," *Slavic Review* 41, no. 2 (1982): 297–305.
19. John McDowell, *Mind and World* (Cambridge, MA: Harvard University Press, 1996), 11.
20. Heidegger, *Being and Time*, trans. John Macquarrie and Edward Robinson (New York: Harper & Row, 1962), 307. Macquarrie and Robinson translate with "ownmost": "Death is Dasein's *ownmost* possibility." I use "distinctive," though it may not be better.
21. George Steiner, *Tolstoy or Dostoevsky: A Study in Contrast* (New York: Open Road, 1980), 222–223.
22. Joseph Conrad, *Nostromo* (Oxford: Oxford University Press, 2009), 50.
23. To be fair, in "A Few Words Apropos the Book *War and Peace*" the narrator claims the privilege, indeed, the superiority of the artist in depicting the totality of history, a most bold and even outrageous claim for the superiority of fiction over the supposed truth of the historians backed up in the novel most notably in the chapter where Lavrushka, the wily servant, meets Napoleon.
24. See Borges, "From Allegories to Novels," in *Selected Non-fictions*, ed. Eliot Weinberger (New York: Penguin, 1999), 337–340.
25. Paul Ricoeur, *Time and Narrative*, trans. Kathleen McLaughlin and David Pellauer, 3 vols. (Chicago: University of Chicago Press, 1990), 1:3–30.
26. M. M. Bakhtin, *The Dialogic Imagination: Four Essays*, trans. Michael Holquist and Caryl Emerson, ed. Michael Holquist (Austin: University of Texas Press, 1982), 30.
27. "Consequently the content and form of epic proper is the entire world-outlook and objective manifestation of a national spirit presented in its self-objectifying shape as an actual event"; see G. W. F. Hegel, *Hegel's Aesthetics*, trans. T. W. Knox, 2 vols. (Oxford: Oxford University Press, 1975), 2:1044.
28. *Hegel's Aesthetics*, 2:1110.

29. Georg Lukács, *The Theory of the Novel*, trans Anna Bostock (Cambridge, MA: MIT Press, 1971), 56.

Works Cited

Aristotle. *Posterior Analytics*. Translated by Jonathan Barnes. Oxford: Oxford University Press, 1993.

Badiou, Alain. *Being and Event*. Translated by Oliver Feltham. London: Continuum, 2006.

Badiou, Alain. *Immanence of Truths*. Translated by Susan Spitzer and Kenneth Reinhard. London: Bloomsbury Academic, 2022.

Badiou, Alain. *L'Infini: Aristote, Spinoza, Hegel*. Paris: Fayard, 2016.

Bakhtin, M. M. *The Dialogic Imagination: Four Essays*. Translated by Michael Holquist and Caryl Emerson. Edited by Michael Holquist. Austin: University of Texas Press, 1982.

Berlin, Isaiah. "The Hedgehog and the Fox." *Russian Thinkers*. Edited by Henry Hardy and Aileen Kelly, 22–81. New York: Penguin, 1978.

Borges, Jorge Luis. "Avatars of the Tortoise." *Labyrinths*. Edited by Donald A. Yates and James E. Irby, 193–198. New York: New Directions, 1962.

Borges, Jorge Luis. "From Allegories to Novels." *Selected Non-fictions*. Edited by Eliot Weinberger, 337–340. New York: Penguin, 1999.

Conrad, Joseph. *Nostromo*. Oxford: Oxford University Press, 2009.

Dauben, Joseph Warren. *Georg Cantor: His Mathematics and Philosophy of the Infinite*. Princeton, NJ: Princeton University Press, 1990.

Hallett, Michael. *Cantorian Set Theory and the Problem of Size*. Oxford: Oxford University Press, 1984.

Hegel, G. W. F. *Hegel's Aesthetics*. Translated by T. W. Knox. 2 vols. Oxford: Oxford University Press, 1975.

Heidegger, Martin. *Being and Time*. Translated by John Macquarrie and Edward Robinson. New York: Harper & Row, 1962.

Heidegger, Martin. *The Fundamental Concepts of Metaphysics*. Translated by William McNeill and Nicholas Walker. Bloomington: Indiana University Press, 1995.

Heidegger, Martin. *The Metaphysical Foundations of Logic*. Translated by Michael Heim. Bloomington: Indiana University Press, 1984.

Heidegger, Martin. *Nietzsche*. Edited by David Farrell Krell. 4 vols. New York: HarperCollins, 1991.

Lukács, Georg. *The Theory of the Novel*. Translated by Anna Bostock. Cambridge, MA: MIT Press, 1971.

McDowell, John. *Mind and World*. Cambridge, MA: Harvard University Press, 1996.

Morson, Gary Saul. *Hidden in Plain View: Narrative and Creative Potentials in "War and Peace"*. Stanford, CA: Stanford University Press, 1988.

Parthé, Kathleen. "Death Masks in Tolstoi." *Slavic Review* 41, no. 2 (Summer 1982): 297–305.

Ricoeur, Paul. *Time and Narrative*. Translated by Kathleen McLaughlin and David Pellauer. 3 vols. Chicago: University of Chicago Press, 1990.

Silbajoris, R. *War and Peace: Tolstoy's Mirror of the World*. Woodbridge, CT: Twayne, 1995.

Spengler, Oswald. *The Decline of the West*. Translated by Charles Francis Atkinson. 2 vols. New York: Knopf, 1926.

Steiner, George. *Tolstoy or Dostoevsky: A Study in Contrast*. New York: Open Road, 1980.

Index

For the benefit of digital users, indexed terms that span two pages (e.g., 52–53) may, on occasion, appear on only one of those pages.

abstraction, 4, 57, 133–34, 159, 185, 194–95
action, 7, 12, 27–28, 30–31, 37–39, 44, 47, 48, 50–51, 56, 102–3, 117, 202–4, 210
agape, 22–23, 161, 188–89
Alexander I, 33, 58–59, 65–67, 75
anarchism, 18, 19, 24–25, 37, 70–71
Anna Karenina, 44, 75–76, 113, 114–15, 167–68
Apocalypse, 194–95
Aquinas, Thomas, 2–3, 206–7
artificiality, 77, 206
Augustine, 2–3, 31, 129
authority, 120–21, 161–62, 165, 216–17

Bakhtin, Mikhail, 213–17
beauty, 144, 153, 154–55, 159–60
Berlin, Isaiah, 195–96, 197, 200
Boyhood, 165, 169, 185
Buber, Martin, 2–3, 12–13, 14

Cantor, Georg, 200–2
Carlyle, Thomas, 14
causation, 196–97, 198–200, 201–2, 208–9
chance, 6, 44, 57–58, 78, 98
Chernyshevsky, Nikolai, 50–52
Childhood, 165
choice, 25–26, 28, 31–34, 76, 155
Christianity, 20–21, 31, 36–37, 133, 161, 165, 173, 185, 187–88

city, 46–47, 48, 112–13, 114, 115–16, 119–20, 122–26, 127–29, 130, 131–32, 133, 134
 See also urbanity
Clausewitz, Carl von, 26
Confession, A, 33–34, 37–39, 167–68, 171–72
contingency, 7, 55–56, 57–58, 157, 160
Cossacks, The, 166–67

Davydov, Denis, 83–89, 90, 91–94, 95, 96–103
death, 13, 149–51, 182–83, 208–9, 211
Decembrists, the, 64–65, 100–1, 167, 173, 189
destiny, 13, 152
determinism, 45, 203–4
 See also indeterminacy
Dostoevsky, Fyodor, 1, 14, 26–27
Druzhinin, Aleksandr Vasil'evich, 83–85

enthusiasm, 166–67, 172–73
essence, 13, 213–14
 of life, 140–41, 154, 158–59, 160
eternity, 7, 185
 See also temporality
Euripides, 18, 26–27, 37–39
experience, 24, 207
 religious, 167–68, 187–88

extraordinary, 2, 5, 211
    and ordinary, 1, 2, 6–7, 152

faith, 155–56, 167–68, 171–72, 216–17
fatalism, 28, 29–30
fate, 30–31, 34, 168–69
fear, 4–5, 6, 188–89, 210–11
fearlessness, 90, 97–99, 131
freedom, 29, 30–31, 32, 33–34, 102–3, 152, 176–77, 199, 202, 203–4, 207, 215

God, 23, 177, 184, 189
Goethe, Johann Wolfgang von, 185–86
good, 21, 37–39, 157, 159–60
Gospel in Brief, The, 189
Grande Armée, 66, 70–71
great men of history, 2, 14, 18, 30, 37–39, 77–78, 82

Hamilton, Edith, 18–19
Hartmann, Nicolai, 8, 9–11
Hegel, Georg Wilhelm Friedrich, 4–5, 7, 14, 197, 215–16
Heidegger, Martin, 4–5, 206–7, 208–9
Herder, Johann Gottfried, 174, 176–77, 188–89
heroism, 2, 14, 78, 92–94, 96–97, 98–100
historicism, 4–5, 7–9
history, 2–3, 7, 18–19, 27–28, 30–31, 47–48, 58–59, 64, 68, 70–71, 72–73, 75–76, 78–79, 84, 98–99, 100–1, 102–3, 123, 124, 150–51, 168–69, 174–75, 195–97, 198–202
Homer, 6, 92, 144, 156
humanity, 2–4, 12, 32, 154–56, 159, 160

ideal, 11–12, 13–14, 133, 160–61, 178, 209–10

immortality, 185, 188–89
indeterminacy, 194–95, 211–12, 214–15, 216, 217
    See also determinism
individuality, 12–13, 52
infinity, 3, 194–97, 198–201, 202, 205, 206, 207–10, 213–14, 217
intelligentsia, 49–50, 52

James, William, 33–34
Jesus, 20–21, 22–23, 24, 37–39, 189
justice, 112, 133, 167, 173
    social, 115–16, 118–19, 128, 129, 131–32, 134, 167
just war theory, 26–27, 37–39

Kafka, Franz, 1
Kant, Immanuel, 7, 11–12, 33–34, 200
Karamzin, Nikolai, 172, 176
killing, 22–23, 27, 31, 36–37
Kingdom of God Is within You, The, 26–27, 37–39
knowledge, 197, 200–1, 202, 206, 207
Kohák, Erazim, 8–9

Law of Love and the Law of Violence, The, 161–62
life, 13, 21–22, 47, 55–56, 114, 117–18, 134, 143, 149–50, 152, 153, 154–55, 157, 158–59, 160, 175, 184–85, 210
    essence of, 140–41, 154, 158–59, 160
    meaning of, 20–21, 22–23, 157, 171
    swarm of, 48, 123
    See also vitality
Life, On, 188–89
literature, 1, 2, 24–25, 31, 63
love, 22–24, 36–37, 140–42, 146, 149–51, 153, 156, 157, 158–59, 160–62, 181–83, 184, 207–8
    devotional, 146–48, 152
    ecstatic, 142–45, 152

of glory, 93, 99–100
of God, 23, 189
Platonic, 37–39, 146
romantic, 22–23, 142–43
sublimated, 150–51, 153–54, 159–60, 161–62
Lukács, Georg, 215–17

Maistre, Joseph de, 173
meaning of life, 20–21, 22–23, 157, 171
memory, 184–85, 189
Merezhkovsky, Dmitry, 75–76
military, 22–23, 27–28, 68, 84
morality, 154–55, 156, 170
of war, 34–35, 37–39, 91–92, 97–98
Murdoch, Iris, 8, 141–42, 154–55, 156, 157, 159–60
music, 180–81, 185–86
mysticism, 11–12, 169–70, 172–74

Napoleon, Bonaparte, 2, 25–26, 27, 31, 54, 66–68, 69, 76–78, 98–99, 122–23, 172, 194–95, 204–5, 212
narrative, 196–97, 207, 210–11, 212–13, 217
nation-state, 24, 25
necessity, 24–25, 30–31, 44, 50–51, 101–2, 176–77, 198–99, 207
nonviolence, 24, 37
novel, 18–19, 51, 63–64, 213–17
epic, 213, 214–16, 217
historical, 167

O'Brien, Tim, 5–6
ordinary, 4–5, 54
and extraordinary, 1, 2, 6–7, 152

pacifism, 18, 20, 24–25, 32, 36–39
Pascal, Blaise, 165–66, 171, 189–90
personality, 12, 51–52

philosophy, 2, 7, 11–12, 34, 165, 184–85
of war, 24–25, 26–27, 37–39
Plato, 37–39, 146, 153, 155, 172–73, 206
presence, 9, 13

rationalism, 45, 46–47, 167–68
reason, 155, 213
religion, 167–68, 169–70, 180–81, 188–89
Resurrection, The, 113–14, 187
Rousseau, Jean-Jacques, 166–67, 169–70, 176

Sartre, Jean-Paul, 32–34
Sassoon, Siegfried, 29
Schleiermacher, Friedrich, 180–81
science, 43–44, 46, 48–49
social, 43, 44, 45–47, 50–51, 53
of warfare, 54, 57, 58
seeing, 9–11
Sevastopol in May, 83–84
skepticism, 59, 78–79, 165, 167–68, 177–78, 197, 201–2
Socrates, 37–39
soul, 14, 150–51, 153, 157, 180, 185
source, 148–49, 150–51, 184, 213
historical, 64, 66–68, 69, 71, 101–3
space, 7, 9–10, 112, 127, 202, 213
spatiality, 7, 9
Spinoza, Baruch de, 176–77, 188–89
spirituality, 20–21, 76, 155, 182, 184, 189
storytelling, 1, 9–10
sublime, 153–55, 157

temporality, 6–7, 8–9, 12, 160, 213–14, 215, 217
See also eternity
time, 4–5, 7, 78
tone, 82–85
truthful, 82–85, 87–88, 101–3
See also voice

Trojan War, the, 25
truth, 14, 83–84, 85, 99–100, 101, 102–3, 146, 149, 197
  historical, 64, 70, 73, 76, 79, 99, 102–3, 173, 197

urbanity, 112–13, 114–16, 118, 121, 122, 123–24, 125, 127–28, 131–32, 133–34
  See also city

value, 2, 8–9, 10–12, 22–23, 154, 159
  objective, 11, 102–3
violence, 26, 75, 119–20
  mob, 121–22
vitality, 148, 152, 161–62, 183, 213, 217
  See also life
voice, 82–83, 84–85, 87–88, 91, 102–3, 130
  See also tone

war, 19, 20, 24–25, 26, 29, 32, 100–1, 156
  morality of, 34–35, 37–39, 91–92, 97–98
  philosophy of, 24–25, 26–27, 37–39
  psychology of, 87, 91–92, 98–99
  science of, 54, 57, 58
What I Believe, 20–21, 26–27, 33–34
What Is Art?, 1
What Is Religion and of What Does Its Essence Consist?, 180–81
What Then Shall We Do?, 114, 115–16, 127–28, 129–30, 133, 134
Wieland, Christoph Martin, 172–73, 179
will, 4, 12, 13, 143, 210
wisdom, 53–54
Wittgenstein, Ludwig, 7–8, 9

Youth, 165, 166–67